AND HE HAD COMPASSION

WILLIAM BARCLAY

Judson Press ®
Valley Forge

To the Members of the Bible Classes
of Trinity Church, Renfrew,
whom it was my privilege to teach
from 1933 to 1946.

AND HE HAD COMPASSION

This revised edition first published in 1975 by The Saint Andrew Press

Judson Press edition 1976
ISBN 0-8170-0686-9
Third Printing, 1978

© William Barclay 1975

Originally published in 1955 by the Church of Scotland Youth Committee as *And He Had Compassion On Them*.

Library of Congress Cataloging in Publication Data

Barclay, William, lecturer in the University of Glasgow.
    And he had compassion.

    Published in 1955 under title: And he had compassion on them.
    Bibliography: p. 271.
    1. Jesus Christ—Miracles.   I. Title.
BT366.B36   1976   232.9′5   75-28099
ISBN 0-8170-0686-9

The name JUDSON PRESS is registered as a trademark in the U.S. Patent Office.

Printed in the U.S.A. by Judson Press, Valley Forge, PA 19481.

CONTENTS

CONTENTS *(continued)*

The Miracles of the Fourth Gospel

PREFACE

I am very grateful to The Saint Andrew Press for republishing this book in a new form. Originally it was a Bible Class Handbook published by the Church of Scotland Youth Committee and the material in it is the substance of talks which were given to a Bible Class in Trinity Church, Renfrew when I was minister of that congregation.

The aim of this book is two-fold. First, I try to explain the Miracles, not explain them away. The purpose of the explanation is to enable the reader to appropriate the wonder-working power of Jesus Christ for himself.

The second aim is to present Jesus as someone, not who *did* things, but who *does* things. The greatest danger in Christianity is to think of Jesus as someone to be remembered. He is someone to be experienced and met. The object of these chapters is to enable people to see the power of the risen Christ in action.

I am deeply indebted to the Rev James Martin MA, BD, of High Carntyne Church, Glasgow for preparing this revised edition for the press; without his invaluable help it would never have appeared at all. I send out this book with the hope that through it men and women may find that Jesus is still mighty to heal and to save.

WILLIAM BARCLAY

CHAPTER ONE

Signs and Wonders

If we are to discuss the miracles of the Bible we must begin by being clear in our minds as to what we mean by a miracle which is not nearly so easy to define as one might think.

In everyday talk we often use miracle in a loose way. For instance, we may talk of someone's recovery from a serious illness as *a miracle*. A friend of his tells us that for years Thomas Hardy would not have the telephone in his house because he regarded it as a rather uncanny *miracle*. We may even at a football match hear an unusually brilliant save by a goalkeeper described as *miraculous*. When we have a very slender hope of passing an examination, we may say: "It will be *a miracle* if I get through." The poets talk to us about *the daily miracle* of night and day. Clearly that is not what we mean when we use the word miracle about certain events in the Bible and, in particular, about certain acts of Jesus. That is a loose use of a great word.

Miracle and knowledge
It is also clear that the state of a person's knowledge will to a great extent decide what he calls a miracle. If someone in the Elizabethan age had been told that a family in Glasgow could watch on a screen attached to a certain instrument a play of Shakespeare's being enacted in London, he would assuredly have called it a *miracle*. If, even a hundred years ago, a man had been told that it would be possible to sit in an arm-chair in his own house and hear a preacher and a choir in a church miles away, he would certainly have called it a *miracle*. If a Roman sailor had been

told of a ship which measured more than one thousand feet in length and weighed more than eighty thousand tons in burthen, he would have classed it as a *miracle*. If even fifty years ago a man had been told that an airman would fly at a speed exceeding that of sound, he would have reckoned it a *miracle*.

When Lawrence brought some of his Arab leaders and chieftains over to this country after the First World War, they were suddenly transported from the desert to the complications of western civilization. It might have been expected that they would have been amazed by things like ocean liners, railway locomotives, fast motor cars and the like; but one thing which left them spellbound in fascinated awe was *a waterfall*. To the men of the waterless desert this was the real *miracle*. It is always necessary to remember that the state of our knowledge and the extent of our experience will condition our idea of a miracle.

The definition of a miracle

Miracle is derived from the Latin verb *mirari, to wonder*. So then, first and foremost, a miracle is something which moves us to wonder. Here we are on the way to a working definition. Let us ask, Why do we wonder at this event we call *a miracle*? The brief first answer is that we wonder at it because we can neither do it ourselves nor understand how it is done. But there are a great many things that most of us cannot do ourselves and do not understand which we do not call miracles. I cannot build a television receiver nor do I understand how it works but I do not call television a miracle. I could not wire my house for electricity nor do I understand how electricity works, but I do not regard electricity as a miracle. This shows us that we have to add something to our definition and say that it is something which no man can perform or explain.

Wonders

With that working definition in our minds, let us turn to the New Testament and see its idea of miracles. It uses two words for the miracles of Jesus and each has something to tell us. First, they are often called *dunameis*, the plural of the Greek word *dunamis*, *power*, from which our *dynamite* is derived. So, then, in a miracle there is *power* which men do not themselves possess. We might put it this way – a miracle is an event in which God's power has made a special entry into our lives. In the gospels we get pictures of men and women to whose needs Jesus brought a power which no one else had.

Signs

Second, the New Testament frequently calls Jesus's miracles *semeia*, the plural of the Greek word *semeion*, a *sign*. They did not only stagger men with their wonder; they *showed* them something. They showed them something of the character of God. Power in itself is neutral. It may be used to help men, and it may equally be used to destroy them. Atomic power, for instance, in itself is neither good nor bad. It can be used to wipe mankind off the face of the globe or it can be used to make life easier and better for all men. Everything depends on the mind and heart of the people using it; and it is always possible to tell something about a person by the way he uses power. That is the point of Jesus's miracles. A miracle was the invasion of men's lives by the power of God. But that power healed the sick and fed the hungry and brought joy to the mourner. In any miracle of Jesus we are meant to see, not only the power of God, but even more his love.

Legends and miracles

This is precisely the difference between the miracles of Jesus, as told to us in the New Testament, and the legendary stories of miracles which later ages produced. The miracles of Jesus in the New Testament are *meaningful*; every one of them tells us something about God. The miracles of the legends add nothing to our knowledge of God; they are simply meaningless marvels. Let us illustrate.

Long after our gospels were written, men wrote what we call the Apocryphal Gospels. Some of these purport to tell the story of the infancy and the boyhood of Jesus. They are works of pious fiction, designed to fill in the gaps in the life of Jesus. One of the most famous is The Gospel of Thomas, which was written sometime in the second century A.D. Here are certain extracts from it.

"This little child Jesus when he was five years old was playing at the ford of a brook: and he gathered together the waters that flowed there into pools, and made them straightway clean, and commanded them by his word alone. And having made soft clay, he fashioned thereof twelve sparrows. And it was the Sabbath day when he did these things. And there were also many other little children playing with him. And a certain Jew when he saw what Jesus did, playing upon the Sabbath day, departed straightway and told his father Joseph: 'Lo, thy child is at the brook, and he hath taken clay and fashioned twelve little birds, and hath polluted the Sabbath day.' And Joseph came to the place and saw, and cried out to him saying: 'Wherefore doest thou these things on the Sabbath, which it is not lawful to do?' But Jesus clapped his hands together and cried out to the sparrows and said to them: 'Go!' And the sparrows took their flight and went away chirping ... But the son of Annas the scribe was standing there with Joseph; and he took a branch of willow and dispersed the waters which Jesus had gathered together. And when Jesus saw what was done, he was wroth and said unto him: 'O evil, ungodly and foolish one, what hurt did the pools and the waters do thee? Behold, now also thou shalt be withered like a tree, and shalt not bear leaves, neither root, nor fruit.' And straightway that lad withered up wholly, but Jesus departed and went unto Joseph's home. . . .

After that again he went through the village, and a child ran and dashed against his shoulder. And Jesus was provoked and said unto him: 'Thou shalt not finish thy course.' And immediately he fell down and died. . . .

Now when he was six years old his mother sendeth him to draw water and bear it into the house, and gave him a pitcher: but in the press he struck it against another and the pitcher was broken. But Jesus spread out the garment which was upon him and filled it with water and brought it to his mother. And when his mother saw what was done she kissed him: and she kept within herself the mysteries which she saw him do. . . .

Now his father was a carpenter and make at that time ploughs and yokes. And there was required of him a bed by a certain rich man, that he should make it for him. And whereas one beam, which is called the shifting one, was too short and Joseph knew not what to do, the young child Jesus said to his father Joseph: 'Lay down the two pieces of wood and make them even at the end next to thee." And Joseph did as the young child said unto him. And Jesus stood at the other end and took hold of the shorter beam and stretched it and made it equal with the other. And his father Joseph saw it and marvelled; and he embraced the young child and kissed him, saying: 'Happy am I for that God hath given me this young child'."

Stories like that do not ring true because they are only glorified conjuring tricks; they fail to do what every miracle of Jesus did – they tell us nothing of the nature of God. In the New Testament sense a miracle has *meaning*; it is a door opening in the eternal to give us a glimpse of God.

Let us pursue this a little further. An amazing handbook called *A Dictionary of Miracles*, by Rev. E. Cobham Brewer, has five hundred and thirty pages of miraculous happenings. In it there are many of the miracle stories which decorate the lives of the mediaeval saints and which became attached to the ancient fathers. Here are two typical specimens:

"Meditating one day on the Saviour's fast, St. Clara resolved to drink nothing for forty days. When brought to the brink of the grave by this abstinence, a cup of gold, filled with a celestial beverage, was brought to her from heaven, and drinking therefrom her thirst was entirely assuaged. Jesus Christ himself brought her, at night, a sweet drink which sufficed for the last twelve years of her life, during all which time she drank nothing except the wine of the Eucharist."

"Agatha Hildegardes was the wife of Count-palatine Paul, who for some motive best known to himself chose to suspect her of infidelity, and locked her up in the castle dungeon. After a long imprisonment, the count one day went to visit her, and, pretending penitence, induced her to walk with him on the keep, and then pushed her from the top of the tower into the foss below. Supposing her dead, he began to wail, and cry for the servants, to whom he said their mistress had fallen over the tower. The servants ran to the foss, fully expecting to find her dead body horribly mangled, but to their amazement they found the countess wholly uninjured; and they thanked God that he had given his angels charge concerning her. The count made the best of the matter he could, confessed his crime, and expiated it with a long penitence."

We have only to read these stories to see the difference between them and the miracles of Jesus. These stories bear their fiction on their face; and they do so because they are essentially *meaningless*. The miracles of Jesus were always *meaningful*; in every one of them is displayed the heart of God.

A miracle is an event in which the power of God is brought to bear on some human situation. But a miracle in the New Testament sense is not only a wonderful work of power; it is an event which allows us to see something of God's attitude of love towards men.

CHAPTER TWO

Can We Believe that the Miracles of Jesus Really Happened?

Whenever we begin to read the stories of the miracles in the gospels, the first question we are bound to ask is, Did these miracles really happen? The more unusual a thing is, the better the evidence must be before we can accept it as an actual historical happening. We must therefore carefully examine the evidence for the miracles before we can be fully convinced that they are not merely legendary stories which gathered around the name of Jesus. This is a matter in which we must be completely honest; we therefore begin with some of the things which are advanced as reasons for regarding the miracles with caution or even for disbelieving in them altogether.

An age of miracle
It is unquestionably true that Christianity came into a world where miracles were a commonplace. We may call it pagan superstition if we like but the fact remains that to these ancient people this world was full of the power of the spirits, the demons and the gods. They believed that every hill, every lake, every river, every tree had its resident demon or spirit or god; and all these gods and demons and spirits were either well or ill-disposed to men. A great scholar puts it this way. "In a time of such vivid belief in the universal presence of divine beings, faith in miracle was a matter of course. . . . In the field of miracle in the second century the heathen could easily match the Christian. With gods in every grove and fountain and on every mountain summit; with gods breathing in the winds and flashing in the lightning, or the ray of the sun and star, heaving in the earthquake or the

November storm in the Aegean, watching over every society of men congregated for any purpose, guarding the solitary hunter or traveller in the Alps or the Sahara, what is called miracle became as natural to the heathen as the rising of the sun."[1] It is the easiest thing in the world to collect so-called examples of pagan miracles from all kinds of sources.

The Roman Emperors were credited with working miraculous cures. Suetonius, the Roman historian, tells of an incident from the life of Vespasian. "Vespasian as yet lacked prestige and a certain divinity, so to speak, since he was an unexpected and still new-made emperor; but these also were given him. A man of the people who was blind, and another who was lame, came to him together as he sat on his tribunal, begging for the help for their disorders which Serapis had promised in a dream; for the god declared that Vespasian would restore the eyes, if he would spit upon them, and give strength to the leg, if he would deign to touch it with his heel. Though he had hardly any faith that this could possibly succeed, and therefore shrank even from making the attempt, he was at last prevailed upon by his friends, and tried both things in public before a large crowd; and with success."[2] When Hadrian was dying, an old blind man from Pannonia touched him and received his sight.[3]

In particular there were two fertile sources of miracle stories in the ancient world. One was the temples of the Egyptian gods and goddesses, especially those of Serapis. The cult of Serapis was introduced into Greece; in the temple of Serapis at Delos there is a third century B.C. inscription which tells how the temple was founded, and there follows it a sixty-five line hymn, written by the priest Apollonius in honour of the god. In it Apollonius says that "he sang of thy miracles every day." [4]

Even more impressive is a papyrus account by an unnamed author, written in Memphis sometime in the second century A.D. The name of the god in this case is Imouthes, and it is the

[1]S. Dill; *Roman Society from Nero to Marcus Aurelius*, pp. 481, 482.
[2]Suetonius; *Life of Vespasian*, 7 (translated by J. C. Rolfe).
[3]*The History of the Caesars*, Hadrian, 25.
[4]Quoted in A. D. Nock, *Conversion*, pp. 51, 52.

personal account of a cure. "It was night, when every living thing save those in pain was at rest, and the deity appeared to me in special power. I was afire with a violent fever and convulsed with difficulty of breathing and cough from the pain arising from my side. Yet in a stupor of pain I was drowsing into sleep, and my mother in great distress at my tortures, as mothers will be for a child (and indeed she is by nature affectionate), sat by me enjoying no sleep at all. Then of a sudden – not in a dream or sleep – for her eyes were immovably open, but they did not discern precisely, for a divine vision came on her, inspiring fear and preventing her from discerning readily, she saw the figure (whether it was the god or his attendant) – anyhow it was someone passing high, of more than human stature, clothed in radiant linen, with a book in his left hand. He did but contemplate me from top to toe twice or three times and vanished. And she came to her senses, and quivering as she still was, tried to waken me. She found me rid of the fever and streaming with sweat, so she gave glory to the god for his appearance, and wiped the sweat off me and brought me to myself. She would fain have told me of the god's miraculous goodness, but I spoke first and told her all; for a dream had revealed to me all that she had seen with her eyes. The pains in my side ceased and the god gave me yet another remedy stilling distress, and I proceeded to proclaim the benefits which he had done to me."[1] The cults of the Egyptian gods produce story after story of miracles, and some of them are told with such a gentle factualness, like the story of Imouthes, that beyond a doubt something happened.

The other great source of miracle stories was the temples of Aesculapius, the Greek god of healing. Men called him the "Saviour of the world," "The great joy to all mortals," "The Lord Healer," "The Gentle One." Two of the great centres of Aesculapius were Epidaurus and Rome; and the shrines of Aesculapius were the Lourdes of the ancient world.

Of Epidaurus, Pausanias, the Greek traveller, historian and antiquarian, said: "Inside the enclosure pillars had been erected: of old there were many, but in my day six still remain, and on

[1]Quoted in A. D. Nock, *Conversion*, pp. 86, 87.

these are inscribed the names of the men and women who had been cured by Aesculapius with the addition of the diseases from which each patient suffered and the means of the cure." Strabo, the Greek geographer, said: "Aesculapius has his temple always full both of the patients and of those engaged in erecting votive tablets inscribed with the cures effected." One thing has to be said – no one goes to the trouble and expense of erecting a stone inscription of a cure *unless something happened*. One of the commonest methods of cure was to spend a night within the precincts of the temple. There is a record of a certain Alketas. "Though blind, he saw the dream-vision; the god seemed to come to him and to open his eyes with his fingers, and he first saw the trees that were in the temple. At daybreak he went away cured."

It was the same in the temple of Aesculapius at Rome. A certain Gaius was blind. "He received his sight in the presence of the people, who congratulated him because living virtues had operated." Lucius, who was "suffering from pleurisy and despaired of by all was cured." "To Julianus who was spitting blood and was given up as hopeless by everyone the god vouchsafed a dream-oracle to come, and from his triple altar to take grains of corn and eat them with honey for three days, and he was cured, and he came and returned thanks publicly before the people." "To Valerius Aper, a blind soldier, the god gave an oracle to come and take blood of a white cock with honey and to mix them into a salve and anoint his eyes for three days, and he received sight and came and gave thanks publicly to the god."[1]

It is beyond all doubt that in the ancient world things happened. We may call it superstition if we will, but men lived in a world where the divine was very near. They were *expecting* things to happen; and therefore they did. So far from discrediting the miracles of Jesus, this makes it even easier to accept and to understand them; for he would find an expectancy that he would never find today in our mechanized and scientific world.

Not only were miracles in the ancient world connected with the gods; there were also in the ancient world men who were

[1]The examples of the Aesculapius cures are taken from S. Angus, *The Religious Quests of the Graeco-Roman World*, pp. 429-433.

somewhere between the saint and the charlatan, and many miracles were accredited to them. One of the most famous was Apollonius of Tyana, who lived just at the beginning of the Christian era. His life was written by a Greek called Philostratus who tells of a series of miracles in India. "There also arrived a man who was lame. He was already thirty years old and a keen hunter of lions; but a lion had sprung on him and dislocated his hip so that he limped with one leg. However, when they massaged with their hands his hip, the youth immediately recovered his upright gait. And another man had had his eyes put out, and he went away having recovered the sight of both of them. Yet another man had his hand paralysed, but left their presence in full possession of the limb."[1]

One of the most notable wonders attributed to Apollonius happened at Rome, or so it was alleged. "Here too is a miracle which Apollonius worked. A girl had died just in the hour of her marriage, and the bridegroom was following her bier lamenting, as was natural, his marriage left unfulfilled, and the whole of Rome was mourning with him, for the maiden belonged to a consular family. Apollonius then, witnessing their grief, said: "Put down the bier for I will stay the tears that you are shedding for this maiden." And withal he asked what was her name. The crowd accordingly thought that he was about to deliver such an oration as is commonly delivered as much to grace the funeral as to stir up lamentation. But he did nothing of the kind, but merely touching her and whispering in secret some spell over her, at once woke up the maiden from her seeming death; and the girl spoke out loud and returned to her father's house, just as Alcestis did when she was brought back to life by Hercules. And the relations of the maiden wanted to present him with 150,000 sesterces, but he said that he would freely present the money to the young lady by way of a dowry. Now whether he detected some spark of life in her, which those who were nursing her had not noticed – for it is said that although it was raining at the time, a vapour went up from her face – or whether life was really extinct and he restored

[1]Philostratus, *Life of Apollonius of Tyana*, iii, 39 (translated F. C. Conybeare).

it by the warmth of his touch, is a mysterious problem which neither I myself nor those who were present could decide."[1]

We do not quote these miracles to set them beside the miracles of Jesus but to show that the age in which Jesus walked this earth was truly one when miracle was a commonplace. So far from making Jesus's miracles less likely, this makes them more likely; for the door of men's hearts was open to receive the divine.

Embroidery and exaggeration

It is further claimed that the stories of the miracles of Jesus come from an age given to embroidery and exaggeration. It is pointed out that there are discrepancies in the New Testament stories and that sometimes the element of wonder is accentuated. That is, at least to some extent, true; but it is not necessary to draw the inference that the miracle stories are works of fiction. The opposite conclusion is at least equally valid.

It is quite true that we can see the embroidery process at work even in the narratives of the Resurrection. In Mark, when the women came to the tomb early in the morning, they saw "a young man sitting on the right in a white robe."[2] In Matthew the figure in the empty tomb was an angel whose " appearance was like lightning and his raiment white as snow."[3] In Luke the women saw two men " in dazzling apparel."[4] In John, Mary Magdalene, as she stood weeping alone, saw "two angels in white where the body of Jesus had lain,"[5] sitting one at the head, and the other at the feet. Two things have to be noted.

(a) The fact of the empty tomb remains constant. The details of the narrative alter but the central fact does not. The one fact that matters remains the same.

(b) It can well be argued that the differences in detail are in fact the best proof of the truth of the narrative. No two people will tell the same story in the same way. If they do, there is at least a probability of collusion. If two witnesses agree in every slightest

---

[1]Philostratus, *Life of Apollonius of Tyana*, iv, 45 (translated F. C. Conybeare).
[2]Mark 16 : 5. [3]Matthew 28 : 2-5. [4]Luke 24 : 4. [5]John 20 : 12.

detail, it is by no means impossible that that agreement has been arranged, for it is not natural.

Collin Brooks in *More Tavern Talk* tells this of Sir James Hope Simpson, the banker. "It was necessary for Sir James Hope Simpson and me to provide one or two specimen signatures for a block-maker. As he signed the little cards, the banker said to me, apropos of nothing, 'Brooks, if ever you want to compare two signatures, and you hold one over the other against a window or a light, and they coincide exactly – one is a forgery'."[1]

A too meticulous correspondence, so far from being a sign of accuracy, could well be the sign of manipulation of the narrative.

The Natural Explanation

It is claimed that certain miracles of Jesus are susceptible of a perfectly natural explanation. That is true.

In the raising of Jairus's daughter all three gospel-writers who tell the story agree that Jesus said that the little girl was not dead but asleep.[2] It is claimed that this saying is to be taken literally and that the story is to be regarded, not as a miracle of healing, but as a masterpiece of diagnosis.

The one miracle which all four gospel-writers relate is the feeding of the five thousand.[3] It is suggested that what happened was this. The crowd was tired and hungry. Jesus suggested that something should be given them to eat. The meagre store the disciples possessed was brought forth; when that happened everyone who had anything, however small, contributed it to the general store and when all was collected there was more than enough for all. The miracle then becomes, not a physical one in which loaves and fish were multiplied, but a spiritual one in which a crowd of selfish people, reluctant to share, was turned into a crowd of generous people, eager to share, by the power of a generous example.

There is no doubt that some sort of explanation can be provided for many of the miracles. In a way that is to be expected.

[1]Collin Brooks, *More Tavern Talk*, p. 70.
[2]Matthew 9 : 24; Mark 5 : 39; Luke 8 : 52.
[3]Matthew 14 : 15-21; Mark 6 : 34-44; Luke 9 : 12-17; John 6 : 1-14.

As we come to understand more and more of the wonders of this amazing world and as we come to see more and more deeply into the mind of Jesus, it is inevitable that we will understand a little better how he worked. But when all is said and done along that line, it is quite impossible to rationalize *all* the miracles. There will always remain a stubborn residue beyond the mind of man to understand or to explain.

William Neil writes in *The Rediscovery of the Bible*: "One of the basic facts of the historical ministry of Jesus, as recorded on page after page of the gospel record, and one which is given pride of place in the earliest preaching, is that by his power countless pain-ridden, blind, deaf, paralysed, deranged mortals were healed of their diseases, restored to sanity, and in a few cases brought back to life. At a word, or with a touch, without preliminary diagnosis, medical treatment or convalescence, the sick and maimed and the mentally deranged were made whole. No amount of rationalization can dispose of this. If the gospel records are not to be dismissed as wholly fraudulent, we have to reckon with someone who had this unique power. The gospels merely give a handful of detailed cases out of what must have been thousands of cures."[1] Explanation can go so far but it cannot go the whole way.

When we add up the case against the miracles it comes to very little. True, Jesus lived and acted in an age when miracles were a commonplace. True, there is sometimes embroidery and sometimes discrepancy. True, natural explanations can be found for some of the miracles. But the miraculous element in the gospels remains. That is not to say that we are bound to accept every story as it stands in the most literal way; but no criticism can alter the fact that Jesus performed deeds which can only be described as miraculous works.

[1]William Neil, *The Rediscovery of the Bible*, p. 205.

CHAPTER THREE

The Case for the Miracles

We have looked at the factors in the situation which have been used to throw doubt on the historicity of the miracles of Jesus. We now look at the factors which entitle us to believe in them.

Before we begin this examination we estimate one argument at its correct value. There are people who dismiss the miracles with a wave of the hand as "impossible." Now "impossible" is a dangerous word to use. A very large number of things have been said to be impossible which have afterwards been done. That which is impossible in one age may become the commonplace of the next. When railways began it was declared impossible to travel at the colossal speed of thirty miles an hour because the human body would not stand it and would simply disintegrate. Not so long ago, it was considered impossible for a man-made machine piloted by a human being to break the sound barrier. Before the invention of proper anaesthetics, many an operation which is routine today was impossible. In ancient Greece any athlete would have said a four-minute mile was an impossibility. To an age without the necessary scientific equipment the ascent of Mount Everest would have been completely impossible.

In the last analysis, the miracles are a matter of *evidence*. It is true that the more unusual a thing is, the better must the evidence be before we can accept it; but if the evidence for an "impossible" thing is strong enough, it must be accepted as having happened.

The evidence of the gospels

It is obvious that the main evidence for the miracles is in the gospels. How far, then, can we regard their evidence as trust-worthy? Modern scholarship is fairly unanimously agreed that the dates of the gospels are: Mark about A.D. 60; Matthew and

__CHAPTER__

Luke between A.D. 80 and 90; John about A.D. 100.[1] For the moment we shall leave John out of the question for, as we shall later see, his gospel is written from a different point of view from the other three. Scholars are also agreed that both Matthew and Luke used Mark as their basis; and therefore the question really reduces itself to whether or not we can believe that Mark is giving us a trustworthy account of the life and works of Jesus.

A.D. 60 is thirty years or so after the death of Jesus, quite a considerable time. Why the delay in setting down a record of the life of Jesus? There were really four reasons for it.

(a) We have to think ourselves back to a time when printing had not been invented. Any book had to be hand written. A book the size of the New Testament would cost no less than the equivalent of two years' wages for a working man in scribes' fees alone; while papyrus, the substance on which books were written, was also very expensive. In those days books were very much rarer than they are today.

(b) Most of the first disciples were Jews. The only non-Jewish writer in the New Testament is Luke. Now the Jewish Rabbis did not write down their teaching. "Commit nothing to writing," was a Rabbinic maxim. Teaching was oral. The Jewish word for instruction is *mishnah* which literally means *repetition*. It was not until long after this time that Jewish teachers thought in terms of writing books. Even a Christian writer of Asia Minor, Papias, could say: "I supposed that the things I learned from books would not help me nearly so much as those I heard from the living and abiding voice."[2] This was neither a book-writing nor a book-reading age, at least in the circles in which Christianity began.

(c) So long as the apostles were alive books were not regarded as necessary. The apostles were at once the repositories and the guarantors of Christian truth and history; and while they were there no printed book was required.

---

[1]Succinct accounts of the formation of the gospels may be found in *Introducing the New Testament,* by A. M. Hunter, and *The Gospels, A Short Introduction,* by Vincent Taylor.

[2]Quoted in Eusebius, *Ecclesiastical History,* iii, 29.

(d) The first Christians vividly expected the Second Coming of Christ at any moment; and, since they were living in an age which was on the brink of passing away, the question of writing books simply did not arise.

The day came when these accounts had to be written down. Christianity left its Jewish cradle and went out into the Greek world and the Greeks were literary people. The apostles could not live for ever. In fact, with the single exception of John, they were all dead by A.D. 70. The Second Coming was obviously not going to be as immediate as they expected and they began to accept the fact that they were living in a more or less permanent situation. Above all, from the very beginning the Church had a missionary character; and the one thing a missionary needs above all is a clear and simple account of the story he tells which he can put into the hands of his converts for them to read it for themselves. Inevitably the written gospels came into being.

The time between

What we may well ask was happening in the time between? Could it not be that the story of Jesus was becoming distorted and embroidered in the years when it was passed from mouth to mouth before it was written down? There are certain things we must remember.

(a) From the very beginning the stories of Jesus's life were the material of the preachers. They would use such stories as illustrations all the way through. There would be an immediate result of that. Very early these stories would become stereotyped in form. The people to whom they were told were simple people, with a certain childlikeness of mind. Anyone who has to do with children knows that a favourite story must be told in exactly the same way every time. If a detail is altered or omitted, the teller must go back and tell it again. The child stereotypes a story and the ancient mind did exactly the same. It is true to say that there was practically no chance of the stories of Jesus being altered. They *had* to be told every time in exactly the same way. Distortion would have been next door to impossible in the circumstances of that age.

(b) It is a fact that the printed book has ruined the human memory. All that the modern man has to do, if he wants to find something, is to turn up the relevant book. But in the ancient world if a man wanted to possess a story or a passage he had to memorize it. The result was that the memory in the time of the early Church was much more retentive than it is today.

In ancient Greece there were many rhapsodists, as they were called, who could recite the whole forty-eight books of Homer's *Iliad* and *Odyssey* by heart. True, they were professionals, but one of the speakers in Xenophon's Symposium tells us that his father compelled him to learn the Homeric poems and that he could still recite them by heart.[1]

The power of memory in the older days can be very widely illustrated. "As late as 1542 Bishop Bonner ordered all the priests of the Diocese of London to learn the whole New Testament by heart. Ten years later Archbishop Holgate enjoined that all the vicars choral of York who were under forty years of age should commit to memory every week, 'One chapiter of Sancte Poule's Epistles in Latyne, after the translation of Erasmus, begynnynge at the first chapiter of the Epistle to the Romanes; and that the queresters do learn withoute booke every weke, or at leaste every fourtenighte, one chapiter of the Gospells, and th'Acctes of the Apostles to th'end, in th'Enlishe tonge, begynnynge at the firste chapitour of Sancte Matheue'."[2] When the Waldensians were being persecuted, an inquisitor, giving evidence at Beziers in 1246, declared: "I myself have seen a young cowherd, who for the space of only a year stayed in the house of a certain Waldensian heretic, who learned by heart and retained with such diligent attention and careful repetition in his mind what he had heard that within that year he had learned and remembered forty of the Sunday gospels (without counting the feast days), and he had learnt all these in his own tongue word for word, apart from other words of sermons and prayers."[3]

[1]Xenophon, *Symposium*, iii, 5; quoted F. G. Kenyon, *Books and Readers in Ancient Greece*, p. 13.
[2]Quoted H. G. G. Herklots, *Back to the Bible*, p. 65.
[3]Ibid, p. 69.

Eusebius met in Palestine a blind Egyptian, who had been exiled from his country, of whom he wrote that "he possessed whole books of the Holy Scriptures not on tablets of stone, as the Divine Apostle says, nor on the skins of beasts or on papyrus, which moth and time can devour, but – in his heart, so that, as from a rich literary treasure, he could, ever as he wished, repeat now passages from the Law and the Prophets, now from the historical books, now from the Gospels and the Apostolic epistles."[1]

When we think that the stories of Jesus were for the first thirty years largely dependent on the memory of men, we must remember that it was the ancient memory and not the modern memory in which they were stored.

The thought of that period of oral tradition, that thirty years in which the stories of Jesus were handed down from lip to lip, need not trouble us. In the nature of the age they would soon be unalterably stereotyped, and they were committed to a memory which as the Rabbis said, was "like a well-plastered cistern which would not lose a drop of water."

The Evidence of Mark

When we come to Mark himself, how shall we evaluate his evidence? In other words, where did he get his information? It would seem that his mother's house was the central meeting place of the Christian Church in its earliest days.[2] Mark would therefore have every chance of hearing stories of Jesus from those who had been with him in the days of his flesh. He had the closest possible relationship with Peter, for Peter can speak of him as "his son."[3]

Mark's gospel has a stronger claim to trustworthiness even than that. We have already referred to Papias, who lived in Asia Minor sometime in the second Christian century and was a great collector of facts about the New Testament and its writers. He says: "Mark, who was Peter's interpreter, wrote down accurately though not in order, all that he recollected of what Christ had said or done. For he was not a hearer of the Lord or a follower of his; he followed Peter, as I have said, at a later date, and Peter

[1]Ibid, p. 96.   [2]cp. Acts, 12 : 12.   [3]I Peter 5 : 13.

adapted his instruction to practical needs, without any attempt to give the Lord's words systematically. So that Mark was not wrong in writing down some things in this way from memory, for his one concern was neither to omit nor to falsify anything he had heard."[1] This means that the Gospel according to St. Mark is to all intents and purposes *the preaching material of Peter* and is therefore essentially *an eye-witness account of the ministry of Jesus*. It is true that Peter was a man of his age; it is true that he might see miracle where a modern, scientifically trained man would not. Even allowing for that, the fact that Mark's gospel embodies the preaching material of Peter puts the fact that Jesus worked miracles beyond all doubt.

There are two further strands of evidence which we may weave into our argument. First, the Jews never attempted to deny the miracles of Jesus. If they could have denied them, they would surely have done so. But in all their attacks on Jesus they never sought to deny that he had performed the most wonderful works. They might and did attribute these works to the power of the devil[2] but they never sought to argue that they did not take place.

Second, about the beginning of the second century a man called Quadratus wrote one of the first defences of Christianity. In an age when Christianity was under fire, many Christians addressed *Apologies* to the Roman government. The Apology of Quadratus is lost except for one fragment, but that one fragment is a notable piece of evidence. Here is what it says: "The works of our Saviour were always present, for they were genuine. I mean, those who were cured and those who did rise from the dead. They were not only seen being cured and rising, but they were also always present. They remained for some considerable time, not only when the Saviour lived among us, but after he had gone from us. So much so was this the case that *the lives of some of them reached down to our own times*."[3] When a man is writing a defence to a government

---

[1] Quoted in James Moffatt, *Introduction to the Literature of the New Testament*, p. 187.

[2] cp. Matthew 12 : 22-24.

[3] The original text is given in M. J. Routh, S.T.P., *Reliquiae Sacrae*, vol. i, p. 75.

he must be sure of his facts; and Quadratus is saying that until his own day men on whom miracles had been worked could actually be produced. If that was untrue nothing would have been easier than for the Roman government to brand it as a lie.

Jesus and his miracles

Before we complete our study of the evidence which can be adduced in support of the miracles we must turn to Jesus himself. There are at least two very significant incidents in his life.

(a) The temptations of Jesus[1] were such as could come only to a person who could do things which other men could not. The temptation to feed the mob or to provide shattering sensations are not temptations to an ordinary person, for he knows he could not do such things. The essence of the story is the temptation to use exceptional powers in a wrong way. The temptation narratives show that from the beginning Jesus was conscious of exceptional powers.

(b) When John the Baptist was in prison and eating his heart out in bleak despair doubts assailed him. He sent his disciples to ask Jesus if he really was the Messiah or if they must look for another. Jesus answered: "Go and tell John what you hear and see: the blind receive their sight, and the lame walk, lepers are cleansed, and the deaf hear, and the dead are raised up, and the poor have good news preached to them."[2] The gospel picture of Jesus is of one who was well aware of his powers.

The sinlessness of Jesus

Here we come on what for many is the one really convincing proof of the miracles. It is the Christian belief that Jesus was sinless. Now if a person is sinless two things are surely certain.

First, he can achieve powers which a sinful man can never reach. There is always a condition attached to any kind of excellence. The student who will not work will never reach the peaks of knowledge. The athlete who allows self indulgences will break no records and win no championships. The musician who will not

[1]Matthew 4 : 1-11; Luke 4 : 1-13.
[2]Matthew 11 : 1-5.

practise will never be a great executant. The painter who paints for money loses the vision. The author who writes simply to hawk his wares will never produce a masterpiece. In all men there is some essential human weakness; *but not in Jesus Christ.* He was without sin and therefore the way was open for him to achieve what sinning man can never rise to.

Second, he can be entrusted with powers which a sinful man can never be given. The Greeks had a symbolic myth of Gyges and his ring. Gyges descended into a chasm in the earth and found there a brazen horse. He opened the side of the horse and inside he found a dead man with a brazen ring on his finger. He drew off the ring and placed it on his own finger, discovering that so long as he wore the ring he was invisible; and he used the gift of invisibility to enter the king's chamber and murder him. It is the plain fact that if any ordinary, sinning man possessed the power to work miracles he would do far more harm than good, being unfit to possess it. But Jesus was sinless and therefore there could reside in him power which other men could never have.

In the last analysis Jesus did the things he did because he was the person he was. The evidence of the miracles is good and well-nigh unanswerable; but the best evidence of all is Jesus himself.

CHAPTER FOUR

The Healing of the Demon-possessed Man in the Synagogue

"THERE was in the synagogue a man with an unclean spirit and he cried out 'What have you to do with us, Jesus of Nazareth? Have you come to destroy us? I know who you are, The Holy One of God.' But Jesus rebuked him saying, 'Be silent and come out of him.' And the unclean spirit, convulsing him and crying with a loud voice, came out of him."   (Mark 1 : 23-26; cp. Luke 4 : 33-35.)

Mark being the earliest of the gospels, it is fitting that we should begin our study of the individual miracles of Jesus by studying the first of which Mark tells us. It is the healing of a demon-possessed man in the synagogue in Capernaum.

All through the gospels we meet people possessed by unclean spirits. In the time of Jesus almost everyone believed implicitly in these demons. They believed that the air was so full of them that it was not possible to insert the point of a needle into the air without touching one. According to some there were seven and a half million of them. A man had ten thousand on his right hand and ten thousand on his left. The ancient peoples lived in a haunted and terrifying world, for always the demons were waiting and watching to do them harm. As Harnack put it: "The whole world and the circumambient atmosphere were filled with devils; not merely idolatry, but every phase and form of life was ruled by them. They sat on thrones, they hovered around cradles. The world was literally a hell."[1]

Where did these demons come from? There were different theories. Some people believed that they were as old as the world itself and had always been there. Some believed that they were the spirits of wicked people who had died and were still carrying on

[1]A. Harnack, *Mission and Expansion of Christianity*, vol. i, p. 161.

their malignant work. The commonest belief connected them with Genesis 6: 1-8. The Jewish Rabbis developed that old story in this way. They said that there were two angels who disobeyed God and came to earth because they were attracted by the beauty of mortal women. Their names were Assael and Shemachsai. One repented and returned to God but the other remained on earth and gratified his lust; and the demons are the children that he begat and their children.

In any event, the universal belief was that the demons were invisible powers, intermediate between God and man, bent on injuring men. (The collective word for demons was *mazzikin*, which meant *those who work harm*.)

The demons, so the ancient peoples believed, could eat and drink and beget children. They lived in unclean places, such as tombs, and in places where there was no cleansing water. They lived in the desert where their howling could be heard; we still speak of *a howling desert*. They were specially dangerous to the lonely traveller, to the woman in childbirth, to the newly married bride and bridegroom, to children who were out after dark, and to voyagers by night. They were specially active both in the midday heat and between sunset and sunrise. They could transfer their own evil gifts to men. For instance, the evil eye which could turn good fortune into bad was a malign gift given to its possessor by a demon. They worked along with certain animals – the serpent, the bull, the donkey and the mosquito. The male demons were known as *shedim*, and the female as *lilin*, after Lilith. The female demons had long hair and were specially dangerous to children. That is why children had their guardian angels.[1]

The demons were responsible for seducing a man into falling to temptation. They were responsible, not only for mental illness and for seizures like epileptic fits, but also for all physical diseases. The Egyptians believed that there were thirty-six different parts of the body and that every one could be occupied by a demon. Commonly the demons settled on a man's food and so got inside him. There was a demon of blindness, a demon of leprosy and a demon of heart disease and of every other disease.

[1]cp. Matthew 18 : 10.

It may sound fantastic to us, but the ancient people believed implicitly in these demons. The strength of their belief is seen in the fact that in very ancient burying places many skulls have been found which have been trepanned. To trepan a skull is to bore a small hole in it. At a time when there were no anaesthetics and no surgical instruments, that must have been a formidable operation. The hole was too small to be of any practical medical use; the proof that it was done during life is that there is bone formation round its edges; and the purpose of the trepanning was to release the demon from the man through the hole in the skull.[1] The fact that doctors would undertake this operation and that patients would submit to it, under the conditions in which it had to be carried out, shows how real was the belief in demons.

One of the earliest medical works in the world is the Ebers Papyrus, which was discovered in Egypt in 1862. It dates back to about 1550 B.C. It has 108 sections of treatments and prescriptions for all sorts of illnesses and diseases. One is entitled, "Words to be spoken in the preparing of medicines for all parts of the body of a person who is ill." It is in the form of a prayer: "May Isis heal me even as she healed Horus of all the pains which his brother Set had inflicted on him when he killed his brother Osiris! O Isis, thou great enchantress, heal me, deliver me, from all evil, bad typhonic things, *from demoniacal and deadly diseases ... that rush upon me.*[2] Even the medical text-books of ancient times accepted the existence and power of the demons.

Exorcism

In view of this, exorcism was a regular practice. The Jews believed that Solomon, the wisest man who ever lived, had received from God the secret of exorcism. Josephus, the Jewish historian, says of him: "God enabled Solomon to learn the arts valid against demons, in order to aid and heal mankind. He composed incantations for the alleviation of disease, and left behind him methods of exorcism by which demons can be finally expelled

[1]cp. A. Rendle Short, M.D., F.R.C.S., *The Bible and Modern Medicine*, p.16
[2]Dorothy Fisk, *Bouquet for the Doctor*, p. 23.

from people, a method of healing which is extremely effective even in our own day."[1]

One of the things which strikes us straight away is the difference between the serene word of authority which Jesus used to cure the man who was demon-possessed and the elaborate spells which Jewish exorcists used. There was a certain magical root called *Baaras* which was supposed to be specially effective. But it was dangerous. When a man approached it, it shrank into the ground unless firmly gripped, and to grip it was certain death. So the ground round it was dug away; a dog was tied to it; the struggles of the dog uprooted it; and when the root was torn up the dog died as a substitute for the man.

Josephus himself in the passage quoted relates how he himself saw a Jewish exorcist, called Eleazar, exorcise a demon from a man in the presence of Vespasian, the Roman Emperor. Eleazar put a ring, entwined with the magical root, below the sufferer's nostrils. He then uttered incantations and drew the demon out through the nostrils with the ring. The proof that the demon had come out was this. A little distance away Eleazar had set a basin of water. He commanded the demon to upset the water as he went away. And in due time the basin was upset!

There is a world of difference between this superstitious mumbo-jumbo and the calm authority of Jesus. So great was the difference that the people who saw Jesus were astonished.

Jesus and the demons

We need not argue whether the demons were realities or not One thing certain is that in the time of Jesus people believed in them with terrified intensity. If a man believes he is ill, he will be ill. If a man believed that he was demon-possessed, then, illusion or no, he was definitely ill in mind and body.

A missionary tells a story from Africa. A lion was terrorising a village. Soldiers were called in to shoot it. The natives believed that if any person was touched by the froth from a lion's mouth he would die. When the lion was killed, one of the natives was accidentally touched by the froth on its mouth. There was not a

[1]Josephus, *The Antiquities of the Jews*, 8, 2, 5.

single diagnosable thing wrong with him, but *he was dead within a week*. He thought he was going to die and he did.

It was like that with demon-possession. With our modern knowledge, we may regard belief in demons and demon-possession as primitive superstitions; but they were real to the Jews of Jesus's day. If a man was mentally or physically ill, he believed a demon was responsible; and, if he got it into his head that a demon had entered him, he would most certainly become ill.

A more difficult question is: "Did Jesus believe in demons?" We may give two different answers to that question.

(a) It may well be that Jesus did. He did not come into this world to give men medical knowledge, and there is no reason to think that his medical knowledge would be any more advanced than that of the people of his day.

(b) Even if that were not so, Jesus would have had to assume the reality of the demons before he could cure those who believed they were possessed by them. A man may have persuaded himself into having a pain; but there is no point in telling him that his pain does not exist. It exists for him, and to cure it, it has to be treated as real. Whatever else may be true, Jesus had to treat the existence of demons as real or he could not even have begun to try to cure the people who were suffering from them.

In the synagogue at Capernaum

One Sabbath very early in his ministry Jesus went into the synagogue at Capernaum. He was speaking to the people with an authority and a wisdom that they had never heard before. In the congregation there was a demon-possessed man. Suddenly he began to cry out that Jesus was the Holy One of God who had come to destroy him. More than once the demon-possessed people are shown as recognizing Jesus for who he was.[1]

The ancients used to say of people whose minds were deranged that the gods had taken their wits away to put divine knowledge into them. But the real reason for the conduct of the demoniacs in the presence of Jesus was this. It was part of the standard belief that when the Messiah came the demons would be conquered and

[1] cp. Matthew 8 : 29.

destroyed. "And there shall be there no spirit of deceit of Beliar (that is, no evil spirit of the devil) for he shall be cast into the fire for ever."[1] The demoniacs heard Jesus speak; they heard his calm voice speaking with a wisdom and an authority that they had never heard before. They had a dim feeling that this was the Messiah; if so, it was the end of them, for man and demon were identified; and they saw in the coming of the Messiah their own destruction. That is why they greeted Jesus with fear.

When the man in the synagogue began his uproar, Jesus did not angrily order him to be ejected. He spoke his word of calm power. We know how the impact of a strong personality can cow an obstreperous person. Often, in a school, the pupils are in the assembly hall and the place is in an uproar; then their respected headmaster walks on to the platform and immediately there is silence. We may have seen a person blazing with anger silenced with a strong word. We may have seen a person, wrought up and hysterical, reduced to calmness by the force of someone else's personality. We may have seen someone shaking with fear become suddenly calm when someone calm and strong arrived on the scene. All these things are indications of what Jesus did. In the presence of his serene authority the demon was banished and the man's sanity restored.

Jesus and the bodies of men

First and foremost, this story tells us that Jesus was interested in the physical health of men. This happened in the synagogue. We might have expected that Jesus would be annoyed to have his address interrupted like this. But he was not only interested in men's souls; he was interested in their bodies too. He wanted to banish physical pain and distress and to help men in every way.

That wise Frenchman Montaigne has certain things to say about how we ought to be educated. He is sure that we ought not only to train our minds but to train our bodies too. He writes of the scholar: "It is not enough to strengthen his mind; his muscles must be strengthened as well. For the mind will be too sorely pressed if not aided by the body, and will have too heavy a task if

[1] *The Testament of Judah*, 25.

it must carry the burden alone." He goes on: "I would have his limbs trained no less than his brains. It is not a mind we are educating, nor a body. It is a man and we must not split him in two."[1]

It is a duty to keep our own bodies fit and to help others to do so, too. Francis Thompson was one of the greatest of English poets but there was a time when he was a homeless beggar, with broken boots and no shirt below his coat, tramping the streets of London starving and sleeping at night on the Embankment. He never forgot a certain Mr. M'Master, a shoemaker of Panton Street in London. One night when he was frozen with cold and sick with hunger, a hand was laid on his shoulder. It was this Mr. M'Master. "Is your soul saved?" said M'Master. Francis Thompson was a proud man even when he was starving. "What right have you," he blazed out, "to ask me that question?" "Ah, well," said M'Master, "if you won't let me save your soul, let me save your body!" And he took Thompson home with him and gave him food and shelter and work to do.

Religion does not mean only trying to save people's souls. It also means helping them to live healthy and happy lives. A man has a body and a soul and Jesus wanted to save both.

Jesus and action
This leads us on to see that Jesus did not confine his help for men to *words*; he turned it into *deeds*. Jesus had preached a most impressive sermon in the synagogue that day; but he did not stop there; he went on to help this suffering man with active kindness. Words without deeds are never enough.

Collin Brooks tells of a certain Quaker. An accident had wrecked the barrow of a street-trader. A crowd had gathered, and everyone was saying how sorry they were. Then the Quaker stepped forward and said to the crowd at large: "Friends, I am sorry £5. How much art thou sorry?"[2]

To be sorry for people is fine; but that sorrow has to be turned into deeds. When Frances Willard became a Christian she entered

[1]Montaigne, *Autobiography*, chapter 3.
[2]Quoted in Collin Brooks, *Tavern Talk*, p. 165.

two things in her diary: (i). "I have learned to believe in God in terms of Christ Jesus. What Paul says of Christ is what I say: the love John felt it is my dearest wish to cherish." (ii). "I shall be twenty years old in September, and I have as yet been of no use in the world."[1] She saw that no one can be a Christian without *doing* something about it.

One of the great missionaries was Adoniram Judson. In 1812 he sailed for Burma. He suffered terribly. The Burmese rulers did everything to stop him. He was starved to a skeleton; he was driven in chains across the desert until he prayed to die; his back was lacerated with the lash; his feet were torn to ribbons. He was two years in a foul prison and his arms and hands were for ever marked by the chains. He was actually under sentence of death. But he always worked on for Christ. After all this he went to the King of Burma to ask permission to go to a certain city to preach. The king said: "I am willing for a dozen preachers to go, but not you. Not with those hands! My people are not such fools as to take notice of your preaching, but they will take notice of *them*.[2] We are never Christian by simply *talking* about Jesus; we must act like him.

So in Mark's first miracle story we see Jesus bringing health to a demon-possessed man; and that story is meant to make us see that Jesus cared both for men's bodies and men's souls and believed that loving words must be turned into loving deeds.

[1]Quoted F. W. Boreham, *A Temple of Topaz*, p. 90.
[2]F. W. Boreham, *A Temple of Topaz*, pp. 136-138. Rita Snowden *If I Open My Door*, p. 230.

CHAPTER FIVE

The Lepers are Cleansed

AND behold, a leper came to him and knelt before him, saying, "Lord, if you will, you can make me clean." And Jesus stretched out his hand and touched him, saying, "I will; be clean." And immediately his leprosy was cleansed. And Jesus said to him, "See that you say nothing to any one; but go, show yourself to the priest, and offer the gift that Moses commanded, for a proof to the people."

(Matthew 8 : 2-4; cp Mark 1 : 40-42; Luke 5 : 12, 13, and for another case of the healing of leprosy, Luke 17 : 11-19.)

There was no disease more terrible than leprosy.[1] It was literally a living death. Josephus declared that the lepers were treated "as if they were, in effect, dead men."[2] For other diseases there were prescribed Rabbinic remedies but for leprosy there was none. If ever the disease did cure itself or was arrested, it was attributed to the direct agency of God.

In the Middle Ages leprosy was the scourge of Christendom. It was first brought into Britain by Roman soldiers who had served in Syria in 61 B.C. – so Pliny tells us; and in the Middle Ages it was very prevalent. For instance, Robert the Bruce, King of Scotland, was a leper.

There are still many lepers in the world. In Britain it is rare; in Palestine there are not many cases; but it still flourishes in India, in China, in Malaya and, worst of all, in Africa. It is still a serious disease in the West Indies and in the tropical parts of America; and almost within the last century it has found its way

---

[1]The facts about leprosy can be studied in the following sources: Leviticus chapters 13 and 14; in the *Mishnah* the tractate entitled *Negaim* deals with leprosy; it is contained in Herbert Danby's edition of the *Mishnah* pp. 676-696; the article on leprosy in Hastings' *Dictionary of Christ and the Gospels*, by E. W. G. Masterman; *The Bible and Modern Medicine*, by A. Rendle Short, pp. 74-83; *The Life and Times of Jesus, the Messiah*, by A. Edersheim, vol. i, pp. 491-496.

[2]Josephus: *The Antiquities of the Jews*, 3, 11, 3.

into the South Sea Islands. It is interesting to note that where it has been defeated it has been by following the Jewish methods of isolation.

In ancient days other nations did not isolate their lepers. Josephus tells us that "there are lepers in many nations, who are yet in honour, and not only free from reproach and avoidance, but who have been great captains of armies, and been entrusted with high offices in the commonwealth, and have had the privilege of entering into holy places and temples."[1] We remember, for instance, the case of Naaman, who was a mighty man although he was a leper, and the story of whose cure at the hand of Elisha is told in 2 Kings 5. But in the case of the Jews the leper was absolutely segregated.

It is of interest to note that the word *quarantine* comes from Jewish practice. In Italy in the fourteenth century people noticed that in times of plague the Jews were much less severely hit than anyone else. They came to the conclusion that the Jewish laws of uncleanness must have something to do with this, especially that which said that a Jew was unclean after he had touched a dead body. So the Italian authorities made a law that anyone who had been in contact with a suspected case of plague must be isolated for forty days. The Italian for *forty* is *quaranta*, hence the word *quarantine*.

As we read of the Jewish treatment of lepers we may think it cruel, as indeed sometimes it was, but it was this strict isolation which in the end defeated the disease. Leprosy is not specially infectious. It is specially dangerous to children and to young people, especially where food is lacking and cleanliness is not observed. But its great problem is that, in order to avoid isolation, people will not seek treatment in its early stages. They wait until it may be too late; and all the time they are a danger to their fellow men.

There are three kinds of leprosy.

(i) There is *nodular* or *tubercular* leprosy. It begins with an unaccountable lethargy and pains in the joints. Then there appear on the body, especially on the back, symmetrical discoloured

[1]Josephus: *The Antiquities of the Jews*, 3, 11, 4.

patches. On them little nodules form, which are at first pink and later turn brown. The skin becomes thick. The nodules gather specially in the folds of the cheek, the nose and the forehead. The whole appearance of the face is changed, until the man loses his human appearance, and, as the ancients said, comes to look like a lion or a satyr. The nodules grow larger and larger; they ulcerate and give out a foul discharge. The eye-brows fall out; the eyes become staring; the vocal chords become ulcerated, the voice becomes hoarse and the breath wheezes. The hands and the feet always ulcerate. Slowly the sufferer becomes a mass of ulcerated growths. The average course of the disease is nine years and it ends in mental decay, coma and death.

(ii) There is *anaesthetic leprosy*. The initial stages are the same; but in this kind the nerve trunks are affected. The affected area loses all sensation. This may happen without the sufferer realizing that it has happened, until he finds that there is no pain where pain should be. As the disease develops the injury to the nerves causes discoloured patches and blisters. The muscles waste away and the tendons contract until the hands become like claws. There is always disfigurement of the finger-nails. There ensues chronic ulceration of the feet and of the hands. There comes the progressive loss of fingers and of toes, until in the end a whole hand or foot may drop off. The duration of the disease is anything from twenty to thirty years. It is a kind of terrible progressive death of the body.

(iii) The third type of leprosy is the commonest of all and in it nodular and anaesthetic leprosy are mixed. A terrible fate came upon the man who suffered from it. There was no cure; he could not even look forward to speedy death; he had to live on while bit by bit his body decayed.

There is no doubt that there were many real lepers in Palestine in the time of Jesus. But leprosy is fully described in Leviticus 13 and 14 and it is clear that, in the time of Jesus, the term was used to describe other skin diseases. In particular it was used to describe *psoriasis*, which is a skin disease which covers the body with white scales. It is not a dangerous disease, although very difficult to cure, but, in the limited knowledge of the time, it was classed with leprosy and would very naturally give rise to the phrase "a leper as white as snow." Ring-worm, too, which was and is very common in the East, was classed with leprosy. The Hebrew word used for leprosy in Leviticus 13 and 14 is *tsaraath*. Now Leviticus 13 : 47 deals with a *tsaraath* of garments and Leviticus 14 : 34 with a *tsaraath* of houses. Such a blemish on a garment would be some kind of mould or fungus; and on a house it would be some kind of dry-rot in the wood or destructive lichen on the stone. It seems that in Jewish terminology the word *tsaraath* covered any kind of creeping skin disease; and, with their limited knowledge, the Jews classed both curable and incurable diseases as leprosy.

The treatment of the leper

Terrible as the disease of leprosy was in itself, it was made doubly terrible by the treatment of the leper. Whenever leprosy was diagnosed on examination by the priest, the leper was banished from human society. "He shall remain unclean as long as he has the disease; he is unclean; he shall dwell alone in a habitation outside the camp" (Leviticus 13 : 46). The leper had to go with rent clothes, dishevelled hair, and with a covering upon his upper lip, and as he went he had to cry, "Unclean, unclean" (Leviticus 13 : 45). In the middle ages when a man became a leper, the priest, having donned his stole and taken his crucifix, brought the man into church and read the burial service over him. For all practical purposes he was dead. In Palestine a leper could not enter the Temple, or go into Jerusalem or any walled city; the penalty for doing so was forty stripes. In the middle ages the leper was banished from all church services but was allowed to watch from outside; and in many old churches there can be seen to this day openings cut in the wall and focused on the Holy Table. They are called leper "squints" and through them the leper might look at the worship of God from afar. In Palestine it seems that, though the leper was barred from Jerusalem and all walled towns, he was not barred from the village synagogues, for the law lays it down that in the synagogue the leper must be the first to

come and the last to go, and that he must be confined to a little isolated chamber called the *Mechitsah*, ten feet high and six feet wide.

Contact with a leper defiled the person who had that contact. The
law enumerated sixty-one different contacts which brought
defilement, and the defilement which contact with a leper brought
was second only to the defilement caused by contact with a dead
body. If a leper so much as put his head inside a house everything
in it became unclean, even to the beams of the roof. It was forbidden to greet a leper even in an open place. No one might stand
nearer to a leper than four cubits away (a cubit is eighteen inches);
and if the wind was blowing from him in the direction of the
other person, the leper must stand at least one hundred cubits
away. A certain Rabbi Meir would not even eat an egg bought in a
street where a leper had passed by; another Rabbi boasted that he
always flung stones at lepers to keep them away; other Rabbis hid
themselves or took to their heels and ran whenever a leper
appeared even in the distance. No disease isolated a man from his
fellow men as leprosy did.

In this miracle we see Jesus healing a leper. Certain things stand
out when we remember what leprosy was like and how a leper was
treated.

First, it is astonishing that the leper came to Jesus at all. Certainly he would never have tried to approach an ordinary Rabbi;
he would have known that he would be treated with disgust.
Clearly the leper saw in Jesus something he had never seen in any
religious teacher before. Few stories tell us more about what Jesus
was like than this one does. It tells us that he was the most
approachable of people. It tells us that even those for whom no
one else cared knew that Jesus cared for them.

Dr. Paul Tournier in *A Doctor's Case Book* tells of a certain
patient's experience.[1] "At the medical conference at Annecy . . .
there was a former patient, M. Jean Gouzy, who told us movingly
of his first interview with the doctor at the sanatorium he had just
entered. This doctor had frankly told him that he must prepare
for a long stay; but he found it possible to add a brief, affectionate

[1] Paul Tournier: *A Doctor's Case Book in the Light of the Bible*, pp. 150, 151

remark that made the patient exclaim within himself: 'Here at last is someone who realizes that I want to live!' "

The leper came to Jesus because he felt that he had found someone who did not merely want to isolate him, but who wanted to give him life back again.

Some of the greatest of all modern missionary stories are of those who gave their lives to the lepers. Perhaps the greatest of all is the story of Joseph Damien. Early in the nineteenth century there were two Belgian brothers training in a certain college. The elder was to be a missionary in the South Sea Islands. But he became ill and it was clear that there was to be no recovery. The younger brother came and said: "Would it make you happier if I were to take your place as a missionary?" The older brother was past words, but his face lit up. So Joseph Damien decided to take his brother's place.

In time he went out to the South Sea Islands, and there he worked until he was thirty-three. Then one day he heard the bishop say that he had no one to send to the leper island of Molokai and that there the lepers were abandoned to their terrible fate without comfort and without help. So Joseph Damien went; and he found the lepers living a life that was no better than that of beasts. For sixteen years he lived among them. He built them a church; he built them better houses; he built them a better water supply; he loved them, cared for them, and when they died, he buried them. The world stood amazed at the Christ-like love of this Belgian priest.

Then one day he spilt some boiling water on his foot and felt no pain. Damien realized that he had developed leprosy. That day he went into the little church where he had preached so often; but this time he began his sermon, not with "My brothers," but with "My fellow-lepers." He was perfectly happy. He said that even if he could be cured by leaving the island he would never leave his lepers. So he worked on with death slowly eating away his body, but with his soul unconquered.

At last the end drew near. Two priests and sisters of charity knelt beside him. "When you are in heaven, Father," said one of the priests, "will you, like Elijah, leave me your mantle?" Joseph

Damien smiled: "What would you do with my mantle?" he said. "It is full of leprosy." And so in 1889 the man who had loved the lepers died.[1]

Damien was like Jesus Christ. He cared for the men for whom no one else cared. The leper saw in Jesus one who wanted him when everyone else would have run away with loathing.

Second, there is one phrase in the narrative which would have come to any orthodox Jew as shocking: "And Jesus put forth his hand and touched him." To touch a leper was to be defiled. We have seen how, even in an open space, there must be six feet between the leper and any other person. We have seen how there were Rabbis who threw stones at lepers to keep them away, who hid when they saw a leper coming, who took to their heels and ran to escape defilement. *And Jesus put forth his hand and touched the leper.*

Here is a picture of Jesus touching the untouchable. Here was not only a new idea of man but a new idea of God. The Jews always connected suffering and sin; they would have considered it as beyond belief that God could have anything to do with a leper. To this day primitive people have the same idea. "Do not missionaries report that disease is a defilement in the eyes of the savage? Even converts to Christianity do not dare to go to Communion when they are ill, because they consider themselves to be spurned by God."[2] Here was Jesus actually touching the man who was untouchable to man and to God alike, as the orthodox of his day believed.

One of the great missionary figures of this present century was Mary Reed. Born in America in 1858 she decided to give her life to work among women in India. For eight years she worked under the most trying conditions in Cawnpore and then her health broke down. She was sent to Pithoragarh in the Himalayas to recuperate. In the district she discovered a gathering of five hundred lepers, absolutely abandoned, without human help or comfort. She returned to Cawnpore, but she could not forget the lepers;

[1] This account of Joseph Damien is based on the story in Arthur Mee's *Children's Encyclopaedia*, vol. ii, p. 1144.

[2] Paul Tournier: *A Doctor's Case Book*, p. 98.

their terrible case haunted her. She worked for another year, and then her health so collapsed that she was sent home to America. Her case baffled the doctors; she had in particular a tingling pain in her forefinger and a strange spot on her face. At last she herself realized what was wrong – *she was a leper*. Then she did an amazing thing. She knelt down and thanked God for the leprosy which meant she might now go and work among the lepers. Only her doctors knew what had happened to her. Without telling even her parents that she was a leper she went back to India. When she got there she went straight to a leper settlement to which no one had ever gone before and told the lepers: "I have been called by God to come and help you." Slowly in Chandag there grew up, in spite of all the difficulties, a settlement and hospital which gave the lepers not only new bodies but new souls; all because one Christlike woman had used tragedy to give her the chance to touch the untouchables.[1]

It is always a Christlike thing to touch the untouchables. One of the most wonderful things Gandhi ever did in India was his work for the "untouchables," men and women of the lowest caste with whom no high-caste Indian would have even the remotest contact. They lived in the utmost poverty and squalor. Gandhi toiled to uplift them. He included them in his own community even when it meant that the orthodox Indians left him and withdrew their support. He gave them a new name; he called them the *Harijan*, which means "God's people."[2]

Jesus by his treatment of that leper that day demonstrated that God loves those whom no one else loves. To a follower of Christ there can be no one who is untouchable.

Satisfying the Law

One thing more we must notice. In Palestine in the time of Jesus there was a ritual through which a man recovered from leprosy must go before he could once again mix with his fellow men. Since real leprosy was incurable, it must in fact have held

[1] The story of Mary Reed is told in *More Yarns on Christian Pioneers* by Ernest H. Hayes, pp. 83-89.
[2] Quoted in *The Eyelids of the Dawn*, by Jack Winslow, p. 87.

good only for those who recovered from some of the other skin diseases which were reckoned as leprosy. It is described in Leviticus 14. The leper was examined by a priest. Two birds were taken and one was killed over running water. In addition there were taken cedar, scarlet and hyssop. These things were taken together with the living bird and dipped in the blood of the dead bird, and then the living bird was allowed to go free. The man washed himself and his clothes and shaved himself. Seven days then passed, and he was re-examined. He had then to shave his hair, his head and his eye-brows. Certain sacrifices were made – two male lambs without blemish, and one ewe lamb; three-tenths deals of fine flour mingled with oil; and one log of oil. (The amounts were less for the poor.) The restored sufferer was touched on the tip of the right ear, the right thumb and the right great toe with blood and oil. He was finally examined, and if he was found to be clear of the disease, he was allowed to go with a certificate that he was cured.

When Jesus had cured the man, he told him to go to the priests and go through this ritual. He was really telling him not to neglect the treatment available to him. We do not get miracles by neglecting the medical and the scientific treatments open to us. It is always necessary for us to do all that a man can do before we can expect the extra power of God to operate. A miracle comes not from a lazy waiting for God to do it all; it comes from the co-operation of the faith-filled effort of man with the divine grace of Almighty God.

CHAPTER SIX

The Healing of Soul and Body

AND when Jesus returned to Capernaum after some days, it was reported that he was at home. And many were gathered together, so that there was no longer room for them, not even about the door; and he was preaching the word to them. And they came, bringing to him a paralytic carried by four men. And when they could not get near him because of the crowd, they removed the roof above him; and when they had made an opening, they let down the pallet on which the paralytic lay. And when Jesus saw their faith, he said to the paralytic, "My son, your sins are forgiven." Now some of the scribes were sitting there, questioning in their hearts, "Why does this man speak thus? It is blasphemy! Who can forgive sins but God alone?" And immediately Jesus, perceiving in his spirit that they thus questioned within themselves, said to them, "Why do you question thus in your hearts? Which is easier, to say to the paralytic, 'Your sins are forgiven,' or to say, 'Rise, take up your pallet and walk'? But that you may know that the Son of man has authority on earth to forgive sins" – he said to the paralytic – "I say to you, rise, take up your pallet and go home." And he rose, and immediately took up the pallet and went out before them all; so that they were all amazed and glorified God, saying, "We never saw anything like this!"

(Mark 2 : 1-12; cp. Matthew 9 : 1-8; Luke 5 : 18-26.)

When Jesus came back to Capernaum, word of his coming soon spread all over the town. The people flocked to listen to his teaching. The houses of the poorer people in Palestine were very small and it would not be long before every available inch of space in the house was taken up. The door of the Palestinian house opened directly on to the street, and round the door the crowd gathered to listen until they had formed a solid mass. In Capernaum were four men who had a friend who was paralysed. They had heard of the wonderful things Jesus was able to do and they made up their minds to take their paralysed friend to him. But by the time they had met each other and got their friend arranged on his bed like a stretcher some little time had passed and when they arrived at the house, it was impossible to get near Jesus.

They were resourceful men, however, and were in no way daunted. Palestinian houses were small and square; to try to get in by the window was hopeless for the window was a little circle not more than eighteen inches across. But Palestinian houses had flat roofs. The roofs were used for many purposes; for storing things; for drying flax; as places of quiet and prayer, for in the crowded little one-room houses there was no other place where a man could be alone. For that reason there was almost always an outside stair up to them. The roof itself was built like this. First, beams were laid from wall to wall, perhaps three feet apart. Timber was usually scarce and the beams had to be sparingly used. Then the spaces between the beams were filled with close-packed reeds and rushes and the branches of thorn bushes. This was filled up and covered over with mortar; and the whole was topped with a covering of marled earth.

It was the easiest thing in the world to get on to the roof; the outside stair was there. It was not difficult to remove the filling between two of the beams; it did very little damage and the roof could easily be repaired. Oddly enough, one of the commonest ways of getting coffins in and out of one of these small houses was through the roof. "When Rabbi Huna died, his coffin could not be carried out through the door; so they determined to send it out through the roof."[1] So the four men decided that, since they could not bring their friend to Jesus through the door, they would bring him through the roof. They did so and let him down at Jesus's feet.

The faith of friends

When Jesus saw their faith, he responded at once. Here is a lovely thing – *this man was saved by the faith of his friends.* All through this story the man is strangely passive. He never speaks; and he never acts, until after he is cured. It may well be that he had come to a stage of utter pessimism in which he was quite

[1] Quoted by J. J. Wetstein in his commentary on the passage.

sure that nothing anyone could do would ever make him well again. His friends may even have carried him to Jesus against his will. In any event, he was saved by the faith of his friends.

That happens quite often in life. It is often those who love us and believe in us who do great things for us. Thomas Carlyle used to say that to the end of his life the greatest influence on him was the voice of his mother coming from the kirkyard in Ecclefechan and saying to him: "Trust in God and do the right." When Augustine, who was to become so great a scholar and saint and preacher, was a young man, he lived anything but a good life. His mother was sorely troubled about it; she wept for him and she prayed for him. She told about her worries, her tears and her prayers to a bishop of the Church. "It is impossible," he said, "that the child of such tears and prayers should perish." It was his mother's efforts which made Augustine what he was. H. G. Wells tells us of a time early in his career. He was just becoming famous and all kinds of new temptations were coming into his life. He had just been married. And he tells us that it was just as well for him that at home there was one who was so pure and sweet that he would have been ashamed to appear before her drunken or unshaven or squalid or base. It was the influence of one whom he loved which kept him right.

One of God's ways of keeping us right and of doing great things for us is through those whom we love and who love us. We can never be sufficiently grateful for them.

Your sins are forgiven

When the man was let down in front of him, Jesus began by saying what sounds very surprising. He did not say anything about the man's paralysis but, "Your sins are forgiven." It seems a queer way to start. But there was good reason why Jesus should start that way. It was the belief of the Jews that all sickness and all misfortune were due to sin. When Job was ill and in misfortune, his friend Eliphaz said to him: "Think now, who that was innocent ever perished? Or where were the upright cut off?"[1] The Psalmist writes: "I have been young and now am old; yet I

[1] Job 4 : 7.

have not seen the righteous forsaken, nor his children begging bread."[1] The Jewish wise men, the Rabbis, said the same thing. Rabbi Ammi said: "There is no death without guilt, no suffering without sin." Rabbi Alexandrai said: "No man gets up from his sickness till God has forgiven all his sins."[2] Rabbi Chija ben Abba said: "No sick person is cured from his sickness until all his sins are forgiven him."[3]

We do not now believe that a man is ill because he has committed some sin; but the Jews believed it. The paralysed man believed it. More than that – it is likely that the paralysed man *had* committed some sin and was haunted by the memory of it. Most likely his paralysis had actually been brought on by the thought of his sin. If a man's mind is sick, his body will be sick, too. Many a physical illness is brought on by a mental state. We can take a very simple example – if we have an appointment that we do not want to keep, we often wake up with a headache or a cold or a sore throat or a lost voice.

The doctors recognize this. Paul Tournier in *A Doctor's Case Book* quotes some amazing instances from his own experience. "There was, for example, the girl whom one of my friends had been treating for several months for anaemia, without much success. As a last resort my colleague decided to send her to the medical officer of the district in which she worked in order to get his permission to send her to a mountain sanatorium. A week later the patient brought word back from the medical officer. He proved to be a good fellow and he had granted the permit, but he added: 'On analysing the blood, however, I do not arrive at anything like the same figures as those you quote.' My friend, somewhat put out, at once took a fresh sample of the blood, and rushed to his laboratory. Sure enough, the blood count had suddenly changed. 'If I had not been the kind of person who keeps carefully to laboratory routine,' my friend's story goes on, 'and if I had not previously checked my figures at each of my patient's visits, I

[1]Psalm 37 : 25.
[2]These sayings are quoted in C. G. Montefiore, *The Synoptic Gospels*, vol. i, pp. 43, 44.
[3]Quoted in J. J. Wetstein's commentary on the passage.

might have thought that I had made a mistake.' He returned to the patient and asked her: 'Has anything out of the ordinary happened in your life since your last visit?' 'Yes, something has happened,' she replied. 'I have suddenly been able to forgive someone against whom I bore a nasty grudge; and all at once I felt as if I could at last say "Yes" to life!' " Her mental attitude was changed and the very state of her blood changed along with it. When her mind was cured, her body was also on the way to being cured. St. Thomas Aquinas said: "Grace flows from the soul to the body."

Dr. Tournier tells of one of his own cases. He was treating a woman for nervous obsessions; she was so nervous that she was in agonizing distress. Then quite suddenly one Good Friday her whole life changed; she felt that God had sent her peace and her anxiety was gone. All the time she had been so mentally upset she had suffered seriously from anaemia. "Throughout all these years preparations of iron and of liver-extract had never succeeded in raising the level of haemoglobin above 55 per cent. Now it is a fact that three weeks after the disappearance of the psychological symptoms, and without her having undergone any further anti-anaemic treatment, the haemoglobin level was found to be 78 per cent."[1]

The extraordinary thing is that when Jesus began the cure of this paralysed man by freeing him from the feeling of guilt, he was treating him in the way which the most up-to-date twentieth century medical knowledge would use. This man had sinned; the sin haunted him and its effect came out in the paralysis of his body. When he knew that his sins were forgiven he was healed.

There is something for everyone to remember here. We can never have a fit body until we have a clean heart and a mind at rest. It is not possible to separate us into parts. Our bodies cannot be cured apart from our minds and our hearts. That is why only Jesus can really make us truly healthy for only he can cleanse us in mind and heart.

[1]These two instances are taken from Paul Tournier, *A Doctor's Case Book in the Light of the Bible*, pp. 151, 152 and 180, 181.

Jesus deals with his opponents

But no sooner had Jesus said to this man: "Your sins are forgiven you," than his enemies began to criticize him. They were saying to themselves: "No one can forgive sins except God. This Jesus is insulting God by claiming to do what only God can do." Jesus knew what they were thinking. So he decided to put the thing to a most practical test. He said: "It is your belief that if a man is ill he must have sinned, isn't it?" They could not deny that. Jesus went on: "Is it easier to say, 'Your sins are forgiven,' or to say, 'Get up and walk'?" They had no answer to that. Then Jesus said to the man, "Get up. Lift up your bed and go away home." And he did. The scribes were baffled because, on their own admission, the man could not be cured until he was forgiven. Now he had been cured and therefore they had to admit that he must have been forgiven. What Jesus did was this. He came to this man and he said to him: "You committed a sin long ago. You have worried about it all your life until you have worried yourself into paralysis. You think that God is angry with you. But he is not. He wants nothing more than to forgive you. He loves you." When the man discovered that, such a weight was lifted off his mind that he was cured. Jesus worked this miracle by telling this man about the miracle of the love of God.

This story reminds us how much we owe to those who love us. It reminds us that we can never be fit in body until we are pure in heart and clean in mind. It reminds us that when we have sinned the miracle of God's love forgives us, and that we could never have known that God was like that unless Jesus had come to live and to die to tell us that it was so.

CHAPTER SEVEN

The Woman in the Crowd

AND there was a woman who had had a flow of blood for twelve years, and who had suffered much under many physicians, and had spent all that she had, and was no better but rather grew worse. She had heard the reports about Jesus, and came up behind him in the crowd and touched his garment. For she said, "If I touch even his garments I shall be made well." And immediately the haemorrhage ceased; and she felt in her body that she was healed of her disease. And Jesus, perceiving in himself that power had gone forth from him, immediately turned about in the crowd, and said, "Who touched my garments?" And his disciples said to him, "You see the crowd pressing around you, and yet you say, 'Who touched me?'" And he looked around to see who had done it. But the woman, knowing what had been done to her, came in fear and trembling and fell down before him, and told him the whole truth. And he said to her, "Daughter, your faith has made you well; go in peace, and be healed of your disease."
(Mark 5 : 25-34; cp. Matthew 9 : 20-22; Luke 8 : 43-48.)

When this incident happened Jesus was in the middle of a crowd. He was on his way to the house of Jairus, the ruler of the synagogue, whose little daughter was desperately ill. In the crowd there was a woman. For twelve years she had suffered from a most distressing trouble, an incurable haemorrhage.

This trouble was very common in Palestine. The Talmud lays down no fewer than eleven different cures for it. Some were tonics and astringents which might have been quite effective in stopping the issue of blood; some were merely superstitious remedies. One was to carry the ashes of an ostrich-egg in a linen bag in summer and a cotton rag in winter. Another was to carry about all the time a barley-corn which had been found in the dung of a white she-ass. We can be sure that this woman had tried every remedy, the real remedies of the physicians and the superstitious remedies, too. The only result was that, so far from being better, she grew worse

The real tragedy of an illness like that was that, according to the Jewish law, it made a woman unclean. That is to say, she could never attend a synagogue service; no one could lie on the same bed as she; no one could even sit on the same chair. She was cut off from all religious and social life. The law regarding this is in Leviticus 15 : 25-27:

> "If a woman has a discharge of blood for many days, not at the time of her impurity, or if she has a discharge beyond the time of her impurity, all the days of the discharge she shall continue in uncleanness, as in the days of her impurity, she shall be unclean. Every bed on which she lies, all the days of her discharge, shall be to her as the bed of her impurity; and everything on which she sits shall be unclean, as in the uncleanness of her impurity. And whoever touches these things shall be unclean, and shall wash his clothes and bathe himself in water, and be unclean until the evening."

So this woman had not only the pain and the trouble of her illness to bear; she had also the loneliness which came from being shut out from the worship of God and from the society of her friends, and even of her family.

A sufferer's last hope

In her distress and pain this woman had heard of Jesus; but her problem was how to make contact with him. She could not go to him and ask him to lay his hands on her, because she was unclean and no one at all should touch her. It was even wrong for her to mingle with the crowd, because everyone she touched in the crowd became unclean from that contact. But her last hope was in Jesus and she could not stay away. So she was in the crowd on this day.

She could not go up to Jesus and tell him what was the matter; she would have been ashamed to make public her affliction. She wondered what she could do. In the crowd she had succeeded in getting close to Jesus, and suddenly she decided what she would do.

Mark (Mark 5 : 27) says that she touched his garment. Matthew (Matthew 9 : 20) is more detailed. He says that she touched *the fringe* of his garment.

In the days of Jesus the devout Jews wore tassels at the corner of their outer garments. They did that in accordance with the law which was laid down in Numbers 15 : 37-41.

> "The Lord said to Moses 'Speak to the people of Israel, and bid them to make tassels on the corners of their garments throughout their generations, and to put upon the tassel of each corner a cord of blue; and it shall be to you a tassel to look upon and remember all the commandments of the Lord, to do them.'"

The fringes were like tassels, and they were put on the edges of the outer garment, so that every time a Jew looked at them, when he put on his clothes in the morning, when he took them off at night, and as he saw them all through the day, he would remember that he was a Jew, one of God's chosen people, and pledged to keep God's commandments.

Jesus had tassels like that on his robe; and it was one of these that this woman dared to touch. No sooner had she touched it than she knew that she was cured. But then there happened what must have been to her a terrible thing. Jesus stopped and demanded who had touched him. There was only one thing to do. It meant advertising her shame. It meant letting everyone know of her illness and how, by touching Jesus's garment and by being in the crowd at all, she had broken the law. Trembling and embarrassed she confessed all; but she found Jesus very kind and he sent her on her way cured because of the faith that she had shown.

Out of the crowd

This miracle shows us two things about Jesus. It shows him, in the midst of a crowd, giving all his attention to one poor woman. When we read this story with insight and with understanding, we cannot help feeling that when the woman was face to face with him, for Jesus the crowd ceased to exist. At that moment this woman was the one person who mattered; she was just one of the crowd but he gave all of himself to her. He might have said that he was on the way to the house of the Ruler of the synagogue and that he had no time to be bothered with her; but no – Jesus had time and courtesy and kindness to give all of himself to one unimportant woman. For Jesus she was not lost in the crowd; because she needed him, she was the one person who mattered at that moment.

One of the signs of a really great person is that he is interested in individuals. James Agate has a description of the character of G. K. Chesterton: "Unlike some other thinkers, Chesterton understood his fellow men; the woes of a jockey were as familiar to him as the worries of a judge. . . . Chesterton more than any man I have ever known had the common touch. He would give the whole of his attention to a boot-black. He had about him that bounty of heart which men call kindness and which makes the whole world kin."[1] On the other hand, Clifford Bax writes of the attitude of that strange mystical writer George Russell, better known as Æ. Russell, who would talk endlessly to anyone who would listen to him. Wonderful talk it was, but Russell was not in the least interested in the person to whom he talked. "People were not real to Æ. Never once did he show any interest in a man's background, in his hopes, in his troubles. We were shadows, shadows and listeners."[2] That is the difference between the Christian and the non-Christian attitude. The Christian is intensely interested in individual men and women; the non-Christian, even if he is a mystic, is not.

Evelyn Bell, in her autobiography, tells two lovely stories which illustrate this interest in individuals which really great men have. She was quite a young girl in London when Kitchener came home after avenging the death of General Gordon in the Sudan. London gave him a triumphant welcome. She went to see it but she was so small that the procession passed and she saw nothing at all. She wandered about disconsolate and some hours later found herself in Portland Square, still sad that she had not seen Kitchener. It was raining. A hansom cab drew up at a door. The

[1] James Agate, *Thursday and Fridays*, p. 66.
[2] Clifford Bax, *Some I knew well*, p. 88.

driver stood by at the salute and two figures emerged from a house. One was little and spare; the other, tall and thin. She recognized them at once from their photographs. The one was Lord Roberts; the other was Kitchener. Impulsively Evelyn Bell ran forward. "Kitchener! Kitchener! Kitchener!" she cried, as she had heard the crowds shout, and she caught Kitchener's hand in hers. Lord Roberts laughed and jumped into the cab. Kitchener paused a moment; then his face relaxed in a smile; he lifted his hat and bowed to the young girl with as much courtesy and elegance as he might have shown to the Queen. "Bare-headed," writes Evelyn Bell, as she remembered, "he stood in the rain; he could not have done more for the Queen. I could never feel ordinary again." Kitchener had this ability to give all of himself to a single unimportant person.

Evelyn Bell was a student of the violin. The famous violinist Kubelik was to give a concert in Queen's Hall in London. Her teacher gave her an introduction to him and she went to ask him for a ticket, for no tickets were to be found. Kubelik told her that he could do nothing, that there was not room for a mouse in Queen's Hall for that concert. "What am I to do about the concert? she said, almost weeping, "If I can't get a ticket, I'll never hear you play." "O, but you will!" said Kubelik. "Sit there!" And Kubelik played his concert programme to an audience of one. There you have this same God-given ability to give the whole self to one person.

Paul Tournier writes: "My patients very often say to me: 'I admire the patience with which you listen to everything I tell you.' It is not patience at all, but interest."[1] Later on he writes: "God says to Moses: 'I know you by name' (Exodus 33 : 17). He says to Cyrus: 'it is I, the Lord, who call you by your name' (Isaiah 45 : 3). These texts express the essence of the personalism of the Bible. One is struck, on reading the Bible, by the importance in it of proper names. Whole chapters are devoted to long genealogies. When I was young I used to think that they could well have been dropped from the Biblical Canon. But I have since realized that these series of proper names bear witness to the fact that, in

[1]Paul Tournier, *A Doctor's Case Book*, p. 40.

the Biblical perspective, man is neither a thing, nor an abstraction, neither a species, nor an idea, that he is not a fraction of the mass, as the Marxists see him, but that he is a person."[1]

As we see Jesus, amidst that crowd, giving the whole of himself to that one, poor, embarrassed woman, we see that he did not think in terms of crowds; he thought in terms of individual men and women. God is like that. As Augustine said long ago: "God loves each one of us as if there was only one of us to love."

The cost of healing

The second thing that this incident tells us about Jesus is that every time he healed someone, it cost him something.

It is impossible to help anyone without cost to oneself. Paul Tournier gives two instances of that. He writes: "Dr. Racanelli of Florence, who has the gift of healing, and who practises the laying on of hands in all kinds of nervous affections, has said that he has a very strong sensation of this force working in him and passing through his hands. Whereas his patients are left with a sense of well-being and calm, he himself experiences such fatigue that he is compelled to observe a strict austerity of life when he is practising this type of treatment, so as not to become exhausted. When we discussed this subject another doctor from Florence told us that he had also practised this kind of healing with success: but, he said, he had to give it up because he himself was too sensitive to it. 'Thus,' he told us, 'for example, my patient suffering from angina would find that his angina had suddenly gone; but I myself at once suffered a similar attack'." Tournier goes on: "When I told my wife about this, we were reminded of a fact we had frequently observed: that we regularly had a quarrel ourselves during the evening of a day in which we had been able to help in the reconciliation of another married couple."[2]

No real help can be given except at the cost of something of oneself. It was said of a rich man who was very generous: "With all his giving, he never gives himself."

[1] Paul Tournier, *A Doctor's Case Book*, pp. 123, 124.
[2] Paul Tournier, *A Doctor's Case Book*, p. 152.

Think what the life of Jesus must have been like. There were days when from morning to evening he was surrounded by sick people begging for his help, and always he freely gave it; and every time he gave it, it cost him something. Once Bernard Shaw said: "I want to be thoroughly used up when I die." All the time Jesus was using himself up. It was not simply wisdom he gave to men; it was not simply healing; it was *himself*. And so with those who would follow in his steps. Their help to others must cost them something or it can have no real effect.

This incident tells us how a woman came in her despair to Jesus, and how the very desperation of her faith gained her the cure she longed for. It shows us that Jesus had this amazing ability to give all of himself to an individual. It shows us what it cost him to help and heal.

CHAPTER EIGHT

The Defeat of the Demons

THEY came to the other side of the sea, to the country of the Gerasenes. And when he had come out of the boat, there met him out of the tombs a man with an unclean spirit, who lived among the tombs; and no one could bind him any more, even with a chain; for he had often been bound with fetters and chains, but the chains he wrenched apart, and the fetters he broke in pieces; and no one had the strength to subdue him. Night and day among the tombs and on the mountains he was always crying out, and bruising himself with stones. And when he saw Jesus from afar, he ran and worshipped him; and crying out with a loud voice, he said, "What have you to do with me, Jesus, Son of the Most High God? I adjure you by God, do not torment me." For Jesus had said to him, "Come out of the man, you unclean spirit!" And Jesus asked him, "What is your name?" He replied, "My name is Legion; for we are many." And he begged Jesus eagerly not to send them out of the country. Now a great herd of swine was feeding there on the hillside; and they begged him, "Send us to the swine, let us enter them." So Jesus gave them leave. And the unclean spirits came out, and entered the swine; and the herd, numbering about two thousand, rushed down the steep bank into the sea, and were drowned in the sea.

The herdsmen fled, and told it in the city and in the country. And people came to see what it was that had happened. And they came to Jesus, and saw the demoniac sitting there, clothed and in his right mind, the man who had had the legion; and they were afraid. And those who had seen it told what had happened to the demoniac and to the swine. And they began to beg Jesus to depart from their neighbourhood. And as he was getting into the boat, the man who had been possessed with demons begged him that he might be with him. But Jesus refused, and said to him, "Go home to your friends, and tell them how much the Lord has done for you, and how he has had mercy on you."

(Mark 5 : 1-19; cp. Matthew 8 : 28-34; Luke 8 : 26-40.)

This miracle happened on the other side of the Sea of Galilee,[1] and later on Mark tells us that it was in the area of Decapolis.[2] Decapolis literally means The Ten Cities. Near to the River

[1]Mark 5 : 1. [2]Mark 5 : 20.

Jordan, and mainly on the eastern side of it, there was a confederation of ten cities. They were Scythopolis, the only one on the western side, Pella, Dion, Gerasa, Philadelphia, Gadara, Raphana, Kanatha, Hippos and Damascus. They were mainly Greek cities and had been founded following upon the campaigns of Alexander the Great. In character and in population they were not Jewish but Greek.

They were actually within the territory of Syria but were very largely independent. They had their own councils and they minted their own coins; they had the right to govern not only themselves but also the area round about them; and they had the right to form a confederation for mutual defence and for purposes of trade and commerce. Down to the times of the Maccabees, in the middle of the second century B.C., they remained independent. At that time they were conquered by the Maccabaean troops and brought under Jewish rule. In 63 B.C. the Roman general Pompey liberated them. Once again they enjoyed a semi-independence, although they were liable to Roman taxation and Roman military service. They were not garrisoned, but they sometimes had to serve as bases for Roman operations in the East. At this time Rome governed this part of the world not by direct rule, but by allowing subject kings to carry on the government of their own states. That meant that Rome was able to give little actual protection to these ten cities and so they were still allowed to band themselves together against both Jewish and Arab attack.

They were all very beautiful cities; they had their temples and their amphi-theatres and their gods. They were stubbornly Greek and proud of it. How Greek they were may be seen from the fact that from Gadara alone came Philodemus, the famous Epicurean philosopher, Meleager, the master of the Greek epigram, Menippus, the famous satirist, and Theodorus, the rhetorician, who was tutor to no less a person than Tiberius, the Roman Emperor.[1] It can be seen that this is more than a miracle story; it is the first foretaste of the going out of the gospel to the Gentile world.

---

[1]Full information about the cities of the Decapolis is to be found in E. Schürer, *The Jewish People in the Time of Jesus Christ*. Division 2, volume 1, pp. 57-149.

The part of the coast of the Sea of Galilee where this miracle happened was a grim place. H. V. Morton describes it: "We made for the opposite bank, where the hills of Gergesa seemed even more terrible and inhospitable as we drew nearer. They looked as they must have looked in the time of Christ: thirsty, burnt-up hills scored with thousands of thin slashes, the marks of dried-up torrents, and invaded by dark gullies in which no man would venture unarmed."[1] In the lime-stone rocks which came down to the lake-side there were many caves and these caves were used as tombs. Here was a fitting place for a demon-possessed man to have his habitation; for it was believed that the demons were specially present in woods and gardens and vineyards and desolate spots, and above all among tombs. No man would have come near this poor, unbalanced sufferer anyway; but the very fact that he dwelt among these grim tombs made doubly sure that no man would approach.

If are we to believe that Mark is telling us his story with due regard to chronological order, the time of this incident makes the whole scene still more eerie. Mark tells us that it was evening when Jesus and his friends began their voyage across the lake.[2] At its widest the Sea of Galilee is 8 miles across and at this point it is about 5 miles. So it would be dark when Jesus and his friends arrived. It would be in the light of the moon that the madman saw him when he was still a good distance away.[3] At such a time popular ideas held that the demons were even more dangerous. It was during the night-time and before cock-crow that they were specially dangerous. It was perilous to greet anyone during the dark hours for he might well be a demon. To go out at night without a lantern or a flaming torch was to court disaster. Even to sleep alone in an empty house was a dangerous thing. It was just at such a time that the demons made their attack.

So, then, the story is set in a grim scene and at an eerie hour.

It is clear that the man was dangerous. Efforts had been made to bring him under control, but there were no fetters which could bind him.[4] He must have been in the habit of wandering about

[1]H. V. Morton, *In the Steps of the Master*, p. 197.
[2]Mark 4 : 35.   [3]Mark 5 : 6.   [4]Mark 5 : 4.

naked, for, when he was cured, the people noted that he was clothed.[1] W. M. Thomson tells how when he journeyed in Palestine such afflicted sufferers were still to be met: "But there are some very similar cases at the present day – furious and dangerous maniacs, who wander about the mountains and sleep in caves and tombs. In their worst paroxysms they are quite unmanageable, and prodigiously strong . . . And it is one of the most common traits of this madness that the victims refuse to wear clothes. I have often seen them absolutely naked in the crowded streets of Beirut and Sidon. There are also cases in which they run wildly about the country and frighten the whole neighbourhood."[2]

The cure

When this man saw Jesus in the distance, he besought Jesus not to torture him. We have already seen that it was to be a feature of the Messianic age that the demons were to be banished and defeated; and the man felt himself to be so identified with the demons whom he believed to be possessing him that the very presence of Jesus made him feel that he would be destroyed.

This is one of the most interesting of all the miracles. It was the most stubborn case Jesus ever handled, so far as his miracles are recorded in the gospels, for he had to make three attempts before he could master the madness which so gripped the man. Jesus began in the way in which he always treated those whose minds were deranged. He began with a calm, strong summons to the demon to come out of the man.[3] But so serious was the man's case that this had no effect. Then Jesus asked the man his name.[4] There was a special point in that. In ancient times it was held that knowledge of a name gave special power over the person whose name it was. Exorcists regularly began with a demand to their patient to tell his name. An ancient magical formula begins: "I adjure thee, every demonic spirit, Say whatsoever thou art."

The man gave a curious answer. He said that his name was Legion. There were very likely two reasons for that. In the ancient

[1] Mark 5 : 15.
[2] W. M. Thomson, *The Land and the Book*, p. 148.
[3] Mark 5 : 8.   [4] Mark 5 : 9.

days men believed that the number of demons was well nigh beyond counting. They were "like the earth that is thrown up around a bed that is sown." There were ten thousand at a man's right hand and ten thousand at his left. Lilith, the queen of the female demons, had no fewer than 180,000 followers. The man was living in an occupied country. Often he had seen a Roman legion clanking along the road in full armour. There were 6,000 men in a legion; and he felt that not one demon but a whole battalion had got inside him.

But there may be another reason why the name Legion sprang to his lips. Ordinarily the Roman legions were well-disciplined. But even these legionaries could sometimes be guilty of what we would now call atrocities. It may well be that sometime, perhaps in his youth, this man had been the victim of such atrocities; and it may well be that it was that experience which drove him mad. It may be that, when he gave his name, he also gave a clue to the very thing that had made him the desperate creature that he was.

Jesus could see now what a difficult human problem he was up against. And yet by this time there was a little breach in the man's defences, for he was speaking – he believed that the demons were speaking in him – and asking Jesus not to send the demons away to destruction. Even if we had to evaluate Jesus on purely human grounds we would have to admit that no one understood the human mind as he did. As a psychologist he would have been great in any age. Paul Tournier speaks of the state of mind of a man who is obsessed by magical ideas. There is no point in saying that his ideas are delusions; to him they are absolutely real, and if he is ever to be cured they must be treated as real. He quotes from the work of Dr. Charles Odier, a great authority on this subject: "Having demonstrated the role of the magical mentality in neuroses, and shown the complete uselessness of rational discussion with such patients, he draws this practical conclusion: 'One magic can be combated successfully only by another'."[1]

Jesus knew quite well that this man was so obsessed with the thought of his legion of demons that nothing on earth would ever

[1] Paul Tournier, *A Doctor's Case Book*, p. 107.

persuade him that *they* were gone *except what he himself would regard as visible demonstration that they were gone*. There was a great herd of swine grazing near by and the man felt that the demons were asking to be sent into them.[1] All the time he had been uttering his queer cries; and suddenly the herd of swine took fright; with one accord they plunged down the slope and were drowned in the sea. "Look!" said Jesus. "Your demons are gone!" The man was cured. It was the only thing that could possibly have cured him. Here was the evidence that alone could convince him that his demons were gone.

A lack of proportion
There have always been people who have cavilled at this miracle. They have been shocked at the destruction of this herd of swine.

Two things have to be said. First, it is not in the least likely that Jesus did destroy the herd of swine. What is far more likely is that he took advantage of their mad stampede to bring conviction to the man's disordered mind. Second, even if the cure of the mad did involve the destruction of the herd of swine, are we going to set the price of a man's sanity beside the value of some swine? Presumably we sometimes eat bacon for breakfast or pork for dinner or sausages for tea; but we do not ordinarily shed tears for the pigs who had to die that we might eat. There is such a thing as a cheap sentimentality which goes into agonies at what happens to an animal and blandly ignores the suffering of men. That is not for one moment to justify cruelty to the animal creation. God loves every creature whom his hands have made. He cares even for the sparrows. But we must preserve a sense of proportion. If it was necessary that the pigs should die that this man should be restored to sanity, it is surely wrong to compare the value of a herd of pigs, who were in any event being kept in order to be slaughtered, with the value of a man's soul.

The characteristics of Jesus
No miracle so shows the characteristics of Jesus's heart.

(i) In dealing with human trouble *Jesus had no fear*. It was a

[1]Mark 5 : 11, 12.

dangerous thing even to approach this violent maniac and yet
Jesus did it with a serene courage which showed that he had no
thought for his own safety. One of the heroic virtues of the doctor
in all ages has been his disregard for personal safety. Every day
in life he risks infection to cure others. Time and time again
doctors have experimented first upon their own bodies that they
might find a cure for others. It was on himself and his colleagues
that Sir James Simpson first tried out chloroform. "The famous
day came in November 1847 when Simpson and two medical
colleagues sat after dinner in the front dining-room of the house
in Queen Street, Edinburgh, overlooking the gardens. . . . Simpson
and his friends filled tumblers with chloroform. They were
enchanted by its seductive, silky aroma, and by the ease with
which a few breaths of its vapour produced a reckless, magical
sense of forgetfulness and relaxation. . . . The faces of the others
danced, and the furniture became dim and rotating. A noise like a
cotton mill roared in their ears. Then followed a blank interval
of time. . . . Simpson seems to have been the first to awake. He
found himself full length on the floor, with the prostrate forms
of his colleagues around him."[1] These doctors might well have
never wakened at all; but they were willing to risk their lives to
save others from pain. The self-forgetful heroism of the medical
profession is its greatest glory; and Jesus is the pattern of it.

(ii) In dealing with human trouble *Jesus showed no repulsion*.
There was not another person in all Decapolis who would have
approached this dreadful madman. Disease is never a pretty thing
and at times it can be loathsome. In every generation the doctor
has been so dominated by the desire to help as to be beyond
repulsion. Love forgets the ugliness because its only desire is to
help. Again Jesus is the pattern of all who have gone to men's
broken and diseased bodies, not with fastidious dislike, but with
skilled hands and loving heart.

(iii) In dealing with human trouble *Jesus showed no superiority*.
He might well have said: "My good man, you are suffering
from delusions. Snap out of it!" But no; with infinite sympathy,

[1]Harley Williams, *Masters of Medicine, the Story of some great Pioneers*
p. 97 (Pan Books Edition).

he entered right into that man's mind in order to heal it. On many an occasion a patient must look to a doctor more like a nervous and ignorant fool than anything else, but the doctor does not look down at him from his superior knowledge. <u>In order to cure it is necessary first to be kind.</u>

In this miracle we see fully displayed the courage, the tenderness and the sympathy of Jesus.

The reaction of the Gerasenes

The healing of the afflicted man was not the end of the story. When the people of the district discovered what had happened, they pleaded with Jesus to leave their country.[1] There is in the story as Mark tells it an almost startling paradox. When the people of the district arrived on the scene they found the man clothed and in his rightful mind; they heard the story; we might expect the next statement to be something like this: "They glorified God for the mighty work that had been done and begged Jesus to stay with them." But the next statement in fact is: "And they began to beg him to depart from their neighbourhood."

The secret of the attitude of the people of the district lies in one phrase: "And those who had seen it told what had happened to the demoniac *and to the swine*." The one thing they were thinking of was not that a demented man had been restored to his rightful mind but that they had lost their pigs.

Exactly the same thing happened to Paul and Silas in Philippi. When they came to Philippi they found a demented girl who had got into the hands of unscrupulous men who used her for the telling of fortunes. Paul and Silas cured her by the power of the name of Jesus. Her masters were so enraged that they had lost their easy way of making money that they had steps taken to see that Paul and Silas were arrested by the authorities.[2]

There have always been people who were more concerned with their own selfish interests than with the welfare of their fellow men. Lord Shaftesbury was the great champion of the children of England in the early days of the industrial revolution. Children

[1]Mark 5 : 17   [2]Acts 16 : 16-24.

were made to work in the mines. "It is an alarming experience for anyone to descend a mine-shaft for the first time, but for a tiny child of four or five years – the age at which work was started in those days – it meant the acutest terror. The air in the mines was damp and close, and water slowly trickled down the sides of the shaft, and at the bottom were dark gruesome passages, thick with black mud and opening out in all directions. The first work of a tiny child was that of a 'trapper', which meant sitting from morning to night holding a piece of string with which to open and shut the doors that divided the coal passages. If these doors were not shut immediately the trolley had passed through, very serious results might follow. If these children moved more than a few feet from their doors, they were discovered and 'strapped.' Children of eight were often set to pump in the pits, standing for twelve or more hours ankle-deep in water. The coal-carrying was nearly always done by girls and women, and it often happened that little children carried half hundredweights of coal up steps that equalled an ascent, fourteen times a day, to the cross on the dome of St. Paul's Cathedral. Even babies were sometimes taken down into the pits to scare rats off their fathers' dinners."[1] One would have thought that such conditions needed only to be brought to light to be condemned; but it took Shaftesbury no less than *fourteen years* to get anything done about them, because mine-owners declared that if anything was done their profits would vanish.

In the country it was the same. "Gangs of boys and girls were employed on the land by farmers under very cruel conditions. They were hired from work-houses. The gang-master would arouse the boys and girls about 5 o'clock in the morning, and march them to the fields, often four to eight miles away. Sometimes all the children in a district were employed by a single gangmaster, and taken by him from farm to farm, as work offered, with no settled home, for they seldom spent more than a few weeks in one village. Mites of six and seven were collected in the morning and marched very quickly to work, their small legs struggling to keep up with the master. On arriving at the fields, they would spread

[1] E. H. Hayes, *Yarns on the Christian Pioneers*, pp. 90, 91.

manure, thin root crops, pick stones or weeds from morning to night, never stopping for school or play At night they trudged back to their miserable quarters, the elder ones dragging and carrying the tinies, to escape the notice of the gang-master, who was often a bully He 'employed' the children, and it is easy to imagine how little of the farmers' money, paid direct to him, ever reached his little victims."[1] Again it might seem that such conditions would need only to be stated to arouse indignation and ensure action. But it actually took Shaftesbury another *six years* to persuade Parliament to pass legislation to deal with it.

It was true in Palestine, it was true in the nineteenth century, and it is true today that there is nothing which so holds up the work of Christ as the selfishness of men. Men hate to be disturbed and often Jesus comes with a disturbing force; the result often is that they try to shut the door on him and bid him be gone.

The reaction of the healed man

But if the people of the district wanted Jesus to be gone, there was one man who wanted to cling to him for ever and that was the man who had been cured. When he saw Jesus about to leave in the boat, he wanted with all his heart to come with him; but Jesus told him to go back home to his friends and to tell everyone what wonderful things God had done for him.[2] It was natural for the man to want to get away from the people who had known him in his evil days and to bear his witness to Jesus among people who had not known him when he was demented. But Jesus said: "No! Go back to the people who knew you at your worst and bear your witness there." It is our duty not to look for some place where it is easier to be a Christian but to be a Christian where we are.

Kipling has a poem called *Mulholland's Contract*.[3] Mulholland was a cattle-man on a ship. Once on a voyage a violent storm broke out and between decks the cattle broke loose; and Mulholland was in imminent danger of death beneath their plunging hooves and horns. So he made a contract with God.

[1] E. H. Hayes, *Yarns on the Christian Pioneers*, p. 92.
[2] Mark 5 : 18, 19.
[3] *The Definitive Edition of Rudyard Kipling's Verse*, pp. 127-129.

"An' by the terms of the Contract, as I have read the same,
If He got me to port alive I would exalt His Name,
An' praise His Holy Majesty till further orders came."

Miraculously he was preserved and he determined to keep his contract.

"An' I spoke to God of our Contract, an' He says to my
  prayer:
'I never puts on my ministers no more than they can bear.
So back you go to the cattle-boats an' preach My Gospel
  there'."

That had not been Mulholland's idea at all; the last thing he wanted to do was to preach on the cattle-boats where everybody knew him, but he was an honest man and he did it.

"I didn't want to do it, for I knew what I should get;
An' I wanted to preach religion, handsome and out of the
  wet;
But the Word of the Lord were laid on me, an' I done what
  I was set."

It is natural for everyone to want to preach religion "handsome and out of the wet," but Jesus says to us what he said to the healed demoniac at Gerasa and what he said to Mulholland: "Go back to the people who know you best and be a Christian there."

The end of the story

Maybe that was not the end of the story. The time passed and we find Jesus in the Decapolis again.[1] And we find him surrounded by a great crowd whom he fed with seven loaves and a few small fishes.[2] Where did that crowd come from? Why were there so many there to come to listen to him in that very area where they had begged him to be gone? Is it not possible that there were at least some who had been brought there by this demoniac whom Jesus had so wonderfully healed? It may well be so; and it will

[1]Mark 7 : 31. [2]Mark 8 : 1-9.

always remain true that the best way in which we can show our gratitude to Jesus for all that he has done for us is to bring others to him that they too may share his friendship and his life and his power and his love.

CHAPTER NINE

The Considerateness of Jesus

THEN Jesus returned from the region of Tyre, and went through Sidon to the Sea of Galilee, through the region of the Decapolis. And they brought to him a man who was deaf and had an impediment in his speech; and they besought him to lay his hands upon him. And taking him aside from the multitude privately, he put his fingers into his ears, and he spat and touched his tongue; and looking up to heaven, he sighed, and said to him, "Ephphatha," that is, "Be opened." And his ears were opened, his tongue was released, and he spoke plainly. And he charged them to tell no one; but the more he charged them, the more zealously they proclaimed it. And they were astonished beyond measure, saying, "He has done all things well; he even makes the deaf hear and the dumb speak."

(Mark 7 : 31-37.)

When Jesus was passing through the Decapolis they brought to him a man who was deaf and had an impediment in his speech. It is probable that the two things went together. He had never heard the voice of another and so, when he tried to speak, he did not know what words should be like and could make only uncouth sounds.

The very first thing that Jesus did was to take the man aside, out of the crowd. At other times he healed people in the full blaze of publicity, in the crowded synagogue and on the thronging streets. But on this occasion he treated the man, as it were, privately. Why?

Scholars have made many different suggestions. The oldest scholars, the Greek fathers, suggested that it was because Jesus wanted to avoid all display. Calvin suggested that it was because he wished to pray with more freedom and intensity than would have been possible in the midst of the crowd. Trench suggested that it was because the man would be more susceptible to Jesus's influence when he was apart than he would have been in the midst of a crowd.[1]

But surely the reason was much simpler and much more human and much more lovely than any of these. Deaf people are easily embarrassed and confused. Quite often they get on not at all badly when there is only one other person present or when there is a small company; but almost invariably when there is a crowd, they become flustered and excited; and the more they strain to hear, the more muddled they become. It is an odd thing that blind people get all the sympathy in the world while deaf people are looked on as something of a nuisance; and yet to be shut out from the world of sound is almost as terrible as to be shut out from the world of sight.

The classic example of what deafness can do to a man's nature is Beethoven. For a musician deafness was the tragedy of tragedies. "My misfortune," he wrote, "is doubly painful because it must lead to my being misunderstood, for me there can be no recreation in the society of my fellows, refined intercourse, mutual exchange of thought, only just as little as the greatest needs command may I mix with society. I must live like an exile."[2] There was a terrible time when he was struggling to conduct an orchestra playing one of his own compositions. He could not hear even the full orchestra. Soon he was beating one time and the orchestra was playing another; and the performance disintegrated in disaster. There is a pathetic picture of him after he had given a piano recital, bent over the keyboard, oblivious to the applause that thundered about him. It has been written of him: "All that easy intercourse with the world which comes, automatically and for the most part unconsciously, through the hearing, was denied him; driven in too much upon himself, he had no immediate social relaxation: far worse, he was made suspicious until he felt like a blind man among enemies or ill-bred mischievous youngsters."[3]

[1] R. C. Trench *Notes on the Miracles of Our Lord,* Pickering and Inglis 1958, pp. 356, 357
[2] Quoted Marion M. Scott, *Beethoven,* p. 49.
[3] E. M. and S. Grew, *Masters of Music,* p. 171.

Anyone who is deaf tends to become awkward, embarrassed, suspicious, and the harder he tries to hear the worse he hears. It would be so with the man in this story; and Jesus drew him out of the crowd simply to get him alone, away from the bewilderment of the crowd. There is no incident in all Jesus's life which so shows his tenderness and consideration for others. No good doctor treats all his patients the same. Neither did Jesus. He knew that, if he was to cure people, it was not enough to be wise; it was at least equally necessary to be kind.

Speaking in actions

Jesus went even further. He put his fingers in the man's ears and touched his tongue.[1] Why did he act like this? The only way in which Jesus could indicate to this deaf man what he was about to do was in dumb-show. Here again we have his infinite consideration. If we had been acting in the capacity in which Jesus was acting, we might well have said, in effect: "Let's get it over as quickly as possible," and have tossed an act of healing at the man as a bone is tossed to a dog. It is easy to be detached and a little inhuman in such a case But Jesus was not like that. No doubt the man was anxious and not very sure what was happening; and Jesus took him with him step by step.

An ancient cure

Now we come to what to us is a strange thing. Jesus spat and with the spittle touched the man's tongue. Twice again we see Jesus doing this — with the blind man at Bethsaida[2] and with the man born blind of John 9 : 6. The ancient world had a curious belief in the healing and protecting power of spittle.

Tacitus recounts a famous incident on the visit of the Roman Emperor Vespasian to Alexandria:

"A plebian of Alexandria, well known to be suffering from disease of the eyes, threw himself down at the Emperor's feet, and besought him with much wailing to heal his

[1]Mark 7 : 33.
[2]Mark 8 : 23.

blindness, praying that he would deign to moisten his eyelids and eyeballs with his spittle, having been moved to this request by the god Serapis, who is worshipped above all other gods, by that most superstitious of nations. Another man with a diseased hand, by the same god's advice, implored the Emperor to trample on it, with the sole of his foot. Vespasian first laughed these petitions to scorn; but at last, when the men persisted, fearing on the one hand to be thought guilty of folly, and on the other hand being led by the men's entreaties and the remarks of flatterers to hope for some result, he ordered the opinion of the physicians to be taken as to whether such cases of blindness or debility could be cured by human help. The doctors gave divers answers; the blind man's sight they said had not been destroyed, and would return if the things obstructing it were removed. In the other case, the crooked limb might be made straight if healing methods were applied. Such perchance might be the will of the gods; and the Emperor might have been chosen to be the divine instrument. And, finally, if the cure were effected, Vespasian would gain all the credit of it; if it failed the ridicule would fall on the sufferers. And so Vespasian, thinking that everything was open to his good fortune, and that nothing was now incredible, put on a smiling face, and amid an eagerly expectant crowd, did what had been asked of him. The hand immediately recovered its power. The blind man saw once more. Both facts are attested to this day, when falsehood can bring no reward, by those who were present on the occasion."[1]

In ancient literature it is Pliny the Elder who gives the classic account of the beliefs of the ancient world about the efficacy of spittle. It is worth quoting in full, in order that we may see just how comprehensive this belief was:

"But it is the fasting spittle of a human being which is the sovereign preservative against the poison of serpents; while,

[1]Tacitus, *Histories* 4 : 81 (translation by G. G. Ramsay). The same incident is related in Suetonius' *Life of Vespasian*, 7.

at the same time, our daily experience may recognize how effective and useful it is in many other respects. We are in the habit, for instance, of spitting as a protection against epilepsy, or, in other words, we repel contagion by so doing. In the same way we repel enchantments, and the evils likely to result from meeting a person lame in the right leg. We ask pardon of the gods by spitting in the lap for entertaining some too presumptuous hope or expectation. On the same principle, it is the practice in all cases where medicine is employed, to spit three times on the ground, and to seek to expel the malady by oath as often, the object being to aid the operation of the remedy employed. It is usual too to mark a boil, when it first appears, three times with fasting spittle. What we are about to say is marvellous, but it may easily be tested by experiment. If a person repents of a blow given to another, either by hand or with a missile, he has nothing to do but to spit at once into the palm of his hand which has inflicted the blow, and all the feelings of resentment will immediately be alleviated in the person struck. This too will often be verified in the case of a beast of burden, when brought on its haunches with blows; for, upon this remedy being adopted, the animal will immediately step out and mend its pace. Some persons before making an effort spit into the hand in the manner above stated, to make the blow more heavy. We may well believe then that lichens and leprous spots may be removed by a constant application of fasting spittle; *that ophthalmia may be cured by anointing, as it were, the eyes every morning with fasting spittle;* that carcinomata may be effectively treated by kneading the root of the plant known as 'apple of the earth' with human spittle; that crick in the neck may be got rid of by carrying fasting spittle to the right knee with the right hand, and to the left with the left; and that when an insect has got into the ear, it is quite sufficient to spit into that organ to make it come out. Among the counter charms too are reckoned the practice of spitting into the urine at the moment it is voided, of spitting into the shoe of the right foot before it is put on, and of spitting while a person is passing a place in which he has incurred any kind of peril. . . . Upon the entry of a stranger, or when a person looks on a sleeping infant, it is usual for the nurse to spit three times upon the ground."[1]

Persius, the Roman poet, speaking of popular superstitious practices, writes:

"See how a granny or an auntie who fears the gods takes baby out of his cradle; skilled in averting the evil eye, she first, with her middle finger applies the lustrous spittle to his forehead and slobbering lips."[2]

In his note on the passage of Tacitus that we have already quoted, Ramsay says that Holman, the blind traveller, tells how mothers in Russia, fearful of the evil eye, would request strangers, before casting an eye on their children, to spit three times on the ground. In India a traveller tells that evil spirits could be averted by spitting three times in a child's face. Mungo Park tells of a journey whose success was achieved by spitting three times on a stone.[3]

It is easy to see how extraordinarily vivid and widespread was belief in the curative and protective power of spittle. Nor is it dead, for there are still those who believe that warts may be removed by licking them with fasting spittle first thing in the morning. It is still the case that a man will spit on his hands before he makes some effort, although doubtless he has no idea why he does so. And it is a first instinct to put a hand into the mouth if it is cut or bruised or burned.

Here, then, we see a most suggestive thing. We see Jesus taking the ordinary means of healing known to men of that time, and charging them with a new power and effectiveness. It is as if Jesus was saying to us today: "Take such means of healing as you possess and use them along with the power that I can give, and wonderful things will happen." The only thing available might be a stump of cheap pencil, but with that a great artist might draw

[1]Pliny the Elder, *Natural History*, 28 : 8.
[2]Persius, *Satires*, 2 : 30-34 (translation by G. G. Ramsay).
[3]G. G. Ramsay, *The Histories of Tacitus*, English translation, p. 389.

a great picture. The only thing available might be the simplest ingredients, but out of them a great cook might prepare a most appetising meal.

One of the greatest of all pictures of the face of Jesus is that by Murillo. When Murillo painted it he was a scullion in a monastery kitchen. He had no canvas but the urge to paint was on him. The cook contemptuously flung him a kitchen towel and said: "Here, paint on that." And on that kitchen towel Murillo painted a masterpiece.

If we take what we have and allow Jesus to use it, there is no limit to what can happen. Jesus took the simple, even superstitious ways of healing that his countrymen knew, and charged them with the power that was his and a miracle resulted. Jesus is always saying: "Let me use what you have and what you know; and with it I will do great things, however simple and poor your knowledge and your power may be." Little is much when that little is in the hands of Jesus.

The power is from God

As Jesus used the simple ways of healing of which men knew, *he looked up to heaven.*[1] We must remember that step by step Jesus was taking this poor man with him. By looking up to heaven, he was showing him that it was the power of God that was about to enter his life. In the end all healing comes from God. There comes a time when man has done what he can and God must do the rest. A man can set a broken limb, but the process which knits the broken ends of the bone together is of God. A great surgeon once said: "I bandage men's wounds; God heals them." With that look Jesus told the man, and tells us, that all health and healing come from God.

The compassion of Jesus

As Jesus touched the man and looked towards God, he sighed, or, as it might be translated, he groaned.[2] Scholars have seen two things in that sigh. Some have seen a prayer so intense that it

[1]Mark 7 : 34.
[2]Mark 7 : 34.

sounded like a desperate cry. Others have seen sheer compassion. As Jesus looked at this poor man in all his wretchedness, a sigh of sympathy was wrung from him for the man's wretched case.

Surely we should see both things here. As Jesus looked at the man's trouble he was moved with deep compassion; and, as he was moved with compassion, he prayed to God to help him to deal with it. We shall never help men unless we are moved with compassion for them; and our compassion will never become effective until we look to God for power to help.

And so in the end Jesus spoke his healing word, "Be opened," and the man heard and spoke. This story tells us of the divine considerateness of Jesus; it tells us how he took the simple human remedies men knew and charged them with his new power; it tells how he looked to God for the things that only God can do. It tells how his compassion joined hands with the power of God and how then a miracle happened.

CHAPTER TEN

The Appeal which Will Not be Silenced

AND they came to Jericho; and as Jesus was leaving Jericho with his disciples and a great multitude, Bartimaeus, a blind beggar, the son of Timaeus, was sitting by the roadside. And when he heard that it was Jesus of Nazareth, he began to cry out and say, "Jesus, Son of David, have mercy on me!" And many rebuked him, telling him to be silent; but he cried out all the more, "Son of David, have mercy on me!" And Jesus stopped and said, "Call him." And they called the blind man, saying to him, "Take heart; rise, he is calling you." And throwing off his mantle, he sprang up and came to Jesus. And Jesus said to him, "What do you want me to do for you?" And the blind man said to him, "Master, let me receive my sight." And Jesus said to him, "Go your way; your faith has made you well." And immediately he received his sight and followed him on the way.

(Mark 10 : 46-52; cp. Matthew 20 : 29-34; Luke 18 : 35-43; Matthew 9 : 27-31.)

In the time of Jesus, Jericho was the loveliest town in Palestine. It was famous for its palm trees; its dates were the most famous in the world and were exported far and wide; it was surrounded by balsam groves and rose gardens so that it was a perfumed city. The climate was so warm that, in the summertime, the people could wear only the lightest of linen garments. Jericho was the last stage on the journey from the north to Jerusalem which was only six hours march farther on.

At the time of this story, Jesus was on his way to Jerusalem for the last contest of all (Mark 10 : 32). Even his disciples could feel the strain and the tension. The final clash was almost on them and there was a sense of destiny in the air. It was the law that all male Jews who lived within reasonable distance of Jerusalem should go up to the holy city for the Passover Feast. To that feast Jesus was on his way. People very seldom went singly to the Passover; they went in companies, travelling in convoys. It is obvious that everyone could not go to the feast. Life had to go on and some had to stay at home and see that it did. But those who were themselves unable to go lined the streets of their towns and villages to greet the pilgrim bands as they passed through and wish them godspeed on their journey.

No doubt, as Jesus passed through, the streets were doubly crowded, for all would come out to see this young Galilaean who said and did such wonderful things. They well knew that he had challenged the orthodox religious authorities of the day and that the final contest was bound to come. He was going either to a kingdom or a cross; and the crowds will always flock to see a man of reckless courage challenging fearful odds. On the day that Jesus passed through Jericho, he was on the last stage of the journey to Jerusalem; the drama was about to reach its crisis; and the streets of Jericho were crowded to see the man who was taking his life in his hands.

As we study this passage we are going to use the material in the other three passages which we have cited with it. At least the first three refer to the same incident and are different accounts of it; and in the fourth there is a strong family resemblance.

As Jesus went through Jericho, there was a blind man sitting at the roadside begging whose name was Bartimaeus. Blindness in Palestine was tragically common, mainly through ophthalmia caused by the strong glare of the sun and aggravated by the fact that in those days people knew nothing of the laws of health. The flies were everywhere and it was the commonest thing to see the matter-encrusted eyes of a blind person covered with them; so infection was carried everywhere and blindness was far more common than it need have been.

The perseverance of Bartimaeus

When Bartimaeus heard that Jesus was passing by he set up something of an uproar. Immediately everyone urged him to be quiet.[1] It was the custom for a Rabbi to teach as he walked and this is what Jesus was doing. Naturally those who were with him wished to hear what he was saying but they could not hear for the

[1]Mark 10 : 47; Matthew 20 : 31; Luke 18 : 38, 39.

roaring of this blind beggar. That is why they angrily told him to be quiet. But they could not silence him; the more they told him to be quiet the more he shouted out his need.

Here is the first element in this miracle. Here was a man who was *determined to persevere*. No obstacles were going to stop him; he had heard what Jesus could do and nothing was going to stop him making contact with him.

When Booker Washington was a young man there was no higher education for negroes. But a university which would take negroes was opened. It meant a walk of seven hundred miles, but he got there. It was only to find, however, that the last place had been filled and that all they could offer him was the job of a servant, sweeping the bedrooms and making the beds. He took it and, in due time, was allowed in as a student; and he went on and on until he became the Principal of Tuskegee University.

Many people miss great things simply because they grow discouraged too soon. It is said that on one occasion Edison carried out more than seven hundred different experiments in seeking to discover a certain way to do something. At the end of them he said: "Now we know seven hundred ways not to do it!" In the end he triumphed and it was sheer perseverance which brought the triumph.

In the beginning of the sixteenth century there was a Frenchman called Bernard Palissy. In those days the art of making cups and saucers and plates of smooth enamelled surface had been lost. Pottery was rough and far from beautiful. Into Palissy's hands came a cup from ancient China where men had possessed the secret. He determined that he would make pottery like that. It took him sixteen years to do it and sometimes he had to burn his furniture to keep his furnaces going. Sixteen years is a long time to keep trying, but Palissy persevered and that is why today even the cheapest cups and saucers are smooth and lovely.

In the middle of the nineteenth century there was a man called Samuel Plimsoll. He was the friend of sailors. In those days ship-owners sent out what came to be known as "coffin ships." They were unseaworthy and loaded in a way which made them highly dangerous. They were sent to sea heavily insured so that even if they foundered, the owners would not lose anything. Plimsoll determined to do something about it, but there was violent opposition from those to whom this iniquitous trade brought wealth. He entered Parliament in 1868 and in 1875 Disraeli promised to introduce a Bill to put things right, but pressure from the ship-owners caused it to be withdrawn. Plimsoll lost his temper and called the House of Commons and the Prime Minister and the ship-owners a set of villains; but public interest and opinion had been so aroused that the Bill was passed in 1876. Eight years is a long time to fight in Parliament a seemingly hopeless battle. It was sheer perseverance which did it and today Plimsoll has his memorial in the line marked on every ship to show maximum permitted depth of loading.

Bartimaeus is the great example of perseverance. He got his miracle because he refused to be discouraged or deterred.

The answer of Jesus

Although the crowd was annoyed with the clamour that Bartimaeus raised, one person was not; and that was Jesus. Immediately he stopped.[1] He was teaching at the moment; but Jesus always knew that people are far more important than words. It was important to teach men but it was still more important to help them.

Kermit Eby, a famous American teacher, taught in every grade from school to university and always believed in being accessible at all times to his pupils and to his students. "There are no office hours in my office," he wrote, "only open house . . . . I know that research is important; yet I know also that a man is more important than a footnote, and a dream more important than either."[2]

Sometimes we may pass a house on which there is a little plate saying: "No hawkers, no circulars, no canvassers." In other words, the occupants of that house might as well put up a notice: "No one in need may call here."

A certain Mrs. Berwick had once done social work for the Salvation Army in Liverpool and in her old age had retired to

[1]Mark 10 : 49; Luke 18 : 40; Matthew 20 : 32.
[2]Kermit Eby, *The God in you*, pp. 32, 33.

London. Then came the war with its terrible air raids. People get queer ideas and some got the idea that somehow they were safe in Mrs. Berwick's poor little house or in her Anderson shelter. Her Liverpool days were far behind but she had the instinct to help. She got together a rough first-aid box and put a notice in her window: "If you need help, knock here."

People come first, before anything else. That is what Jesus showed on that day when he gladly interrupted his teaching to listen to Bartimaeus. The others found Bartimaeus an intrusion; to Jesus he was a human being needing help.

The man who knew what he wanted

When Bartimaeus came up to him, Jesus asked him what he wanted and, like a shot, back came the answer: " Master, let me receive my sight."[1]

(i) Bartimaeus knew exactly what he wanted. He did not come to Jesus with a kind of vague, sentimental longing; he came with a perfectly definite request. In every sphere of life, the way to get anything is to know what we want. A person who knows what he wants goes into a shop and gets it; a person who does not really know what he wants goes in and wanders about to the waste of his own time and everyone else's, and very likely comes out with nothing. A student who goes to university with a clear idea of why he is there will get far more than the student who goes with no specific aim. It is the same with a church service. If we go wanting something, we will get it; if we go wanting nothing, the probability is that we will get nothing. It is so with prayer. The thing that really makes it effective is a sense of need.

(ii) When Bartimaeus came to Jesus, he pitched his demand high. He did not ask for alms; he asked for *sight*. The simple fact is that when we come to Jesus we cannot ask for too much. As John Newton said in his hymn:

> "Thou art coming to a King;
> Large petitions with thee bring;
> For his grace and power are such,
> None can ever ask too much."

[1]Mark 10 : 51; Matthew 20 : 33; Luke 18 : 41.

The biggest thing we can ask is that Jesus should change us and make us strong instead of weak, good instead of bad.

The Man of Faith

In Matthew 9 : 27-31 there is one little extra bit not definitely stated in the other stories, although implied. Jesus asked the blind men a question: "Do you believe that I am able to do this?" They answered: "Yes, Lord."[1] They came with *faith*.[2]

Any doctor will agree that the man who has faith in the treatment prescribed has a far better chance of recovery than the man who has not. It is almost true to say that a man can grow well and live or grow worse and die according to his own belief and determination. Neville Chamberlain was Prime Minister when Britain entered upon the Second World War, but the time came when he was removed from office. Not long afterwards he died. Margot Asquith tells how she talked about Chamberlain and his death to Lord Horder who was his doctor. "You can't be much of a doctor," she said, "as Neville Chamberlain was only a few years older than Winston Churchill, and I should have said he was a strong man. Were you fond of him?" Lord Horder replied: "I was very fond of him. I like all unlovable men. I have seen too many of the other kind. Chamberlain suffered from shyness. He did not want to live; and when a man says *that,* no doctor can save him."[3] The man died because he had no determination to live.

The blind man came to Jesus with the belief that he was able to make him see. In every sphere of life, what we believe makes all the difference. If we enter upon a game believing that we will lose, the chances are that we will. If we engage upon any enterprise sure that we will fail, in all probability we will. If we seek treatment for any ailment with the conviction that the treatment will be useless, all the likelihood is that it will be. Belief makes all the difference. When we seek the help of Jesus, we must be confident that he can help. History tells us how he has done great things for

[1]Matthew 9 : 28.
[2]Mark 10 : 52; Luke 18 : 42.
[3]The Countess of Oxford and Asquith, *Off the Record*, p. 81.

those who really believed in him – and he will do the same for us if we believe that he can.

The cure and the gratitude

Jesus cured this blind man and, when he was cured, he followed Jesus.[1] There was only one way in which he could show his gratitude and that was by becoming one of Jesus's followers. There are many people who go to someone with a request and, when they have got what they want, go away, and that is the last that is seen of them. Ingratitude is an ugly thing. We can never repay what Jesus has done for us but we can show our gratitude by giving to him the love of our hearts and the service of our lives.

In this miracle the determination, the sense of definite need and the believing faith of Bartimaeus met the compassion and the power of Jesus; and healing resulted. When our determination and our belief meet the power of Jesus great things can happen for us, also.

[1]Mark 10 : 52 ; Matthew 20 : 34 ; Luke 18 : 43.

CHAPTER ELEVEN

The End of Worry and of Fear

ON that day, when evening had come, Jesus said to them, "Let us go across to the other side." And leaving the crowd, they took him with them just as he was, in the boat. And other boats were with him. And a great storm of wind arose, and the waves beat into the boat, so that the boat was already filling. But he was in the stern, asleep on the cushion; and they woke him and said to him, "Teacher, do you not care if we perish?" And he awoke and rebuked the wind, and said to the sea, "Peace! Be still!" And the wind ceased, and there was a great calm. He said to them, "Why are you afraid? Have you no faith?" And they were filled with awe, and said to one another, "Who then is this, that even wind and sea obey him?"

(Mark 4 : 36-41; cp. Matthew 8 : 23-27; Luke 8 : 22-25.)

The country surrounding the Sea of Galilee is largely bare and deserted now but in the time of Jesus it was one of the busiest and most beautiful places in the world. There were many famous sayings of the Jews and their Rabbis about the beauty of Galilee. The Sea of Galilee was also called the Lake of Tiberias, because Tiberias was the largest town on its shore; and it was said that "The shores of Tiberias form one of the gardens of the world." Sometimes it was called the Lake of Gennesaret after the plain which bordered on its western shore; and it was said that that plain was "the unparalleled garden of God." One of the Rabbis said: "God created seven seas but the Sea of Gennesaret is his delight."

Josephus was at one time governor of Galilee and knew the country round the Sea of Galilee well. He said that in his time there were 204 towns in Galilee, none with a population of fewer than 15,000 people; and Galilee is only 50 miles from north to south, and 25 miles from west to east. He said that "the soil is universally rich and fruitful, and full of plantations of trees of all sorts, insomuch that it invites the laziest to take pains to cultivate it, because of its fruitfulness."[1] He said that the climate was such that in Galilee were found all kinds of trees which were never found together in other places. There was the walnut, which needed a cool climate; there were the palms, which needed heat; there were the fig-trees and the olives, which needed a temperate climate. The seasons seemed to conspire and compete to make it possible for every kind of tree to grow.[2]

Galilee was indeed a land flowing with milk and honey. A modern writer gives a list of the unique number of trees which grew in Galilee – the vine, the olive, the fig, the oak, the walnut, the terebinth, the palm, the cedar, the cypress, the balsam, the fir-tree, the pine, the sycamore, the bay-tree, the myrtle, the almond, the pomegranate, the citron, the oleander.[3] Nowadays the climate has changed because the country was recklessly and unwisely deforested; but in the time of Jesus, Galilee was one of the fairest places in the world. The Jews had three derivations for this name Gennesaret by which the lake was sometimes known. They derived it from *kinnor*, which means *a harp*, because "its fruit is as sweet as the sound of the harp." They derived it from the *gan*, which means *a garden*, and *sar*, which means *a prince*, and so they called it *The Prince of Gardens*. They derived it from *gan* and from *asher*, which means *riches*, and so they called it "the garden that is rich in fertility."

The lake and its storms

The district of Galilee and the Sea of Galilee owed both their loveliness and their peril to their position. The surface of the Sea of Galilee is 680 feet below sea level. The lake and the area round it is like a deep basin in the earth. It is because it is so far below sea level that the climate is almost tropical. But for that very reason the Sea of Galilee is a dangerous sheet of water. It was not large, only 13 miles from north to south and 8 miles from east to west at its widest. It is surrounded by deep wadis or gorges

[1] Josephus, *Wars of the Jews*, 3, 3, 2.
[2] Josephus, *Wars of the Jews*, 3, 10, 8.
[3] S. Merrill, *Galilee in the Time of Christ*, p. 21.

in the surrounding hills. If a cold wind comes from the west, it rushes down these narrow gorges and leaps out on the lake with startling suddenness, and the calm of one moment may well be the raging storm of the next. All landlocked lakes and lochs have this danger, but the Sea of Galilee is specially subject to these squalls, which are all the more dangerous because of their suddenness. A nineteenth century traveller tells of his personal experience near the Sea of Galilee.

"My experience in this region enables me to sympathize with the disciples in their long night's contest with the wind. I spent a night in that Wadi Shukaiyif. . . . The sun had scarcely set when the wind began to rush down to the lake, and it continued all night long with constantly increasing violence, so that when we reached the shore next morning the face of the lake was like a huge boiling cauldron. The wind howled down every wadi from the north-east and east with such fury that no efforts of rowers could have brought a boat to shore at any point along that coast. . . . To understand the cause of these sudden and violent tempests we must remember the lake lies low – six hundred feet lower than the ocean; that the vast and naked plateaux of the Jaulan rise to a great height spreading backward to the wilds of Hauran, and upward to snowy Hermon; that the water-courses have cut out profound ravines and wild gorges, converging to the head of this lake, and that these act like gigantic *funnels* to draw down the cold winds from the mountains. On the occasion referred to, we subsequently pitched our tents at the shore, and remained for three days and nights exposed to this tremendous wind. We had to double-pin all the tent-ropes, and frequently were obliged to hang with our whole weight upon them to keep the quivering tabernacle from being carried up bodily into the air. . . . The whole lake as we had it was lashed into fury; the waves repeatedly rolled up to our tent door, tumbling over the ropes with such violence as to carry away the tent-pins. And, moreover, these winds are not only violent, but they come down suddenly, and often when the sky is perfectly clear. I once went to swim near the hot baths, and, before I was aware, a wind came rushing over the cliffs with such force that it was with great difficulty that I could regain the shore."[1]

W. M. Christie, who spent many years in Galilee, says: "The storms on the Sea of Galilee are in many ways peculiar, and sometimes the wind seems to blow from various directions at one time, tossing the boat about. This arises from the fact that the winds blow violently down the narrow gorges and strike the Sea at an angle, stirring the waters to a great depth. Many of the storms, too, are quite local in their character. . . . All may be smooth along the shores to the north and south of Tiberias and for a mile out, but there we may pass in a moment from the region of perfect calm into a gale so violent that the only chance of safety is to run before the wind to the eastern shore." He tells of an occasion when "a company of visitors were standing on the shore at Tiberias, and, noting the glassy surface of the water and the smallness of the Lake, they expressed doubts as to the possibility of such storms as those described in the gospels. Almost immediately the wind sprang up. In twenty minutes the sea was white with foam-crested waves. Great billows broke over the towers at the corners of the city walls, and the visitors were compelled to seek shelter from the blinding spray, though now 200 yards from the Lake side."[2]

The placid sunshine of the lake can turn to a raging storm in less than half an hour. H. V. Morton tells of his experience in Galilee.

"There was not a breath of wind. The sky was blue. But Abdul, the young fisherman, sniffed the air and, looking to the south, said that a storm was coming. This is, and always has been, one of the peculiarities of the Lake of Galilee. Sudden storms swoop swiftly over this low-lying sheet of water whipping the surface of the lake with fury and covering it with waves that frequently swamp the small rowing-boats.

[1] W. M. Thomson, *The Land and the Book,* pp. 374, 375.
[2] James Hastings, *A Dictionary of Christ and the Gospels,* vol. ii, Article on the Sea of Galilee, by W. M. Christie, p. 591.

The reason is that winds from the west passing over the highlands come swirling down through a hundred gorges and narrow valleys into the deep pit in which the lake lies. The water is smooth one moment, and the next it is a raging sea in which men battle for life. Three men had recently been drowned in such a storm, said Abdul, and their bodies had not yet been recovered."[1]

In the time of Jesus the Sea of Galilee must have been crowded with boats. Josephus tells how on one occasion, when it was necessary to assemble an armada of small boats to deal with a rebellion at Tiberias, he succeeded in mobilising no fewer than two hundred and thirty such ships.[2] Many of Jesus's friends were fishermen and sometimes, when he wanted a little peace and quiet to refresh his soul, he would sail with them to the other side of the lake. So on this occasion they embarked and set sail. The boats of the Galilaean fishermen were quite large and a little unwieldy, with one mast and one great triangular sail. At the stern of the boat, just in front of the helmsman, there was a little platform-like deck and on it a cushion; and it was the custom that distinguished guests sat there while the boat sailed.

Jesus was sitting in the stern of the boat; he was tired and he fell asleep. That tells us two things about him. It tells us how exhausting his work of preaching and healing was; it literally took it out of him. And it shows us how much he trusted his men. He knew the dangers of the Sea of Galilee as well as any man did and yet he slept in peace because he trusted the skill and the resources of his fishermen friends.

They had not gone far before one of these sudden tremendous squalls hit the boat. So fierce were the seas and so high was the wind that they were in danger of their lives, but Jesus slept on. In their terror, the disciples awoke him, asking if it was nothing to him that they were all like to die. Jesus stilled the waves and the wind with a word; and there was a calm. Then he asked them where their faith was and why they had lost their nerve like that.

[1]H. V. Morton, *In the Steps of the Master*, p. 196.
[2]Josephus, *The Wars of the Jews*, 2, 21, 8.

The stilling of the storm

There is far more in this miracle than simply that once on a day in Galilee Jesus stilled a tempestuous storm. If that was all this story would certainly be very wonderful but it would have nothing very practical to do with us. But this story means something which affects every one of us. It means that whenever Jesus comes into life, its storms become a calm; it means that he can and does and will bring peace to us in the midst of any of the storms that come upon us.

The storms of life

There are *the storms of temptation*. Sometimes we are very seriously tempted to do something which we know is wrong; the tide of temptation is like to sweep us away from our moorings. At such a time there is no safety like the memory of Jesus. We might do some shameful thing if we were absolutely alone, but never if we thought that we might turn round and see the hurt eyes of someone we loved looking at us. When the storm of temptation comes, we must remember that Jesus is there to see us and to help us. That will bring peace in the storm.

There are *the storms of passion*. Sometimes we are apt to be carried away in the heat of the moment, especially if we have hot tempers and strong feelings. There was a French courtier who had a very ungovernable temper. He was always doing and saying things for which he was sorry afterwards. A friend of his knew just the kind of thing which annoyed him. One day, when this courtier was in the king's presence, one of these annoying things happened, but he kept his temper. Afterwards his friend said to him: "When that thing happened, I was surprised to see how well you kept your temper." The courtier answered, "I had to. The king was there, and I couldn't lose my temper in front of him." His friend said quietly: "I wish that you would remember that, wherever you are, you are in the presence of the King of kings." If we remember that Jesus is always with us, it will bring a new calm to us when the storms of our own passionate natures threaten to sweep us away.

There are *the storms of worry and fear*. It is almost impossible to go through life without being frightened sometimes. It is always easier to face something in company than when we are alone. Henry J. Taylor, famous American journalist, tells of a thing he never forgot. His father was a mine-owner. A new elevator was being installed; and before the proper cage was fitted, a descent had to be made in a barrel at the end of a rope. His father took him down with him in the barrel. It was a terrifying experience with the barrel swaying at the end of the rope and knocking against the sides of the shaft. Henry was terrified. But his father's strong arm was around him and his father's voice was saying: "Don't be afraid, son." They got to the foot of the shaft. Everything was strange and frightening. A miner came up and warned them to be careful of gas, and the warning made things worse. Then, Henry Taylor said, someone came up to him and said: "Aren't you frightened?" "Well," he answered honestly, "I'd be awfully scared except my father is with me."[1]

Gene Tunney tells a thing from his own experience. Before his fight with Jack Dempsey, all the newspapers said that Dempsey would half kill him and perhaps even maim him for life. One night he woke and felt the bed shaking. Gradually it dawned on him that the bed was shaking because he was trembling so much. One thing cured him, *and that one thing was prayer*. He did not pray to win; he prayed not to be afraid; and he willingly bears his testimony: "You can pray away your terrors, if you have enough faith."

Prayer simply means realizing that Jesus is there, remembering that there is nowhere we can go and nothing which can happen to us without Jesus being with us. Gene Tunney knew John M'Cormack, the great tenor singer, intimately. When he visited Ireland he saw a great deal of him and M'Cormack's favourite good-bye was: "May God keep you in the palm of his hand."[2]

That is exactly what God does. We can never be separated from the love of God nor from the presence of Jesus; and if we remember that Jesus is always with us, we will find the storms of life become a calm.

[1]Norman Vincent Peale, *Guideposts*, 8.
[2]Norman Vincent Peale, *Guideposts*, pp. 1-5.

CHAPTER TWELVE

The Priority of Human Need

On another sabbath, when Jesus entered the synagogue and taught, a man was there whose right hand was withered. And the scribes and the Pharisees watched him, to see whether he would heal on the sabbath, so that they might find an accusation against him. But he knew their thoughts, and he said to the man who had the withered hand, "Come and stand here." And he rose and stood there. And Jesus said to them, "I ask you, is it lawful on the sabbath to do good or to do harm, to save life or to destroy it?" And he looked around on them all, and said to him, "Stretch out your hand." And he did so, and his hand was restored. But they were filled with fury and discussed with one another what they might do to Jesus.

    (Luke 6: 6-11; cp. Mark 3 : 1-6; Matthew 12 : 9-14. For other miracles which Jesus worked on the Sabbath day cp. Luke 13 : 11-13; Luke 14 : 1-6; John 9; John 5 : 1-16.)

There is a whole series of miracles in the gospels in which Jesus is depicted as healing people on the Sabbath day and thereby making himself liable to the bitter hostility of the scribes and Pharisees and orthodox Jews. In the time of Jesus the Sabbath had become a tyranny with hundreds of rules and regulations which laid down what a man might and might not do. The development of the Jewish law had followed an amazing course. Originally the law had been the first five books of the Old Testament whose centre was the Ten Commandments. The Ten Commandments are not rules and regulations but great principles which a man must take into his heart and then apply for himself to the situations of life as he finds them. But the Jews were not content with that. They believed that the law was the direct word of God. If so, *it must contain everything*. If a thing was not there explicitly, it must be there implicitly.

So there arose a body of men whose duty it was to study the law and to extract from its great principles a rule and a regulation for every possible man in every possible situation in life. All this elaboration was known as the *Oral Law*. It was the work of the scribes to extract it from the scriptures of the Old

Testament and then to pass it down from generation to generation by word of mouth. A good scribe was said to be like a well-plastered cistern which never lost a drop of water. It was not until after the time of Jesus that this vast mass of oral laws was written down. A summary of them was made and the summary is known as the Mishnah: in its English translation the Mishnah makes a book of almost 800 pages.[1] The scribes and the scholars still went on writing long commentaries on the Mishnah; these are known as the Talmuds. Of the Jerusalem Talmud there are twelve printed volumes and of the Babylonian Talmud there are sixty printed volumes. An orthodox Jew had to govern his life by these thousands of rules and regulations.

The Sabbath law was particularly elaborate. In the Mishnah the section on the Sabbath has twenty-four chapters. In the Jerusalem Talmud the commentary on the Sabbath section of the Mishnah runs to sixty-four and a half columns; and in the Babylonian Talmud it extends to one hundred and fifty-six double folio pages. It was with this mass of rules and regulations that Jesus collided again and again.

In the Old Testament the law which governs the Sabbath is a great, wide principle. "Remember the sabbath day to keep it holy. Six days you shall labour and do all your work; but the seventh day is a sabbath to the Lord your God; in it you shall not do any work, you, or your son, or your daughter, your man-servant, or your maidservant, or your cattle, or the sojourner who is within your gates."[2] A man has to apply this principle to the various circumstances of life.

Let us see what the scribes did with it.[3] First of all they insisted on defining what work is; and they laid down thirty-nine different *fathers of work*, general classifications of things which

[1] The best English translation is, *The Mishnah, translated from the Hebrew with Introduction and brief Explanatory Notes,* by Herbert Danby.

[2] Exodus 20 : 8-11.

[3] The Sabbath regulations may be found in the chapter of the Mishnah entitled Shabbath, in Danby's edition of the *Mishnah* pp. 100-121. The best summary of the Sabbath law, including the development in the Talmuds, is in A. Edersheim, *The Life and Times of Jesus the Messiah.* vol. ii, Pickering & Inglis, 1959, Appendix xvii, pp. 777-787.

constitute work. Not content with that, they divided and sub-divided each of these thirty-nine different classifications. To take an example, one of the kinds of work forbidden was *the carrying of a burden*. But the scribes were not content with that; they had to go on to define a burden. It was "food equal in weight to a dried fig, enough wine for mixing in a goblet, milk enough for one swallow, honey enough to put upon a wound, oil enough to anoint a small member, water enough to moisten an eye-salve, paper enough to write a customs house notice upon, parchment enough to write, 'Hear, O Israel,' ink enough to write two letters of the alphabet, reed enough to make one pen," and so on and on with-out end. Everything was defined; everything was reduced to rules and regulations.

The Sabbath was encompassed with an endless series of these prohibitions. It must be remembered that the orthodox Jew of the day identified these rules and regulations with goodness; to keep them was to please God; to break them was to be guilty of the gravest sin. Now one of the things that was forbidden on the Sabbath was *to heal*. The law was quite definite about this. To heal on the Sabbath was to work; to work was to break the law; to break the law was to sin; therefore to heal on the Sabbath was to sin. It is true that if there was danger to life medical attention might be given. For instance, a woman in childbirth might be helped; any trouble of the eye, the nose, the ear and the throat might be helped. "If a man has a pain in his throat they may drop medicine into his mouth on the Sabbath, since there is doubt whether life is in danger, and wherever there is doubt whether life is in danger this overrides the Sabbath."[1]

Even at this the law was quite clear that steps could be taken *only to keep a man from getting worse*, not to make him any better. An artificial emetic might not be used; a broken limb could be made comfortable but not set; a dislocated hand or foot might be washed, but cold water might not be poured over it.[2] A plain bandage might be put on a cut, but not a medicated bandage; plain cotton wool might be put into a painful ear, but not medi-

[1]*Mishnah*, tractate *Yoma*, 8, 6, Danby, p. 172.
[2]*Mishnah*, tractate, *Shabbath*, 22, 6, Danby, p. 119.

cated cotton wool. There were three kinds of drink which all had medicinal qualities – Greek hyssop, pennyroyal and knotgrass water. Healthy people often drank the second two because they were pleasant to take; the first was used only in sickness. On the Sabbath the second two might be drunk but not the first, because it was used exclusively as a medicine and might therefore improve a man's health. There was a liquid known as purgative water; on the Sabbath, if a man was thirsty and had nothing else to drink, he might drink it, but he might not drink it if he was using it as a purge.[1] If a man had toothache on the Sabbath, he might take vinegar with a meal in the ordinary way as a relish, but he might not suck it through his teeth. If a man's body pained him, he might anoint himself with oil, because it was the daily custom to use oil to anoint the body, but he might not use wine or vinegar or rose-oil which all had curative properties.[2] If, on the Sabbath, a building fell down on a man – walls sometimes collapsed as a man was passing by – and there was a doubt whether the man was actually under it or not, or whether he was dead or alive, or whether he was a Gentile or a Jew, enough might be cleared away to let him be seen. If he was alive, he might be released; if he was dead or a Gentile, he must be left.[3]

It is against that background that we must read the story of the healings which Jesus performed on the Sabbath day. He knew the Sabbath law perfectly well, and deliberately and publicly broke it. The orthodox Jews of the day regarded these laws as a matter of life and death, however fantastic they may appear to us; and, therefore, they regarded Jesus as a law-breaker whose example was an evil and blasphemous thing, which had to be eliminated as quickly as possible. It was from that point that the opposition to Jesus started. With this in our minds let us turn to the miracle itself.

The scene
The miracle happened in the synagogue during the service

[1] *Mishnah*, tractate *Shabbath*, 13, 3, Danby, p. 119.
[2] *Mishnah*, tractate *Shabbath*, 14, 4, Danby, p. 113.
[3] *Mishnah*, tractate *Yoma*, 8, 7, Danby, p. 172.

(Luke 6 : 6). There is no question here of anything like a disturbance of a church service. In the synagogue service there was a certain informality. After the prayers had been said and scripture had been read came the sermon; but there was no one person to preach; any Rabbi or distinguished stranger might do so upon the invitation of the President or Ruler of the synagogue; and after he had preached there was time for discussion and argument. We may take it that it was during the informal part of the service that this scene took place.

At the service there were the scribes and Pharisees (Luke 6 : 7). We have seen that the scribes were the men whose duty it was to draw out of the great principles of the law the rules and regulations. The Pharisees were men who made it the one business of their lives to observe them all. It may be that the name *Pharisee* means *the separated one*. No one could observe all the rules and regulations and go on with the routine business of living; to obey every regulation of the law was a whole-time job. The Pharisees were those who *separated* themselves from ordinary affairs in order to observe every detail of the law.

These scribes and Pharisees had not come to worship and to learn; they had come to spy upon Jesus (Luke 6 : 7). They would be occupying the front seats, the seats of honour, sitting with critical faces and ready to start a heresy hunt at the slightest opportunity. It is always awkward and embarrassing to do something in front of a critical audience. Once a friend was speaking to a very famous surgeon. When a great surgeon operates, the galleries of the operating theatre are sometimes filled with students who intently study the technique of the master surgeon. The friend was thinking how very difficult it is in ordinary things to avoid awkwardness when one's every action is being watched intently. "I don't know," he said to the surgeon, "how you manage to carry on with all these eyes gazing intently at your hands." "When I operate," said the surgeon, "as far as I am concerned, there are only three people in the theatre." "Yes?" said the friend. "There are just myself and the patient I am seeking to help," said the surgeon. "What about the third person you mentioned?" said the friend, thinking it was perhaps the anaesthetist or some other who had an intimate connection with the operation. "The third," said the surgeon quietly, "is God."

That is why Jesus was able to speak and act in that synagogue with a complete disregard of the hostile eyes of the scribes and Pharisees. He was not thinking that they were watching him; he was thinking only that God was watching him. He was able to act with courage and with decision because for him the only spectator of life who mattered was God.

The man

In the synagogue there was a man with a paralysed hand. It is interesting to note that Luke, the doctor, is the only one of the gospel writers who says that it was the man's *right* hand that was paralysed.[1] In the story as our gospels tell it the man does not speak. But there is an old gospel called *The Gospel to the Hebrews*. It failed to gain an entry into the New Testament and is lost except for a few fragments. When the fifth century Christian scholar Jerome was writing about Matthew's account of this incident he said that in *The Gospel to the Hebrews* it is related that the man appealed to Jesus to help him. "I was a stone mason," said the man, "seeking to earn my living with my hands: I pray you, Jesus, give me back my health, that I may not have to beg my bread in shame."[2]

So then Jesus was faced with two things. He was faced with the critical faces of the scribes and Pharisees; and he was faced with the appeal of human need. He knew that if he answered the appeal of human need, he would play right into the hands of the hostile watchers. He knew that he would do exactly what they were waiting for him to do, that he would give them an opportunity to brand him as a Sabbath-breaker and do it so publicly as to burn his boats for ever. Not for one moment did he hesitate. For him there was no priority above that of human need.

Jesus's first words to the man were a command that he should rise from his place and stand in the middle of the synagogue where

---

[1]Luke 6 : 6; cp. Matthew 12 : 10; Mark 3 : 1.

[2]The fragments of *The Gospel to the Hebrews* are given in M. R. James, *The Apocryphal New Testament*, pp. 1-8. This saying is on pp. 4, 5.

everyone could see him.[1] Very likely there were two reasons for this. First, it was to demonstrate to the watching scribes and Pharisees that, whatever he was going to do, he was not going to do in a corner. He was quite prepared to meet the challenge of the scribes and Pharisees. There comes a time when a man has to show beyond a doubt where he stands.

There is a story which tells how one of John Wesley's early preachers came to a town where the people were hostile to the new evangelism. He hired the bellman to go round the town announcing the time and the place of the meeting. The bellman, knowing the hostility of the people, made the announcement in a very quiet voice that no one could hear. Thereupon the Methodist preacher took the bell from the bellman and made the announcement that so and so would preach in such and such a place and at such and such a time, "and," he said, "I am the man."

The action of Jesus in bidding the man to stand forth was his way of saying that he defied the scribes and Pharisees to do their worst. But it may be that he had another reason. It may be that he was making an attempt to kindle sympathy in the hearts of the onlookers. It may be that he was saying by his action: "Are you going to allow your rules and regulations to stand between this man and the healing he so much longs for?"

The scribes and the Pharisees

If Jesus healed this man he definitely broke the law; to heal was to work. No one could say that this man's life was in danger or that he would get any worse if the healing was left until the next day. But Jesus did not see why any man should have to wait even one day longer than necessary for the help that he could bring. We must look not only at this incident but also at the incident of the healing of the crooked woman[2] and of the man with dropsy[3] to see how Jesus dealt with the scribes and Pharisees.

In this case he turned to the scribes and Pharisees and said: "Is it lawful on the Sabbath day to do good, or to do evil? to save life, or to destroy it?" Here was a personal challenge indeed. What Jesus was really saying was this: "I am in this synagogue

[1]Luke 6 : 8.   [2]Luke 13 : 11-13.   [3]Luke 14 : 1-6.

and I am trying to help a man regain his health, his strength, his self-respect. You are in this synagogue and you are trying to find a way to destroy me. In the sight of God who do you think is right – I, who am seeking to save a life, or you, who are seeking to destroy one?"

When it came to acuteness of argument Jesus could meet the Rabbis on their own ground in skill. When he healed the woman who had had a curvature of the spine for eighteen years, the ruler of the synagogue found fault with him because he had healed on the Sabbath and not left the matter to an ordinary day of the week. Jesus pointed out that the very scribal law permitted cattle to be loosed from their stalls on the Sabbath day and to be led out to be watered. If it was lawful to loosen the tether of an animal on the Sabbath, how much more must it be lawful to loosen the bond with which Satan had bound this poor woman? (Luke 13 : 15, 16). When he healed the man with the dropsy on the Sabbath day and the scribes and Pharisees critized him for it, Jesus pointed out that if an ass or an ox fell into a pit on the Sabbath day the law would not prohibit help from being given. If it is lawful to help an animal, surely it is still more lawful to help a human being?

To Jesus any law which prohibited help being given to any man on any day was an irreverent absurdity. The man who is really obeying the commandment of God is not he who rigidly observes legalistic rules and regulations but he whose one desire is to bring help to his fellow men. In effect Jesus was saying to the scribes and Pharisees: "It is not rules and regulations you ought to love but men and women. Nothing takes priority over human need."

The man's share in the miracle
Jesus defied the men who had come to catch him out. He turned to the man and uttered one command: "Stretch out your hand" (Luke 6 : 10). Here was the test. The man might have answered: "Don't you see that my hand is paralysed? That's the very thing that I can't do." But that is just what the man did not say. No matter what Jesus told him to do he was prepared to try it. And that is precisely the way to experience a miracle. The first

essential is to banish the word impossible from our thought. There are two sides to every miracle; God's power and our response; without our response not even God's power can act. We never know what is possible until we try to do it.

William James, the American philosopher, held that none of us had ever really put out more than one-tenth of our physical and mental effort. The man who begins a task with the conviction that it is impossible need never start it. But there are no limits to what we can do if we set out with the idea that with God all things are possible. Jesus Christ can do anything with the man who is willing to try. Amos Wells has a poem which sings of the joy which came to the man who received his health back again because he was prepared to attempt the impossible:

"Praise God! Praise God! Give me my tools again!
    Oh! Let me grasp a hammer and a saw!
    Bring me a nail, and any piece of wood,
    Come, see me shut my hand and open it,
    And watch my nimble fingers twirl a ring.
    How good are solids! – oak, and stone, and iron,
    And rough and smooth and straight and curved and round!
    Here, Rachel: for these long and weary years
    My hand has ached to smooth your shining hair
    And touch your dimpled cheek. Come, wife, and see
    I am a man again, a man for work,
    A man for earning bread and clothes and home –
    A man no more a bandaged cumberer
    And did you hear them muttering at him?
    And did you see them looking sour at me?
    They'll cast me from the synagogue, perchance:
    But let them: I've a hand, a hand, a hand!
    And, ah, dear wife, to think he goes about
    so quietly, and does such things as this,
    Making poor half men whole. . . ."[1]

[1]Quoted in Rita F. Snowden, *If I open my Door*, p. 132.

CHAPTER THIRTEEN

Fulfilling the Obligations of a Citizen

WHEN they came to Capernaum, the collectors of the half-shekel tax
went up to Peter and said, "Does not your teacher pay the tax?"
He said, "Yes." And when he came home, Jesus spoke to him first,
saying, "What do you think, Simon? From whom do kings of the
earth take toll or tribute? From their sons or from others?" And
when he said, "From others," Jesus said to him, "Then the sons
are free. However, not to give offence to them, go to the sea and cast
a hook, and take the first fish that comes up, and when you open its
mouth you will find a shekel; take that and give it to them for me
and for yourself."

(Matthew 17 : 24-27.)

The Temple at Jerusalem did not run itself for nothing. The
ritual and the sacrifices were costly things.

Many of the sacrifices were offered by the worshippers out of
their own private means; when a man wished to make some offering to God, he naturally paid for it himself. But certain sacrifices
were made for the whole nation every day. Morning and evening
three offerings were made – a male lamb one year old, a meat
offering of flour and oil, and a drink offering of wine. The full
regulations are in Exodus 29 : 38-41:

> "Now this is what you shall offer upon the altar: two lambs
> a year old day by day continually. One lamb you shall offer
> in the morning, and the other lamb you shall offer in the
> evening; and with the first lamb a tenth measure of fine
> flour mingled with a fourth of a hin of beaten oil, and a
> fourth of a hin of wine for a libation. And the other lamb
> you shall offer in the evening, and shall offer with it a cereal
> offering and its libation, as in the morning, for a pleasing
> odour, an offering by fire to the Lord."[1]

[1] cp. Numbers 28 : 3-8; 1 Chronicles 16 : 40; 2 Chronicles 13 : 11.
For a full description of the daily sacrifices see E. Schürer, *A History of
the Jewish People*, 2, 1, 273-298. A *deal* was the same as an ephah, and
was equal to 8 gallons; a *hin* was about $1\frac{1}{2}$ gallons.

As long as the Temple stood, even in days of siege and starvation, this daily sacrifice was never omitted.

In addition to the expense of the daily sacrifices, there was the expense of the incense which was burned before the morning and after the evening sacrifice; the expense of wood for the altar fires and oil for the lamps; the expense of the robes of the priests and the hangings and curtains of the Temple courts; the expense of continually beautifying and constantly administering the sanctuary.

To meet all this there was the Temple tax.[1] In ancient times the expense of the sacrifices had been defrayed by the kings. "It shall be the prince's duty to furnish the burnt offerings, cereal offerings, and drink offerings ... at all the appointed feasts of the house of Israel."[2] But long before the time of Jesus this had become a national expense. The regulations regarding the Temple tax were taken right back to the building of the Tabernacle.[3] That was no doubt a reading back of a later regulation into earlier times, for it was characteristic of the Jews to wish to give to all their practices the earliest possible origin. That regulation was certainly operative in the days of Nehemiah (Neh. 10:32). The tax itself was one half-shekel, which was roughly equivalent to two denarii. In the time of Jesus a working man's wage was a denarius a day, so that the Temple tax was the equivalent of two days' wages, and that at a time when wages were low. The tax was almost universally imposed. "From whom did they exact pledges? From levites, Israelites, proselytes, and freed slaves, but not from women slaves or minors."[4] A man became liable for the tax at twenty years of age. In the early days the tax was voluntary, but in the year 78 B.C. it had become compulsory, and the Temple authorities had the right to distrain upon a man's property if it was not paid.

[1]For full information concerning the Temple tax and its payment, see E. Schürer, *The Jewish People in the Time of Jesus Christ*, 2, 1, 249-251; A. Edersheim, *The Temple, its Ministry and services as they were in the Time of Jesus Christ*, 71-75.
[2]Ezekiel 45 : 17. [3]Exodus 30 : 11-16.
[4]*The Mishnah*, Tractate *Shekalim* (The Shekel Dues), 1, 3, Danby's translation, p. 152.

This Temple tax brought into the Temple no less than £76,000 a year. It was usually paid by a village or a community as a whole. On the first day of the month Adar – that is about the middle of March – proclamation was made that the time of the tax payment had come. On the fifteenth day of Adar stalls where the tax could be paid were set up in all the villages and towns and communities. On the twenty-fifth day of Adar the stalls were removed and thereafter the tax could be paid only in the Temple itself. Not only did the Jews of Palestine pay this tax; the Jews dispersed all over the world also paid it. It was one of their great links with the Temple and the Holy City.

Sometimes that payment caused trouble. There were many Jews in Phrygia. The Roman governor of the province was alarmed at the amount of money which was leaving the province and he banned the export of currency. His name was Flaccus and the date was 62 B.C. In spite of his orders, the Jews of Laodicaea made their collection and sent it off. The result was that twenty pounds weight of gold was seized as contraband. Twenty pounds weight of gold would be equal to 15,000 drachmae. The tax was equal to two drachmae and that means that about 7,500 Jews sent home the Temple tax from Laodicaea alone.[1] It is known that the Jews of the district in Asia Minor around Hierapolis sent as much as £7,500 in tax to the Temple in one year.

Every devout Jew throughout the world gladly paid his tax to the Temple he loved so well; and in Palestine every Jew paid whether he liked it or not.

Jesus and the Temple tax
It was that Temple tax which was in question in this incident. Jesus and his friends were in Capernaum where the booths for the payment of the tax had been set up. The authorities asked Peter if Jesus was in the habit of paying this tax. It is probable that they hoped Jesus would refuse to pay the tax so that they would have another reason to accuse him of being a law-breaker. Jesus knew that this question had been put and, when Peter came

[1] Sir W. M. Ramsay, *The Letters to the Seven Churches*, p. 420.

into the house where they were staying, he asked him a question. "Peter," he said, "do kings usually exact taxes and tribute from their own people or from foreigners?"

In those days nations had little idea of benefiting the peoples whom they conquered. Especially in the East, the regular custom was to exploit conquered nations. The conquerors did not pay any taxes but financed the expenses of their government by extracting taxes from their subject nations. There was a quite common class of people called the *paroikoi* or *metoikoi*, what we might call *resident aliens*. Strangers who had come to settle in a town, they did not become citizens but paid what was called an *alien tax*. In the ancient world it was only foreigners and strangers who had taxes to pay.

Now this tax which had just been demanded from Jesus was the *Temple* tax; the Temple was the house of God; and God was in a very special sense the Father of Jesus. The Temple was, therefore, his Father's house.[1] There was no necessity for him to pay a tax to his own Father's house; but, for all that, Jesus was willing to pay. He claimed no special exemptions. He would give no man a chance to say that he was lax in the discharge of his duty to God.

The coin in the fish's mouth
The tax was half a shekel, two silver drachmae, if Jesus was to pay the tax for himself and for Peter, he must find a stater, a four-drachmae piece, and that was a lot of money. As Matthew tells the story, Jesus told Peter to go to the lakeside and cast a line into the sea, and the first fish he hooked would have a four-drachmae piece in its mouth with which he would pay the Temple tax.

If we take this story literally, it is the strangest miracle Jesus ever performed and quite unlike any of the others. The other miracles were done for other people. If this one is taken literally, it is merely an easy way out of a practical difficulty for Jesus himself.

[1] Luke 2 : 49 would be more correctly translated: "Did you know that I must be in my Father's house?"

There can be little doubt how we are meant to read this story. When Jesus was confronted with the demand for the Temple tax, he said: "Peter, this tax must be paid. Get out your boat and your nets. Go back to the fishing for a day and that will earn enough for us to pay the tax." The coin was to come from the fish's mouth all right – but Peter was to catch the fish.

For Jesus simply to have produced a coin whenever he wanted one would have been quite wrong. It is a first principle of life that God will never do for us what we are well able to do for ourselves. That would be to encourage laziness on our part. For Jesus to have used his miraculous power to produce money would have been to misuse his power. This story is a vivid eastern way of telling us that when Jesus and his men needed money to fulfil their obligations they got it at their trade.

The Christian duty

We have always to remember that the New Testament stories are handed down, not simply as stories, but as guides in the matter of daily life and living. Thomas Arnold, the great headmaster of Rugby, once said in a sermon: "O that we would know and remember to search the Scriptures, not for truths, but for lessons!"[1] What does this story teach us?

It so happens that the preservation of this story comes out of a definite set of circumstances. The Gospel according to St. Matthew was written somewhere between A.D. 80 and 90. Just at that time a puzzling situation had arisen for the Jews; and, because the Roman government found it difficult to distinguish between Christians and Jews, it involved the Christians, too. In A.D. 70 the city of Jerusalem was taken and destroyed by the Romans; the Temple was left a heap of ruins. To this day the Temple has never been rebuilt. The Romans laid it down that the Jews' Temple tax should now be paid to them to support the temple of Jupiter Capitolinus in Rome. Josephus tells us: "He (that is, the Roman Emperor Vespasian) laid a tribute on the Jews, wheresoever they were, and enjoined every one of them to bring two drachmae every year into the Capitol, as they

[1] Quoted F. J. Woodward, *The Doctor's Disciples*, p. 6.

used to pay the same to the Temple at Jerusalem."[1] Suetonius, the Roman historian, tells us that in the reign of Domitian, "besides other taxes, that on the Jews was levied with the utmost rigour." He goes on to say that those who lived as Jews without acknowledging the Jewish faith and without paying the tribute to the Jewish Temple, were also brought under tribute.[2] By these he means the Christians, because he thought that they were a sect of the Jews since Christianity originated in Palestine.

When that demand was made of the Jews and Christians, naturally many of them would rebel and refuse to pay the taxes which the Roman government imposed. If that had gone on, the Christians would simply have acquired the reputation of being disloyal citizens and Christianity would have been much damaged. So when the Gospel according to St. Matthew was written, the writer put in this incident to show that Jesus fulfilled all the obligations which the law of citizenship laid down.

First and foremost this story teaches us that a Christian must be a good citizen. There has always been a tendency for Christians to be so taken up with heaven that they forget their duties to this earth. Sometimes the Christians wrote and spoke as if they did not care what happened to the community in which they lived. Tertullian wrote: "The Christian knows that on earth he has a pilgrimage but that his dignity is in heaven." "Nothing is of any importance to us in this world except to depart from it as quickly as possible."[3] Clement of Alexandria wrote: "We have no fatherland on earth."[4] Augustine wrote: "We are sojourners unable to live happily exiled from our fatherland; we desire means to help us to end our sorrows and to return to our native country."[5] In a certain sense this is true: our citizenship, as Paul said, is in heaven (Phil. 3 : 20). But the danger is that, if this kind of point of view is overstressed, it might end in the belief that the Christian has no duties at all as a citizen and as

---

[1]Josephus, *Wars of the Jews*, 7, 6, 6.
[2]Suetonius, *The Lives of the Caesars*, Domitian, 12.
[3]Tertullian, *Apology* 1 and 41.
[4]Clement of Alexandria, *Paedagogos*, 3, 8, 1.
[5]Augustine, *Concerning Christian Doctrine*, 2, 4.

a member of the community.

In point of fact a Christian should be a better citizen than anyone else and the first to shoulder his obligations. One of the great tragedies of modern life is that it is just here that Christians on the whole have failed. Town councils, trade unions and the like are often dominated by people who are indifferent or hostile to Christianity. But if Christians will not take office and shoulder their responsibilities they are at fault if, for instance, Communists have too much power in certain circles.

The necessity of work
This story teaches an even wider lesson. If we take it in the way that we have suggested, Jesus was saying to Peter: "Peter, we need some money; go and work for it." This story teaches us that nothing in this world can be obtained without work. Jesus is saying to us: "You can fulfil your obligations to life only by using the gifts God gave to you."

CHAPTER FOURTEEN

The Defeat of Death

The Raising of the Daughter of Jairus and of the Son of the Widow of Nain

THEN came one of the rulers of the synagogue, Jairus by name, and seeing Jesus, he fell at his feet, and besougnt him, saying, "My little daughter is at the point of death. Come and lay your hands on her, so that she may be made well, and live." And he went with him.

While he was still speaking, there came from the ruler's house some who said, "Your daughter is dead. Why trouble the Teacher any further?" But ignoring what they said, Jesus said to the ruler of the synagogue, "Do not fear, only believe." And he allowed no one to follow him except Peter and James and John the brother of James. When they came to the house of the ruler of the synagogue, he saw a tumult, and people weeping and wailing loudly. And when he had entered, he said to them, "Why do you make a tumult and weep? The child is not dead but sleeping." And they laughed at him. But he put them all outside, and took the child's father and mother and those who were with him, and went in where the child was. Taking her by the hand he said to her, "Talitha cumi"; which means, "Little girl, I say to you, arise." And immediately the girl got up and walked; for she was twelve years old. And immediately they were overcome with amazement. And Jesus strictly charged them that no one should know this, and told them to give her something to eat.

(Mark 5 : 22-24, 35-43; cp. Matthew 9 : 18, 19, 23-25; Luke 8 : 41, 42, 49-56.)

SOON afterwards Jesus went to a city called Nain, and his disciples and a great crowd went with him. As he drew near to the gate of the city, behold, a man who had died was being carried out, the only son of his mother, and she was a widow; and a large crowd from the city was with her. And when the Lord saw her, he had compassion on her and said to her; "Do not weep." And he came and touched the bier, and the bearers stood still. And he said, "Young man, I say to you, arise." And the dead man sat up, and began to speak. And he gave him to his mother.

(Luke 7 : 11-15.)

In the first three gospels there are two stories which tell how
Jesus rescued people from death, the daughter of Jairus and the
son of the widow of Nain; and they are two of the loveliest
stories in the whole New Testament. However they are explained,
these remain two of the most moving and precious stories about
the life and power of Jesus.

A man in need

Jairus was a most important man. He was one of the rulers of
the synagogue, the men responsible for the correct administration of the synagogue and the reverent conduct of its services.
They administered all the synagogue's financial affairs and material
undertakings. They might not actually share in the conduct of
the services themselves but they decided who was to take the
prayers and who was to preach the sermon. The rulers of the
synagogue were looked up to by all.

Jairus had a daughter who was so ill that there seemed no hope
of her recovery; and she was only twelve years of age. In the East
young people grow up far more quickly and twelve was just the
age when a girl was likely to get married.[1] This girl was just
on the threshold of womanhood, with life opening out before her.
All the resources that the physicians could command seemed
helpless to save her; and then Jairus took an extraordinary step –
he decided to go to Jesus for help. We must remember that by
this time Jesus had incurred the hatred of the Jewish religious
authorities. He had begun by preaching in the synagogue; but
in the synagogue he had healed the man with the withered hand
on the Sabbath day and thus broken the law. The consequence
was that the religious leaders were out for his life so that he had to
leave the synagogues and take to the open country (Mark 3 : 1-7).
In his hour of need Jairus turned to the man whom he and his
colleagues had already branded as a heretic and a sinner.

This very fact tells us something about Jairus and something

[1]A. C. Bouquet, *Everyday Life in New Testament Times*, p. 145.
"Marriage could be at a very early age, say eleven or twelve, and
sometimes even nine."

about Jesus. It tells us that *Jairus was a man who was prepared to swallow his pride*. He was prepared to ask help from the man whom he had despised. Nothing can so readily bring a man to disaster as the pride which will not ask for help. One of the great legends of the world is a kind of parable on that. One of Charlemagne's greatest paladins was Roland, and Roland had an inseparable friend called Oliver. Charlemagne, so the legend runs, was returning from fighting against the Moors in Spain, and Roland was in command of the rearguard of the army. All unexpectedly the rearguard was attacked by a force of Moors who out-numbered them by a hundred to one. Now Roland had a horn of such tremendous power that it could be heard miles away. It was so powerful that its blast killed the birds as they flew in the sky. Oliver said to Roland: "Blow your horn, and Charlemagne will hear it and return with help." But Roland was too proud to ask for help. He would fight and conquer these Moors alone. For long the battle raged, and ever fresh reinforcements kept coming to the Moors. In the end Roland's little force was cut to pieces. Oliver was dead and he himself was mortally wounded. Then he put his horn to his lips and blew it, and Charlemagne far away heard the note of the horn and came back. But it was too late, for Roland and Oliver and all their men were dead. Roland was too proud to ask for help and his pride brought him to disaster and to death.

Jairus was not too proud to ask for help, even from this Jesus whom he had once despised. That is why he received his daughter back, rescued from death. If we want to keep from many a mistake, and perhaps from spoiling our lives altogether, we should never be too proud to ask for advice and help when we need them; and always humble enough to accept them when we receive them.

Equally this story tells us something about Jesus. It tells us that he *bore no grudges.* It would have been easy for him to say: "You banished me from your synagogues; you insulted me by calling me a sinner and a heretic; and now that you are in trouble you want me. I want nothing to do with you." But that is exactly what Jesus did not do.

George Sava, the famous surgeon, tells a story in one of his books. During the Second World War, a continental surgeon had escaped from Prague and was using his skill to serve the wounded in a London hospital. News filtered through to England that Prague had been savagely bombed; and the surgeon learned that his mother and father were among the dead. There was an air raid in London. The telephone rang and the surgeon was summoned to hospital to carry out an emergency operation. When he reached the hospital he found that the person on whom he was to operate was a German air force officer whose plane had been shot down in flames and who had been dreadfully injured in the crash. A thought came into the surgeon's mind. This man was a member of the air force which had killed his father and his mother; for all he knew, the very man who had dropped the bomb which killed them. The man was so badly injured that no one would be surprised if he died. Only the most superlative surgery could save him, and even that was only a chance. It would be so easy just to see that he did not recover. The surgeon dressed and went into the operating room. Hours later he emerged, looked at his assistant, smiled and said, "I think he'll live." Here was a man who could not bear a grudge. What the German had done made no difference. All that mattered was that he needed his skill.

One of the things which embitters life and divides people is the bearing of grudges. Jesus never bore a grudge; neither must we.

The house of mourning

Jesus was detained on the way to Jairus's house; he stopped to comfort the poor frightened woman with the haemorrhage who had touched his robe and been healed (Mark 5 : 25-34). Just as he was setting out on the way again messengers came from Jairus's house to say that the girl was dead and that there was no point in Jesus's coming now. But Jesus insisted on going on. He told Jairus not to fear, and to keep on believing.

Jesus well knew what he would find in that house of grief.[1] The Jews regarded the expression of sorrow for the dead as one of the most sacred duties, the omission of which brought the direst consequences. The Rabbis said: "Whoever is remiss in mourning over the death of a wise man, deserves to be burned alive." "The tears dropped over the death of a virtuous man are counted by the Holy One, blessed be he! And they are laid by in his treasuries." "Children die young because their fathers have not mourned over the death of a virtuous man." The most definite steps were taken to see that mourning was carried out; but the steps were such that a house of mourning must have been more like pandemonium than anything else.

There were three customs which would be found in every house of mourning. All of them must have been going on in the house of Jairus when Jesus arrived on the scene.

The rent garments

There was the rending of garments. There were no fewer than thirty-nine different laws which prescribed just how garments were to be rent. The rent was to be made standing. Clothes were to be rent to the heart so that the skin was exposed. For a father or mother the rent was to be exactly over the heart; for others the rent was on the right hand side. The rent must be big enough to put a fist through. For the seven days of deep mourning the rent was to be left gaping open; for the thirty days of lighter mourning it was to be roughly stitched up, in such a way that it could still be seen that the garment was rent; only after that

[1]For information regarding Jewish mourning customs, the following may be consulted. A. Edersheim, *Sketches of Jewish Social Life*, chapter x, *In death and after death*, pp. 161-182; H. B. Tristram, *Eastern Customs in Bible Lands*, chapter v, *Marriage and Burial Customs*, pp. 89-109; K. E. Keith, *The Social Life of a Jew in the Time of Christ*, chapter x, *Death and Burial*, pp. 84-93; W. M. Thomson, *The Land and the Book*, pp. 104-108; G. Robinson Lees, *Village Life in Palestine*, pp. 128-133; J. Hastings, *Dictionary of Christ and the Gospels;* the following articles: *Mourning*, by W. H. Rankine, vol. ii, pp. 208, 209; *Rending Garments*, by W. H. Rankine, vol. ii, p. 496; *Wailing*, by T. Gregory, vol. ii, p. 811; *Flute-playing*, by W. Taylor Smith, vol. i, p. 603.

might the rent be permanently repaired. It would obviously have been immodest for women to rend their garments in such a way that the breast was exposed. So it was laid down that a woman should rend her inner garment in private; she must then reverse it and wear it back to front; and then in public she must rend the outer garment. Thus her garments were rent but her body was not exposed to view.

Wailing for the dead

All the time that the body of the dead person was in the house an incessant wailing was kept up. Matthew talks about the people "making a tumult."[1] Mark talks about the ado and the weeping.[2] Luke says that they wept and bewailed her.[3] There must indeed have been a tumult for the verb used to describe this weeping really means howling. There were women who carried out this duty professionally. Jeremiah[4] mentions them when he bids the people call the mourning women. "Let them make haste and raise a wailing over us, that our eyes may run down with tears, and our eyelids gush with water." The *Talmud* lays it down: "The husband is bound to bury his dead wife, and to make lamentations and mourning for her, according to the custom of all countries. And also the very poorest amongst the Israelites will not allow her less than two pipes and one mourning woman; but if he be rich, let all things be done according to his quality." There would not be a house of mourning in Palestine where these wailing women were not present. This wailing is still a sign of sorrow in the East. Tristram describes it: "The breath has scarcely left the body when the professional mourners appear. These are the old women and gossips of the village or neighbourhood, who seem always to be in waiting and need no summons."[5] Thomson gives us an even clearer and more detailed picture: "There are in every city and community women exceedingly cunning in this business. They are always sent for, and kept in readiness. When a fresh company of sympathisers comes

[1]Matthew 9 : 23.   [2]Mark 5 : 39.   [3]Luke 8 : 52.
[4]Jeremiah 9 : 17, 18.
[5]H. B. Tristram, *Eastern Customs in Bible Lands*, p. 95.

in, these women make haste to take up a wailing, that the newly come may the more easily unite their tears with the mourners. They know the domestic history of every person, and immediately strike up an impromptu lamentation, in which they introduce the names of their relatives who have recently died, touching some tender chord in every heart; and thus each one weeps for his own dead, and the performance which would otherwise be difficult or impossible comes easy and natural."[1] To us there is something almost revolting in this artificial sorrow. When Jesus arrived in the house of Jairus the mourning women would already be there and the wailing would already have begun.

Flute playing

There would be the flute-players; Matthew speaks about *the minstrels*.[2] In ancient times flute-players with their wailing tunes were an integral part of mourning in every country. "Flutes for a corpse" was a regular phrase. Josephus[3] tells us that, when in A.D. 67 news reached Jerusalem of the disastrous capture of Jotapata by the Romans, "most people engaged flute-players to lead their lamentations." And we know that even at the funeral of the Roman Emperor Claudius in A.D. 54 flute-players were present.

The scene in a house of mourning must have been an astonishing thing. It went to pattern and to plan. No doubt there would be in the hearts of those who loved the departed a spontaneous and genuine grief often beyond words and beyond tears. But into every house of sorrow there came the artificial paraphernalia of mourning; the carefully arranged rending of the garments, the deliberate wailing of the professional wailing women and the shrill, sad melody of the flutes. And it was into such a home that Jesus came when he entered the house of Jairus.

He asked what all the disturbance was about and said that the girl was not dead, but only asleep. The crowd of mourners laughed at him. They thought they knew better. Jesus put them all out; into the room he took the father and mother of the girl,

---

[1] W. M. Thomson, *The Land and the Book*, p. 103.
[2] Matthew 9 : 23.   [3] Josephus, *The Wars of the Jews*, 3, 9, 5.

and Peter, James and John. He stood over the girl and said with gentleness and authority combined: "Child, awake!" At once she arose and walked about. As father and mother gazed in astonishment at their daughter come back to life, Jesus told them to give her some food so that they might see that the cure was real.

Sleep or death?

There is undoubtedly a problem in this miracle. To put it in a sentence it is: Was Jesus speaking literally when he said that the girl was asleep or was he using sleep to mean death? The difficulty is accentuated by the fact that there are little differences in the narrative as given by Mark and Matthew and Luke. Mark's is the earliest account and, we believe, goes directly back to the memory of Peter. If we had only Mark's account, we would most naturally come to the conclusion that the girl was not dead but in a coma. Vincent Taylor quotes Turner as saying: "If we could read Mark without presuppositions from Matthew and Luke we should take the meaning to be coma."[1] Alan Menzies writes: "If Mark's account stood alone, there could be little doubt as to the purport of the story. Here the child is not really but only apparently dead; her spirit has not departed definitely but only for a time."[2]

We ought carefully to read the three accounts.[3] That of Mark is by far the longest and the fullest and its whole tone is that Jesus steadfastly refuses to believe that the girl is dead. In Mark 5 : 23 Jairus arrives saying that his daughter is *at the point of death*. In Luke 8 : 41, 42 Jairus comes saying that his daughter *is dying*. But only in Matthew 9 : 18 is Jairus depicted as saying that his daughter is *even now dead*, that is to say, that she has just died. Again, in Mark 5 : 40, Matthew 9 : 24 and Luke 8 : 53, all three say that the mourners laughed at Jesus when he said that the girl was asleep but only Luke adds the phrase "knowing that she was dead." The curious thing is that only Mark never actually says that the girl is dead.

[1]Vincent Taylor, *The Gospel according to St. Mark*, p. 295.
[2]Alan Menzies, *The Earliest Gospel*, p. 131.
[3]Mark 5:22-24, 35-43; Matthew 9 : 18, 19, 23-25; Luke 8 : 41, 42, 49-56.

Burial in the East takes place with astonishing quickness because of the hot climate. Tristram says: "Interments always take place at latest on the evening of the day of death, and frequently at night, if the deceased have lived till after sunset."[1] Further it is a matter of medical history that in the ancient world the signs of the occurrence of death were not so scientifically known as they are now.[2] Between the speed of burial, necessitated by the climate, and the rudimentary medical knowledge, it was by no means impossible that mistakes should happen and that people who were in a coma or trance should be buried alive. The evidence of eastern tombs confirms that this did happen.

In fact there are occasions in much more recent times of the same kind of thing. J. M. Thompson[3] quotes an astonishing instance from the daily newspapers of December 30, 1910: "A remarkable story of a Boy Scout's dramatic reappearance after his supposed death following a surgical operation came from Nottingham last night. At a social gathering of the Nottingham Wesley Mission Boy Scouts on Wednesday night a letter was received by Mr. D. Wright, the scoutmaster, stating that a member of the company had died. It contained a farewell message from the boy and a note from the nurse that the funeral arrangements would be sent later. It was known that the boy had to undergo a surgical operation and a week previously he had attended service at the mission, when prayers were offered for his recovery. On receipt of intimation of the boy's death, the scout leader decided to postpone the festivities but a profound sensation was caused by the sudden appearance of the supposed dead boy himself. 'It was all a mistake,' he explained. 'They thought I was dead and laid me out, but when the doctor came later he saw a slight flush on my cheek, and then discovered I was breathing slightly. Within an hour or two I was well enough to get up, and when nurse told me a letter had been sent I determined to come here myself.' The boy stated he had no recollection of what

[1] H. B. Tristram, *Eastern Customs in Bible Lands*, p. 94.

[2] Alan Menzies quotes an article in the *Expository Times*, xii (March, 1901), p. 256, on this aspect of the subject.

[3] J. M. Thompson, *Miracles in the New Testament*, p. 44, footnote.

occurred during the twelve hours he lay in a trance, except that he lay covered only with a counterpane. He is still in a weak condition. On several previous occasions the boy has, it is stated, been seized with faints, during which for a considerable interval life has appeared to be extinct."

That is an amazing story; and if that could happen in England in the twentieth century, it is certainly possible that something like it could happen in Palestine in the first century. Of this miracle J. H. Bernard wrote: "Even those who reject all miracles need find no difficulty in Mark 5: 35 or Luke 7: 11.[1] And Vincent Taylor wisely says of it: "In these circumstances I do not think that a modern reader need feel disquieted if he finds himself inclined now to this opinion and now to that."[2] If the girl was in a trance and Jesus raised her from it, it would mean that he saw what no one else could see and, in the most real sense, rescued her from a dreadful death. To believe this is in no way to detract from the wonderful knowledge and compassionate love of Jesus Christ.

The eternal truth of the story
Whatever we deduce to have happened in the house of Jairus, one thing is certain – the writers tell this as the story of a girl who was raised from the dead. But they tell it for a purpose. No gospel story is told simply for its own sake but always to illustrate great Christian truth. This story has two great truths to tell us, truths closely allied to each other.[3]

First, *death is a sleep and from a sleep there is an awakening*. It is continually as a sleep that the New Testament speaks of death. At the end of Stephen's terrible martyrdom, he fell asleep.[4] David, after he had served his day and generation, fell asleep.[5] Some of those who were witnesses of the Resurrection are now asleep.[6] Those who have died are those who have fallen asleep.[7]

[1] J. H. Bernard, *St. John*, vol. i, p. clxxxiv.
[2] Vincent Taylor, *The Gospel according to St. Mark*, p. 286.
[3] For the following interpretation of the teaching of the raising of Jairus's daughter see Alan Richardson, *The Miracle Stories of the Gospels*, pp. 74, 75.
[4] Acts 7: 60.   [5] Acts 13: 36.   [6] 1 Corinthians 15: 6.
[7] 1 Corinthians 15: 18, 20.

The dead are those who are asleep in Christ.[1] All over the New Testament there is this certainty that death is not an obliteration but a sleep.

Second, if that be so, *there is no cause for mourning in death.* Jesus put the wailing women and the flute-players outside; they had no right to be there. When someone dies, it is natural and inevitable to be sad; but our sorrow is for ourselves and not for those who have died. If we believe that death is only a sleep from which we wake to be in heaven, we cannot be sorry for those who have died. So far from being sorry, we ought to be glad that they have entered into a far greater life.

In the early Church the Christian martyrs called the day of their death their *birth-day*. It was the day which ushered them into real life. John Ruskin once said: "I will not wear black for the guests of God." An incomprehensible thing is the way we wear the colour of deepest gloom in honour of those who have passed into the greatest glory.

Gertrude Knevels wrote this lovely poem when sorrow came to her:

> "Shall I wear mourning for my soldier dead,
> I – a believer? Give me red,
> Or give me royal purple for the King
> At whose high court my love is visiting.
> Dress me in green for growth, for life made new;
> For skies his dear feet march, dress me in blue,
> In white for his dear soul; robe me in gold
> For all the pride that his new rank shall hold.
> In earth's dim gardens blooms no hue too bright
> To dress me for my love who walks in light."[2]

Nain

We now turn to the other story which tells of Jesus's power to rescue from death, the raising of the son of the widow of Nain.

Nain is about 25 miles from Capernaum. It would actually

[1] 1 Thessalonians 4 : 13-15.
[2] Quoted by Rita F. Snowden in *If I open my Door*, p. 66.

be in sight from the hill-top above Nazareth and Jesus would know it well. Its name means *The Pleasant Place*[1] and it was in the time of Jesus a lovely place. It was said by the Rabbis that it was Nain of which he was thinking when Issacher said of his inheritance: "He saw the land that it was pleasant."[2] Nowadays Nain is an undistinguished village; but the burying-place to which the funeral cortege was going is still to be seen. Tristram writes: "Thus at Nain the approach to the place is from the north-east, the Tiberias road, by which our Lord would travel; and on this road, a little distance from what once were walls, is the burying place still used by the Moslems, with a few whitened sepulchres, and many oblong piles of stones, marking the humbler graves. This, from its situation, must have been the ancient cemetery; and there is no trace of any other."[3] It is interesting and suggestive to note that Nain is near Shunem where Elisha also raised a widow's only son.[4]

In Palestine cemeteries were always outside the city boundaries and as Jesus entered into Nain, there met him a grief-stricken funeral procession, for a widow's only son was being borne out to his tomb.

---

[1] A. Edersheim, *The Life and Times of Jesus the Messiah*, vol. i, p. 553.

[2] Genesis 49 : 15.

[3] H. B. Tristram, *Eastern Customs in Bible Lands*, pp. 100, 101. Tristram tells rather a lovely story about an experience of his own at Nain. "Just outside the ruins of the wall is an ancient fountain or well. . . . While we were examining it there was an Arab girl standing by who had just been filling her pitcher. We asked her for a drink. Unlike the woman of Samaria, she set down her tall water-jar and readily gave it. On our offering her a small present, she declined it. Tears filled her eyes, and she said she did not give it for money . . . but she gave it to the strangers for the memory of her mother, who had lately died and been buried over there (pointing to the cemetery), for charity, and for the love of God. In vain we pressed it. Who could not but feel a touch of sympathy? The poor single-hearted girl kissed our hands, and we passed on." Surely no lovelier way of commemorating a mother could be found than to give thirsty strangers a drink of water.

[4] 2 Kings 4.

We have already seen how unrestrained was the grief in a house of mourning; and it was the same on the way to burial.[1] When a person died, the corpse was kissed, the eyes were closed and the head was bound in a napkin to keep the jaws from dropping open. The body was washed and anointed and wrapped in elaborate clothes. The hair and the nails were cut. Then the funeral procession started out. The body was carried on a bier in a wicker-work basket. The face was left uncovered and the hands were folded on the breast, as if the dead person was lying asleep. In front of the procession went the professional wailing women; then the mourners; then the bier; and then a crowd of men and boys. Every one who possibly could joined the procession, for not to do so was said to be a sin as serious as mocking one's Creator. The professional mourners worked themselves up to an hysterical condition. Tristram writes: "They fling up their arms, tear their hair, with the wildest gesticulations of grief, and shriek forth the name of the deceased, with lamentations that God has taken him." Thomson tells how the women toss their arms, swing their kerchiefs and shriek at the top of their voices. He says that they get themselves into such a wrought-up state that generally someone goes off into convulsions and, foaming at the mouth like an epileptic, falls to the ground senseless.

That was the kind of procession which met Jesus at the entrance to Nain. With a gesture of authority, he stopped it. With a word of authority he spoke to the young man on the bier. The young man sat up – Luke uses the medical word which is regularly used of a patient sitting up in bed – and began to speak. Then follows the loveliest sentence in the New Testament: "He gave him back to his mother."

The eternal truths
We need not stay to discuss whether the young man was dead or in a coma. All we have said of the daughter of Jairus applies

[1]For an account of Burial Customs see: K. E. Keith, *The Social Life of a Jew in the Time of Christ*, pp. 88-94; A. Edersheim, *The Life and Times of Jesus the Messiah*, vol. i, pp. 554-557; H. B. Tristram, *Eastern Customs in Bible Lands*, pp. 98-104; W. M. Thomson, *The Land and the Book*, pp. 99, 100.

equally here. It is perfectly possible that the young man was in some kind of coma and, if we wish to think of it in that way, we may; but certainly Luke tells the story as a raising from the dead. However we take it, the story tells us certain precious things about Jesus.

The compassion of Jesus

First of all, it tells of his *compassion*. When Jesus saw that sorrowing widow woman, he had compassion on her. The word used for *he had compassion* is the strongest word in the Greek language. It is *splagchnizesthai*. The *splagchna* are *the bowels*; and *splagchnizesthai* means *to be moved to the very depths of one's being*.

This word is repeatedly used of Jesus in the gospel story. When he saw the multitude with all their sick people, he was moved with compassion.[1] When he saw the crowds like sheep without a shepherd, he was moved with compassion.[2] When he saw the hungry people, far from home, he was moved with compassion.[3] The interesting thing is that in the gospels the word is never used of anyone except Jesus; it is characteristic of him. He could not see anyone in trouble without being moved to compassion; and always his compassion moved him to action. It never evaporated in a feeling.

Here is a test for ourselves. When we see someone in distress, does it leave us unmoved? Or does it move us to compassion? And, if it does move us to compassion, do we do anything practical about it. If we are to follow the example of Jesus, we can never see another's trouble without pity flooding our hearts; and we can never feel pity without translating it into action.

The willingness to take a risk

Second, *Jesus was prepared to take a risk to help the person in trouble*. He touched the bier. To us that means nothing special but to a Jew it did. A dead body or anything that dead body had touched was unclean, and anyone who touched a body or anything

[1]Matthew 14 : 14.   [2]Mark 6 : 34; Matthew 9 : 36.
[3]Mark 8 : 2; Matthew 15 : 32.

the body had touched also became unclean. The law was clear: "He who touches the dead body of any person shall be unclean seven days,"[1] and cleansing was a complicated process. Jesus knew this quite well but without hesitation he touched the untouchable. He took a risk in order to help.

So many of the world's great cures would never have been discovered unless someone had been prepared to take a risk. In the eighteenth century small-pox was a fatal scourge. Nowadays vaccination has practically eliminated it. The method of vaccination was discovered in 1796 by a doctor called Edward Jenner. Involved in the discovery was a lad named James Phipps whose name deserves to be rescued from oblivion. Cow-pox at that time was very common, and quite harmless; but Jenner believed that, if a person was vaccinated from the matter of cow-pox, he would be immune to small-pox. A dairymaid in Jenner's practice, Sarah Nelmes by name, developed cow-pox. Jenner punctured one of the spots on her hand and let the fluid run into a goose quill. Then he scratched some of this fluid into the skin of a healthy boy called James Phipps. In due time Phipps developed cow-pox and, of course, recovered quickly and completely. But there was only one way to prove that this method of vaccination was effective and that was to inoculate the boy with matter from a case of small-pox. This was done, the lad took no harm and so vaccination was proved effective. James Phipps took a risk and by that risk millions of lives were saved.

When Sir James Simpson was searching for a simple anaesthetic he tried out ether. One of his biographers goes on to say quite simply: "Simpson saw the disadvantages of ether and occupied the summer of 1847 *in trying out on himself* various other chemical compounds."[2]

If we are always thinking of what it will cost to help someone else, we will never help at all. If we are to be like Jesus, we must help first and think of the consequences afterwards.

[1] Numbers 19 : 11.

[2] The case of James Phipps and the experiments of Sir James Simpson are described, together with many similar experiments in Harley Williams, *Masters of Medicine*.

The note of authority

Third, we see in a very special sense *the authority of Jesus*. Everyone would have expected Jesus to join the funeral procession, or even the stranger was supposed to do so. But he stopped that procession with a gesture. There is nothing more vivid in all the gospel story than the sight of Jesus with one gesture bringing this screaming mob to a silent halt. And his authority went further. It called this young man back from death or rescued him from the terrible death he might have undergone. Jesus always speaks with authority. Sometimes we disregard his voice but, when we do, we run the risk of missing the miracle.

The tenderness of Jesus

Fourth, we must see most of all *the tenderness of Jesus*. The story closes with the lovely words: "He gave him to his mother." Jesus used his power, not to glorify himself but to give a son back to his mother. Whatever gifts God has given us we must use them like that, not for self, not to impress others, not for prestige, not for gain, but to make life happier for someone else.

It has been often noted that the three stories in the four gospels of Jesus raising people from the dead seem to have a kind of progression in them.[1] In the case of the daughter of Jairus, Jesus raised her from her *death-bed*. In the case of the son of the widow at Nain, he raised him from his *bier*. In the case of Lazarus, he raised him from the *tomb*. We cannot tell whether or not this progression is deliberate; but it does show us that there is nothing too difficult for Jesus. No matter how lost a man may be to goodness, no matter how much a slave to the wrong things, no matter how dead to sin, Jesus can raise him to life anew; and when the last enemy, death, has come, Jesus can conquer even that.

[1]A. Plummer, *St. Luke*, p. 200; J. M. Creed, *The Gospel according to St. Luke*, p. 102; Alan Richardson, *The Miracle Stories of the Gospels*, p. 114.

CHAPTER FIFTEEN

A Warning from Nature

The Blasting of the Fruitless Fig-tree

ON the following day, when they came from Bethany, Jesus was hungry. And seeing in the distance a fig tree in leaf, he went to see if he could find anything on it. When he came to it, he found nothing but leaves, for it was not the season for figs. And he said to it, "May no one ever eat fruit from you again." And his disciples heard it. . . . As they passed by in the morning they saw the fig tree withered away to its roots.   (Mark 11 : 12-14, 20; cp. Matthew 21 : 17-19.)

Of all the miracles of Jesus this has caused most difficulty.

We must begin with some facts without a knowledge of which it is impossible to see the point of the miracle. The fig-tree was together with the vine the best known and best loved tree in all Palestine.[1] It grew to a height of fifteen to twenty feet; but its branches spread from twenty-five to thirty feet. It was therefore treasured not only for its fruit but also for its shade. In the Old Testament it is again and again a kind of symbol of civilization and of peace. The promised land, amongst all its other bounties, was to be a land of fig-trees.[2] In the days of Solomon and in the dream of the golden age peace was such that a man would sit "under his own vine and his own fig-tree."[3]

The fig-tree is unique in the way it grows. In the early spring, before the leaves have come, the ends of the branches expand into little green nobs, called *paggim,* which later mature into the figs. After that the leaf buds expand and the flower comes. The fruit is the first thing to be seen on the fig-tree.

The fig-tree bears two crops. The first crop is borne on the old wood. The fruit buds which have been dormant all winter

[1]For the fig-tree and its culture see the article *Fig-tree* in J. Hastings' *Dictionary of Christ and the Gospels,* vol. i, pp. 592-595, by B. W. Bacon; the article *Fig-tree* in the *Encyclopaedia Biblica,* by N. Maclean, Sir W. T. Thistleton-Dyer, and T. K. Cheyne, vol, ii, columns 1519-1522; H. B. Tristram, *Eastern Customs in Bible Lands,* pp. 149-151; W. M. Thomson, *The Land and the Book,* pp. 349, 350.
[2]Deuteronomy 8 : 8.   [3]1 Kings 4 : 25; Micah 4 : 4.

expand and mature. This happens in the month of April. But there are never any eatable figs until the month of June. The new and better crop is borne on the new wood, and comes to maturity in the autumn.

It is to be noted that the little green nobs which the fig-tree bears and which in time mature into the full-grown fruit are not eatable. It is also to be noted that very occasionally the autumn fruit remains on the tree all through the winter until the next springtime; but by that time it is small and hard and uneatable.

We must specially bear in mind that a fig-tree in full flourish would be expected to be bearing figs; but we must also note that no fig-tree ever does bear figs until the month of June.

The blasting of the fig-tree

Now, with the habits of the fig-tree in mind, we come to our story. Even in the story itself there are difficulties. According to Matthew's version, when Jesus cursed the fig-tree the withering was immediate. "And the fig-tree withered at once."[1] In Mark's version the withering is not seen until the next morning.[2] That shows that there has indisputably been some development in the story. It seems wisest to accept Mark's version because his is the earliest gospel and nearest the events. The story tells that Jesus was on his way into Jerusalem. He was hungry; and he saw a fig-tree in full leaf.[3] The time was Passover, that is to say, early April. As we have seen, no fig-tree ever bore fruit until June in Judaea; as Mark himself says: "For it was not the season for figs."[4] This Jesus well knew. In spite of that he went to the

[1] Matthew 21 : 19.   [2] Mark 11 : 20.   [3] Mark 11 : 13.

[4] Jesus was perfectly entitled to eat the figs from the tree, if there had been any. The law lays it down in Deuteronomy 23 : 24, 25 that both in a vineyard and in a cornfield the passer-by might eat of the fruit and of the crop so long as he did not take an undue amount of it. Josephus expands this law: "You are not to prohibit those who pass by, when your fruits are ripe, to touch them, but to give them leave to fill themselves full of what you have" (quoted W. M. Thomson *The Land and the Book*, p. 349). Thomson goes on to say that the custom of plucking figs from wayside trees is to this day universal and that after September the figs that remain on the trees are common property and the poor may come in and gather them.

fig-tree to look for figs. When he found none, he cursed the fig-tree and said that no man would ever eat figs from it again. When they passed the same way next day the fig-tree was blasted and completely withered.

The problem of this miracle is acute. It is not the question of its possibility which troubles the mind. No wise man will ever be dogmatic about what is and is not possible. The problem is a *moral* problem. If we take this story literally, then Jesus used his power to blast a fig-tree for not doing what it was unable to do; an action which was completely unjust. Further, it is again and again plain that Jesus never used his miraculous power for his own sake. His first temptation, to turn the stones into bread and so satisfy his hunger, was precisely the temptation to do that, and he refused.[1] And yet here we find him using his power to blast a fig-tree from which he had failed to find fruit. In all honesty and reverence we are bound to say that in anyone else we would have called this petulant irritation.

Parable or miracle?

Some scholars explain the problem in this way. In Luke 13 : 6-9 there is the parable of the fig-tree which failed to bear fruit. The gardener asked mercy for it and twice mercy was given; but in the end, because it was fruitless, it was destroyed. The interesting thing is this. Both Matthew and Mark have the story of the blasting of the fig-tree but not the parable of the fig-tree; Luke has the parable of the fig-tree but not the story of the blasting of the fig-tree. Beyond a doubt Luke knew Mark's gospel and used it as one of the foundations of his own; therefore he deliberately omitted this story. It looks very much as if the gospel writers regarded the parable of the fig-tree and the blasting of the fig-tree as two versions of the same story; and felt that if they included one they did not need to include the other. It may well be that the story of the blasting of the fig-tree is a development of the parable. It is a fact that many people have insisted that the parables are stories of actual historical happenings. Sir Philip Sidney, for instance, was surprised that some theologians

[1]Matthew 4 : 3, 4.

regarded the story of the good Samaritan as fictitious and not as the record of an actual happening.[1] On this theory the story of the blasting of the fig-tree would be a later attempt to turn the parable of the fruitless fig-tree into an historical incident. That is possible but we find it hard to believe.

As we see it, there can be no doubt that the story of the blasting of the fig-tree goes back to some perfectly definite historical incident. We cannot be certain what happened but it may have been something like this. As Jesus came into Jerusalem, he saw a fig-tree in full flourish at a quite unnatural time of the year. If the tree was in full leaf, there *ought* to have been fruit but there was not. For the absence of fruit there could be two reasons either that the tree had reverted to its wild state or that there was something radically wrong with it. In either case no man would ever eat figs from that tree again and Jesus said so. One commentator put it this way: "Then said he who knew human nature and the human heart, 'This tree will soon wither'; for a fig-tree with full leaf in early spring without fruit is a diseased tree."[2] Jesus recognised that tree's state and knew its fate. By the next day it was clear that he was right; the fig-tree was dead.

But there is far more to it than that. This was not simply a horticultural verdict of Jesus on a diseased tree. One of the great customs of the Old Testament prophets was to use symbolic actions. When people would not listen to their words, they dramatized their message into some vivid action which people were bound to see. When Ahijah wished to tell Jeroboam that the Kingdom of Israel would be split into two, he stopped him, took his new robe and rent it into twelve pieces, handed him ten and kept two. This was a picture that ten of the twelve tribes would be given him to govern and rule.[3] Jeremiah used the dramatic picture of the marring of the girdle buried by the river bank to tell the people how the pride of Judah would be marred; and he

[1] This instance is quoted by T. K. Cheyne, *Encyclopaedia Biblica*, vol. iii, column 1521.

[2] Quoted in *The Gospel of Matthew*, by A. B. Bruce, in the *Expositor's Greek Testament*, p. 264.

[3] 1 Kings 11 : 29-32.

used the symbols of the yokes, one of which he himself wore in public, to show how the nation for its folly would be subjected to a foreign yoke.[1] Again and again Ezekiel put his message into dramatic form. For instance, he took a brick and on it made a model of the siege of Jerusalem to show how the city would fall.[2] This custom was by no means extinct in New Testament times. When Paul was on his last journey to Jerusalem, Agabus the prophet came to Caesarea to meet him. With Paul's girdle he bound his own hands and feet as a dramatic sign that Paul's journey was to end in imprisonment (Acts 21 : 10, 11).

To Jesus the inevitable death of that fig-tree was far more than the death of a diseased tree. It was a symbolic event. That doomed tree stood in Jesus's eyes for two great truths.

Uselessness invites disaster

First, uselessness invites disaster. When any person or thing fails to fulfil the function it ought to fulfil, that thing or person is doomed. The function of a fig-tree in leaf is to bear fruit; that particular tree did not bear fruit; it was therefore destroyed.

This is a universal truth. When a business fails to fulfil any useful function to the community, bankruptcy is assured. When a once useful custom becomes superfluous, it is bound sooner or later to be eliminated. When a subject in the curriculum of a school or college is left behind by the march of knowledge and events, it is bound to be deleted. When a person no longer fulfils a useful purpose, he becomes redundant. We were sent into the world to fulfil a purpose; if we fail to fulfil it there can be nothing but disaster.

For Jesus there was an immediate truth here. The leaders of the Jews had received their position for one reason only. It was their function to guide, teach and direct the people in such a way that they would recognize and accept God's Anointed One when he came. That they had failed to do; they were in fact bent on his destruction.

[1] Jeremiah 13 : 1-9; 27 : 1-11.
[2] Chapters 4 and 5 of Ezekiel are a succession of such symbolic actions.

Profession and performance

Second, the destruction of the fig-tree was a symbol that profession without performance is doomed. That was one of Jesus's basic principles. "Not everyone who says to me, Lord, Lord, shall enter the kingdom of heaven, but he who does the will of my father who is in heaven" (Matt. 7 : 21-23). Dick Sheppard tells that when he was a student at Oxford, he was thinking of entering the ministry but nearly abandoned the whole idea because he saw a bishop lose his temper at a game of tennis. In his autobiography Gandhi tells that during his early days in South Africa he enquired into Christianity. He attended a certain church in Pretoria for several Sundays; but "the congregation did not strike me as being particularly religious; they were not an assembly of devout souls, but appeared rather to be worldly minded people going to church for recreation and in conformity to custom." He therefore concluded that there was nothing in Christianity which he did not already possess. Gandhi was driven away from Christianity – and with what staggering consequences – by the fact that the performance of Christians fell far short of their profession.[1]

Jesus saw the Jewish authorities claiming to be men of God and living lives of selfishness and arrogance and legalism which belied every word of their profession. Of them the fig-tree was a symbol and of their doom the destruction of the fig-tree was a sign. Here is a terrible warning against giving no more than lip-service to Christ.

This story is one of the great warning beacons of the New Testament. It is far from being the story of how Jesus in a moment's petulance destroyed a fig-tree because he found no figs on it. It is the story of how he used the destruction of a diseased and deceiving tree to warn men from the useless and the hypocritical life. It is in the spirit of self examination that we should study it.

[1]Both these instances are cited by G. T. Bellhouse, *The Hand of Glory*, pp. 7, 8.

CHAPTER SIXTEEN

The Fishers and the Catch

The Draught of Fishes

AND when he had ceased speaking, he said to Simon, "Put out into the deep and let down your nets for a catch." And Simon answered, "Master, we toiled all night and took nothing! But at your word I will let down the nets." And when they had done this, they enclosed a great shoal of fish; and as their nets were breaking, they beckoned to their partners in the other boat to come and help them. And they came and filled both the boats, so that they began to sink. But when Simon Peter saw it, he fell down at Jesus' knees saying, "Depart from me, for I am a sinful man, O Lord." For he was astonished, and all that were with him, at the catch of fish which they had taken; and so also were James and John, sons of Zebedee, who were partners with Simon. And Jesus said to Simon, "Do not be afraid; henceforth you will be catching men."

(Luke 5 : 4-10; cp. John 21 : 1-11.)

Although these two miracles come from widely separate parts of Jesus's life, one before and the other after the Resurrection, we take them together because the events they describe are very similar and the lessons they teach are closely inter-related.

In ancient times the Sea of Galilee must have been almost crowded with shipping. Josephus tells that, when he had to collect ships for a military exploit against the Romans, he had no difficulty in assembling no fewer than 240 from the neighbourhood of Tarichaea alone.[1]

The number of fish in the Sea of Galilee is almost incredible. One traveller talks about "dense masses of fishes," while another says: "The density of the shoals of fish in the Lake of Galilee can

[1] Josephus, *The Wars of the Jews*, 2, 22, 1.

scarcely be conceived by those who have not witnessed them. They sometimes cover an acre or more on the surface in one dense mass."[1] Such catches as are described here are by no means impossible and were by no means uncommon.

It is not necessary to suppose that in this case Jesus created a special shoal of fishes for his disciples to catch. H. V. Morton describes the method of fishing he witnessed still in use on the lake and his description illuminates this passage.[2] The commonest net, the net which is said to be cast, is like a circular cone of fine mesh. The open circular edge of the cone is weighted with pellets of lead all round. The net is skilfully and beautifully cast into the sea and drawn towards the fisherman; the fish are caught in the cone and the mesh is too fine for them to escape. Morton describes two Arab fishermen at work. The one was casting the net some distance out in the lake; the other was watching from the shore. Repeated casts brought no catch. The man on the bank shouted to cast to the left. The cast was made; and the net was drawn in full of fish. The caster of the net is often too close to see where the fish are, while the person farther away can see them and direct the cast. That is what happened here. Jesus with his skilled and clear-sighted eyes saw exactly where the net should be cast and when his friends obeyed him the net was filled.

The conditions of a miracle

Let us first of all look at Luke's story. Peter and his friends had been toiling all night long. Night fishing is still done. W. M. Thomson describes it: "There are certain kinds of fishing always carried out at night. It is a beautiful sight. With blazing torch, the boat glides over the flashing sea, and the men stand gazing keenly into it until their prey is sighted, when, quick as lightning, they fling their net or fly their spear; and often you see tired fishermen come sullenly into harbour in the morning, having toiled all night in vain."[3] Peter and his friends had had a night of ill success; but

[1] Quoted B. F. Westcott, *The Gospel of John*, p. 300, and A. Plummer, *St. Luke*, p. 144.

[2] H. V. Morton, *In the Steps of the Master*, p. 199.

[3] W. M. Thomson, *The Land and the Book*, p. 402.

when they followed the instructions of Jesus, their nets overflowed with fish.

The fishermen disciples would never have experienced this wonder catch except upon certain conditions.

(i) They were willing to try again even when they were tired. Peter's answer is very illuminating: "Lord," he said, "we have been at this job all night; but, if you say so, we'll have another go." It is impossible to overestimate the number of people who have lost something precious because they were too tired or too discouraged or even too lazy to try again. It could well be argued that the most useful of all the virtues is the unromantic one of perseverance.

In 1875 people laughed at the idea of laying a telegraphic cable between England and America. A small team of scientists under Sir Charles Bright was certain it could be done. The first line broke when they were only 4 miles out; the second broke when they were 226 miles out. Next year they decided to try a new method. Two ships were to meet in the middle of the Atlantic; the two ends of the cable were to be joined there; and then each ship was to sail for its own coast paying out the cable. Twice the joint broke. A third time it broke and 500 miles of cable were lost. Supplies gave out and the expedition had to be abandoned; still another failed, and people began to talk of the whole conception as impossible. But at last an expedition succeeded and on the 5th August, 1878 England spoke with America across the ocean, because someone had refused to accept failure as final.

On 25th July 1909, Louis Bleriot was the first man to fly an aeroplane across the English Channel from France to England. Before he succeeded he built ten aeroplanes every one of which crashed. It was in his eleventh machine that he was finally successful. Kepler, the first of the modern astronomers, spent seventeen years in study and research and tested no fewer than nineteen different theories before he succeeded in discovering the explanation of the movements of the earth and other planets in their motion round the sun. Once Edmund Burke had made a memorable speech in the House of Commons. Someone afterwards came upon his brother Richard in deep thought. "I have been wondering," said Richard, "how it comes about that Ned has contrived to monopolise all the talents of our family; but then again I remember that when we were at play he was always at work."[1]

The man with the gift of perseverance and who refuses to accept any failure as final is the man who gains the wonderful thing.

(ii) They were willing to obey the orders of Jesus even when they seemed to launch them on a hopeless task. Peter and his friends might so easily have said: "We have been at this job all night and have met with no success. It's hopeless to try again. What's the use of wasting time?" Instead, they attempted the hopeless task and succeeded. All progress depends on the elimination of the word *impossible*.

Oliver Baldwin in a magazine article on David Lloyd-George tells of his contacts with that famous Prime Minister. "My happiest memory of him was a week-end I spent at his house in Churt. He loved to show people over his farm, and he took a real pride in the fact that he had grown prize apples on soil the experts had told him was unsuitable for such fruit. 'Experts,' he snorted. 'When they tell you a thing can't be done, that is the time to start'." Baldwin goes on: "I never forgot that remark, and sixteen years later, I recalled it when in the West Indian Island of Antigua. I was told by experts there was no underground water in the place. I thereupon sent to Jamaica for a water-diviner, and we found a-plenty."

Again and again Jesus has told men to do the impossible. He has sent lonely men with a fire in their bones to the hopeless task of converting continents where the Gospel has never been heard. He has sent social reformers to fight some evil which seemed to be backed by the embattled might of invincible armies. For many of us it will not be nearly so dramatic as that; but if at his command we go out to face some seemingly impossible task, we may well find that the difference between the difficult and the impossible, as someone has said, is only that the impossible takes a little longer.

[1]These illustrations have been taken from Maud M. Higham, *Torches for Teachers*, pp. 120, 122.

Fishers of men

There is a further point in this story. We have seen that Jesus, as the prophets did, made use of symbolic actions. Now when Jesus originally called his disciples, he made them an offer: "Follow me," he said, "and I will make you fishers of men,"[1] It may well be that in this story he was dramatically repeating that call. "Henceforth you will be catching men," he said.[2] Jesus was saying in effect: "You were given this amazing catch because you cast your net where I told you. If you obey me in your greater task as you have obeyed me in your smaller task, you will also catch men with equal success."

The disciples were not the only ones to be given the duty of catching men for Jesus and bringing them into his friendship. Every Christian has that duty, too.

The symbolic number

We now turn to John's very similar story. Its details are almost the same. But John gives one very curious detail. The fishes numbered 153. Since nothing in John's gospel is pointless, that number has meaning. It has been suggested that the sole point is that the disciples counted out the fish because they intended to share the catch equally among each other and that the sole reason the number has come down is that they were impressed with the size of the catch.[3] But surely it is in the last degree unlikely that the disciples would be fussing about the counting of fish for business purposes in the presence of the Risen Christ. They may at times have been dull and insensitive but not so much as to act like that with the wonder of the Resurrection in their hearts. Assuredly John meant more than that.

There have been many many explanations. One of the earliest and best is that of Jerome. He declared that the standard works on fish gave the number of different kinds as 153.[4] In that case the 153 would stand for completeness. Just as the net contained

[1]Mark 1 : 16; Matthew 4 : 19.   [2]Luke 5 : 10.
[3]J. H. Bernard, *St. John*, vol. ii, p. 699.
[4]Jerome, *Commentary on Ezekiel* 47 : 9-12, quoted in full in E. Hoskyns and F. N. Davey, *The Fourth Gospel*.

every kind of fish, so in the end the kingdom of Jesus will contain every man. Augustine has a more elaborate explanation.[1] He says that the 10 is the number of the Law for there are ten commandments; 7 is the number of the Spirit, for the gifts of the Spirit are sevenfold. $10+7=17$; and 153 is the sum of all the numbers from 1 to 17 added together. Therefore 153 stands again for the inclusiveness of the kingdom of Christ, which consists of all who come to the gospel by law and by grace combined, that is to say, of Jews and Gentiles alike.

The 153 stands for the all-embracing character of the kingdom of Christ. It is indeed true that that kingdom is imperfect until it becomes complete.

Rita Snowden has a wonderfully beautiful story. A new church was built, to be called the Church of the Christchild. The people planning it wished a stained glass window to dramatize and summarize the love of Christ for the children. The theme was to be:

> "Around the throne of God in Heaven
> Thousands of children stand,
> Children whose sins are all forgiven,
> A holy, happy band,
> Singing Glory! Glory! Glory!"

They employed an artist to draw the picture for the window; and he produced a picture which he thought the best thing he had ever done. When the picture was finished he went to bed. He was awakened, as he thought, by a noise in the studio. He went there and found a stranger with palette in his hand altering his picture. "Stop!" he cried. "You'll ruin it." The stranger answered: "*You* have already ruined it." The artist looked his question. "You have five colours on your palette," said the stranger, "yet you have made the faces of all the children white. Who told you that their faces were all white in heaven?" I have simply used the colours you omitted to use and made some of the faces yellow and some

---

[1] This is given in Augustine's *Sermons on John* 122. This, and other ingenious explanations, are given in B. F. Westcott, *The Gospel of John*, Additional Note on chapter 21, pp. 306, 307.

brown, some black and some red. For these little ones have come from many, many lands in answer to my call." "Your call?" said the artist. "What call was that, sir?" And the stranger's voice said: "Suffer little children to come unto me."[1]

[1]This is a much abridged version of the story in Rita Snowden, *If I open my Door*, pp. 68-71.

CHAPTER SEVENTEEN

The Unique Faith

The Healing of the Centurion's Servant

After he had ended all his sayings in the hearing of the people he entered Capernaum. Now a centurion had a slave who was dear to him, who was sick and at the point of death. When he heard of Jesus, he sent to him elders of the Jews, asking him to come and heal his slave. And when they came to Jesus, they besought him earnestly, saying, "He is worthy to have you do this for him, for he loves our nation, and he built us our synagogue." And Jesus went with them.

When he was not far from the house, the centurion sent friends to him, saying to him, "Lord, do not trouble yourself, for I am not worthy to have you come under my roof; therefore I did not presume to come to you. But say the word, and let my servant be healed. For I am a man set under authority, with soldiers under me: and I say to one, 'Go,' and he goes; and to another, 'Come,' and he comes; and to my slave, 'Do this,' and he does it." When Jesus heard this he marvelled at him, and turned and said to the multitude that followed him, "I tell you, not even in Israel have I found such faith." And when those who had been sent returned to the house, they found the slave well.

(Luke 7 : 1-10; cp. Matthew 8 : 5-13; Matthew 15 : 21-28; John 4 : 46-54.)

We have suggested that this miracle be taken along with the healing of the nobleman's son and the healing of the daughter of the Syro-Phoenician woman because all three miracles have a common characteristic – they were performed at a distance. Jesus did not touch or speak to or even see the person healed. But it is with the healing of the centurion's servant that we are mainly concerned.

Jesus had come to Capernaum. In the town there was a centurion whose servant was gravely ill. The centurion had heard of Jesus but he did not wish to approach Jesus himself and so he asked the elders to make the approach for him. This the elders were delighted to do, for the centurion was a friend of the Jewish people. To such lengths did his friendship go that he had actually built them a synagogue in which to worship. Jesus responded immediately to the appeal for help and started out for the centurion's house; but, as he went along the street, messengers arrived to say that the centurion was well aware that his house was not a fit place for Jesus to enter. He knew the authority that even his comparatively subordinate position gave him; he could give his soldiers or his servants an order and be sure that it would be carried out. If Jesus would but give the order, he was sure that his servant would be healed. Jesus turned to the crowd which was following. "I tell you," he said, "not even in Israel have I found such faith." When the centurion's friends returned home, they found the servant cured.

The centurion

Let us look at this centurion whose faith Jesus called unique. That he was a centurion is proof of his worth as a soldier and a man. A Roman legion consisted of 6,000 men and was divided into sixty centuries each under the command of a centurion. The centurions were the backbone of the Roman army. They were regular soldiers who had signed on for twenty years. They were the men who held the army together. They had different degrees of honour and authority; but most honoured of all was the centurion who had charge of the eagle which was the standard of the legion.[1] To reach the position of standard-bearer of the regiment was the peak of a centurion's career. Centurions were responsible for the discipline of the regiment.[2] Both in war and in peace the morale of the Roman army depended on them.

It is most suggestive that every centurion mentioned in the New Testament is mentioned with honour. There was the centurion who at the Cross recognized Jesus as the Son of God; there was Cornelius, the first Gentile convert of the Church; there was the centurion who suddenly discovered that Paul was a

[1] Juvenal, *Satires* 14 : 197.
[2] Juvenal, *Satires* 16 : 14-24.

Roman citizen and promptly protected him; there was the centurion who received news of the plot to kill Paul between Jerusalem and Caesarea and saw that steps were taken to foil it; there
was the centurion whom Felix ordered to look after Paul; there
was the centurion who was with Paul on his last journey to Rome
and treated him with courtesy and accepted him as leader when
the storm struck the ship.[1] Polybius, the Greek historian, in his
section on the Roman army, has a character study of the centurion. "They must not be so much venturesome seekers after
danger, as men who can command, steady in action, and reliable;
they ought not to be over-anxious to rush into the fight, but
when hard pressed, they must be ready to hold their ground, and
die at their posts."[2]

This centurion from Capernaum would be a man among men.

Further, it is clear that he was a Gentile. "I am not worthy to
have you come under my roof," his message to Jesus ran.[3] This
is exactly the course that Cornelius took when Peter came to him
after the vision.[4] As Peter said, it was not lawful for a Jew to
enter into a Gentile's house.[5] The Jewish law was quite definite
about this. The *Mishnah* lays it down: "The dwelling-places of
Gentiles are unclean."[6] The centurion could not even have been
a convert to Judaism or this law would not have applied.

What he was doing in Capernaum and what his nationality was
must remain doubtful. He may have been a Roman soldier, because
the Romans may have kept a detachment of troops at Capernaum,
a most important customs centre. More likely he was in the service
of Herod. At that time Herod was king of that part of Palestine
which included Galilee. He was not independent; he was subject
to the Romans; but he had his own troops and among them were
men from as far away as Thrace and Gaul and Germany. He also
often recruited his forces from the people of Samaria and from the
Gentiles who lived in Caesarea.[7] This centurion may have been a
Gentile from far away.

[1]Matthew 27 : 54; Acts 10; 22 : 26; 23 : 17, 23, 24; 24 : 23; 27.
[2]Polybius 6 : 24.   [3]Luke 7 : 6.
[4]Acts 10 : 24.   [5]Acts 10 : 28.
[6]*Mishnah*, Tractate Oholoth, 18 : 7, in Danby's translation p. 675.
[7]Josephus, *The Antiquities of the Jews* 17, 8, 3.

Even apart from this, we would have known that he could not be a Jew. There were no Jews in the Roman armies. The Romans had a kind of compulsory military service, but from it Jews were exempt. They were exempt because the law forbade them to carry arms on the Sabbath day; to do so would have been to carry a burden. The *Mishnah* lays it down: "A man may not go out with a sword or a bow or a shield or a club or a spear on the Sabbath; if he went out with the like of these he is liable to a sin-offering."[1]

Twice at least rigid adherence to this principle nearly brought the Jews to disaster. When Pompey invaded Palestine in 63 B.C. he laid siege to Jerusalem. Jerusalem with its high ramparts was difficult to take. When a general was confronted with such a situation in ancient times, he built a huge mound overlooking the ramparts of the besieged city and from it used his primitive artillery to pour missiles into the city. It was of course the aim of the garrison to stop this mound being built. But Pompey discovered that the Jews were so rigid in their keeping of the Sabbath that his soldiers could build unmolested on the Sabbath; and in the end Jerusalem was taken.[2]

The same thing had happened a hundred years before. Antiochus Epiphanes had tried to destroy the Jewish faith and to coerce the Jews into Hellenism. Under the Maccabees the Jewish opposition flared into open revolt. The first people to revolt took to the hills and the Syrian troops pursued them. The Jews took refuge in caves. At first the Syrians tried to persuade them to surrender but when they would not, "they fought against them on the Sabbath day, and they burned them as they were in the caves, without resistance and without so much as stopping up the mouths of the caves. They did not even need to defend themselves on that day, because the Jews were not willing to break in upon the honour they owed the Sabbath, even in such distresses; for our law requires that we rest upon that day."[3]

In view of this absolute refusal of the Jews to fight or to bear arms on the Sabbath day, the Romans had exempted them from

[1]*Mishnah*, Tractate Shabbath 6 : 4, Danby's translation, p. 105.
[2]Josephus, *The Wars of the Jews* 1, 7, 3.
[3]Josephus, *The Antiquities of the Jews*, 12, 6, 2.

military service. Josephus quotes an edict of Dolabella, the governor of Asia, giving this exemption: he says that the Jewish envoy came to Dolabella and told him that his countrymen could not go into the Roman armies because they were forbidden either to travel or to fight on the Sabbath day, and because their laws about food could not be kept in army circumstances. Dolabella decreed: "I do therefore grant them a freedom from going into the army, as the former prefects have done,"[1]

There are two further facts about this centurion which to any Jew or Gentile reading the gospels for the first time would have appeared frankly incredible. He is said to have loved the Jewish nation.[2] There can have been few Gentiles who ever loved the Jews. They were the most hated nation in the world. Cicero called the Jewish religion a "barbarous superstition."[3] Tacitus called the Jews "the vilest of people."[4]

To some extent the Gentile hatred of the Jews merely returned the Jewish hatred of the Gentiles. The Gentiles, not without reason, regarded the Jews as haters of all mankind. Tacitus said of them that "their loyalty among themselves was stubborn: the help they gave to each other was prompt; but against all others they bore a hostile hatred." He said that if ever a Gentile became a Jewish proselyte the first thing he was taught to do was to despise the gods, to repudiate his nationality and to hold worthless his parents, children and friends.[5] Juvenal said that if they were asked the way by anyone, they would refuse to give any information except to a fellow-Jew and that if anyone was looking for a well in order to drink, they would refuse to direct him or bring him to it unless he was circumcised.[6] In Alexandria the story went that the Jews had taken a deliberate oath never to show kindness to any Gentile, and it was even said that the Jewish religious ceremonies involved the yearly sacrifice of a Gentile.[7] The Jew

---

[1] The whole edict is quoted in Josephus, *The Antiquities of the Jews,* 14 10, 12.
[2] Luke 7 : 5.
[3] *barbara superstitio,* Cicero, *Pro Flacco* 28.
[4] *taeterrima gens,* Tacitus, *Histories* 5 : 8.
[5] Tacitus, *Histories* 5 : 5.   [6] Juvenal, *Satire* 14 : 103, 105.
[7] These charges are quoted in Josephus, *Against Apion* 2 : 10; 2 : 8.

did look down on the Gentile; and the Gentile repaid exclusiveness with bitter hatred. The friends of Antiochus Sidetes urged him to exterminate the Jews because "alone of all nations they refuse all fellowship and intercourse with any other nation, and suppose all men to be enemies." Moses, it is said, laid down for the Jews the most misanthropic and lawless laws.[1] Josephus quotes the charge of a certain Lysimachus that Moses charged the Jews to show good will to no man, never to give good, but always evil counsel to others, and to overturn and destroy whatever altars and temples of the gods they might encounter. Apion himself affirmed that the Jews swore by the God of heaven and earth and sea never to show goodwill to a man of another nation, and especially never to do so to the Greeks.[2] The Jews were a notoriously hated nation, because they were notoriously hating.

Further, the Jews were hated for the exclusiveness of their religion. In the sphere of religion the Romans were essentially tolerant. They could not understand any nation claiming to have the *only* religion. Cicero said to Laelius as a principle: "To each state its own religion, ours to us."[3] When the Roman Emperor Claudius gave religious toleration to the Jews, he wrote: "And now I charge them to use my kindness with consideration for others, and not to despise the religions of other nations."[4]

Again, certain Jewish religious customs seemed to the Gentiles the height of foolishness. They laughed at the Jewish abstention from swine's flesh. "A long established clemency allows pigs to reach old age," mocked Juvenal. It seemed to him that to them the flesh of the pig was as sacred as the flesh of a human being.[5] Plutarch quite seriously discussed whether the Jews abstained from pig's flesh because the pig was their god?[6]

Moreover, the Gentiles found the Jewish Sabbath incomprehensible. Juvenal talks of them as "giving up every seventh day to idleness."[7] Augustine quotes Seneca as insisting that, because

---

[1]Diodorus Siculus 31, 1, 1, 3.
[2]Josephus, *Against Apion* 1 : 34; 2 : 10.   [3]Cicero, *Pro Flacco* 69.
[4]Quoted in Josephus, *The Antiquities of the Jews* 19, 5, 3.
[5]Juvenal, *Satires* 6 : 160; 14 : 98.   [6]Plutarch, *Symposium* 4 : 5.
[7]Juvenal, *Satire* 14 : 104, 105.

the Jews rested every seventh day, they had in fact thrown away one-seventh of their lives.[1] It is true that in the end the day of rest conquered the world and became recognized as a human as well as a divine necessity, but in ancient times it seemed to the Gentiles an astonishing and shocking display of laziness.

The Gentiles had their own slanderous accounts of the origin of the Jewish religion. Even Tacitus hands on the popular account of the way in which the Jewish faith began.[2] The story was that the Jews were banished from Egypt because they were infected with leprosy. They were sent to the stone quarries in the desert. There Moses, a renegade Egyptian priest from Heliopolis, persuaded them to abandon the Egyptian religion and accept a religion of his own. He led them across the desert to Palestine where they settled as invaders. Tacitus says that the Jews abstained from swine's flesh because it caused an itch from which they suffered. The ancient world believed – or professed to believe – that the Jews worshipped an ass's head and that an ass's head was in the Holy of Holies.[3] Tacitus retails the story that that worship was due to the fact that when the Jews were dying of thirst in the desert they found water by following a herd of wild asses. Their use of unleavened bread was ascribed to the fact that they had stolen corn when they left Egypt. Their custom of observing the Sabbath was traced to the fact that it was on that day they had given up work for good in Egypt and that they had liked their idleness so much that they had consecrated a day to remember and repeat it for ever.[4]

There never has been any people so hated, so misunderstood, so misrepresented, so persecuted as the Jews. As Glover writes of the heathen point of view: "Why should the Jew not intermarry with other races? Why should he not eat with them? Why should he insist on one idle day in every seven? Why circumcision? Why

[1]Augustine, *The City of God* 6 : 11.

[2]Tacitus, *Histories* 5 : 5.

[3]Josephus, *Against Apion*, 2 : 7.

[4]The opening chapters of Tacitus, *Histories* 5, are a good summary of what even the educated Gentiles believed about the Jews. The material on the Gentile attitude to the Jews will be found collected in E. Schürer, *The Jewish People in the Time of Jesus Christ*, vol. ii, section ii, pp. 292-297.

his eternal fussiness about obviously wholesome food? . . . All these points of difference were at once obvious and to the common man ludicrous."[1]

Yet the Roman centurion of this story loved the Jewish people. Clearly he was no ordinary man.

A master and his servant

There was another respect in which this centurion was a quite unusual man and that was the length to which he went to help his slave. The ancient world was founded on the institution of slavery. Many masters were kind to their slaves and many slaves loved their masters, but the fact remains that a slave was a thing.

Aristotle, talking about the relationships which exist in life, and the possibilities of friendship, writes: "There can be no friendship nor justice towards inanimate things; indeed, not even towards a horse or an ox, nor yet towards a slave as a slave. For master and slave have nothing in common: a slave is a living tool, just as a tool is an inanimate slave."[2] The master could treat his slave exactly as he would treat a thing. "Over all these persons, so long as they are slaves, the owner possesses absolute power. He can box their ears or condemn them to hard labour – making them for instance work in chains upon his lands in the country or in a sort of prison-factory; or he may punish them with blows of the rod, the lash or the knout; he can brand them upon the forehead if they are thieves or runaways, or, in the end, if they prove irreclaimable, he can crucify them."[3] A slave had no legal rights. He could not own anything. He was not even allowed the right of marriage; and, when two slaves cohabited, the children of the union belonged to the master and not to the parents.

The principle was that as the lambs of the flock belong to the shepherd and not to the sheep, so the children of slaves belong to the master and not to the slaves. Gaius, the Roman lawyer, states the matter in his *Institutes*: "We may note that it is universally

[1] T. R. Glover, *The World of the New Testament*, pp. 88, 89.
[2] Aristotle, *Nicomachean Ethics* 8, 11, 6 (1161^{b}4).
[3] T. G. Tucker, *Life in the Roman World of Nero and St. Paul*, p. 203.

accepted that the master possesses the power of life and death over the slave, and whatever is acquired through a slave is acquired by the master."[1] Varro, the Roman writer on agriculture, has a passage which divides the instruments of agriculture into three classes – the articulate, inarticulate and the mute: "the articulate comprising the slaves, the inarticulate comprising the cattle, and the mute comprising the vehicles."[2] The only difference between a slave and a beast or a wagon was that the slave could talk. Cato, an older writer on agriculture, gives advice for the putting into order of a farm which had been slackly administered. "When slaves were sick, such large rations should not have been issued." "Look over the livestock and hold a sale. Sell your oil, if the price is satisfactory, and sell the surplus of your wine and grain. Sell worn-out oxen, blemished cattle, blemished sheep, wool, hides, an old wagon, old tools, an old slave, a sickly-slave, and whatever else is superfluous."[3] The worn-out slave is classed with the broken tool and the useless beasts and is to be got rid of.

But the real terror for the slave was that he was subject to the caprice of his master. There were good masters and public opinion condemned the man who was cruel to his slaves. But insecurity and terror of life were always there for the slave. The elder Pliny tells how a master called Vedius Pollio treated a slave. The slave was bringing in some precious goblets while his master and his guests sat in the courtyard. He dropped and broke one; there and then Vedius Pollio had him thrown into the fishpool which was in the middle of the courtyard where he was torn in pieces by the savage lampreys which were kept in there.[4] Juvenal draws a picture of the domineering wife whose every whim has to be satisfied. " 'Crucify the slave,' says the wife. 'But what crime worthy of death has he committed?' asks the husband. 'Where are the witnesses? Who informed against him? Give him a hearing at least. No delay can be too long when a man's life is at stake!' 'What, you numskull?' says the wife. 'You call a slave a man, do you? He has done no wrong, you say? Be it so; but this

[1] Gaius, *Institutes* 1 : 52.
[2] Varro, *On Agriculture* 17 : 1.
[3] Cato, *On Agriculture* 2 : 7.
[4] Pliny, *Natural History* 9 : 23.

is my will and my command: let my will be the voucher for the deed'."[1] It often happened that the female slaves suffered from the caprices of the mistress of the house even more than the male slaves did from the caprice of the master and Juvenal also draws a picture of the unreasonable mistress: " Her household is governed as cruelly as the Sicilian court. If she has an appointment and wishes to be turned out more nicely than usual, and is in a hurry to meet someone waiting for her in the gardens, or more likely near the chapel of the wanton Isis, the unhappy maid who does her hair will have her own hair torn, and the clothes stripped off her shoulders and her breasts. 'Why is this curl standing up?' she asks, and then down comes a thong of bull's hide to inflict chastisement for the offending ringlet."[2] Juvenal writes, too, of the master who "delights in the sound of a cruel flogging, deeming it sweeter than any siren's song," and of the master who is never happy "until he has summoned a torturer and he can brand some-one with a hot iron for stealing a couple of towels" and "who revels in clanking chains."[3]

The matter is summed up by a writer called Petrus Chrysologus: "Whatever a master does to a slave, undeservedly, in anger, willingly, unwillingly, in forgetfulness, after careful thought, knowingly, unknowingly, is judgment, justice and law."[4] It is difficult to imagine what life must have been like for the slave who was a living tool, who had not one single right in all the world, who was at the mercy of the caprice of an unreasonable, and even sadistic, master or mistress. But the centurion of this story loved his slave.

The qualities of the man whom Jesus admired
This centurion is one of the few people in the New Testament to whom Jesus gave unstinted praise. Let us note the qualities of the man whom Jesus so much admired.

---

[1]Juvenal, *Satires* 6 : 218-222.   [2]Juvenal, *Satires* 6 : 486-492.
[3]Juvenal, *Satires* 14 : 16-22.
[4]Petrus Chrysologus, *Serm.* 141. The material regarding slaves is well collected in W. A. Becker, *Gallus, or Roman Scenes of the Times of Augustus* pp. 217-225.

(i) The centurion was *a man of humility*. As one who was probably in command of the soldiers in Capernaum, he might have stormed up and demanded help as a right; but his humility was such that he did not even presume to come to Jesus himself, but sent his request to others who, as he thought, had a better right to speak. Humility and greatness always go hand in hand.

(ii) The centurion was *a man of courtesy*. He knew that a strict Jew might not enter the house of a Gentile and he tried to save Jesus from possible embarrassment.

(iii) The centurion was *a man of faith*. His confidence in Jesus was such that he believed that he had only to speak the word and his servant would be healed.

The gospel stories always have a far deeper meaning than lies on the surface; and that is so here.[1] It is the feature of this story that Jesus healed the centurion's servant at a distance. There is a great truth here. The centurion stands for all the Gentiles who never saw Jesus in the flesh but who, through faith, experienced the blessings he can bring. The centurion had not seen, yet he believed. It will be well with us if we bring to Jesus a like humility, a like trust and a like faith.

Beyond the senses

Now we have to face the problem of this story. What are we to think and say of the fact that Jesus could heal at a distance, not having seen or made contact with the sufferer at all? The strange thing is that modern investigation has made these stories of miracles wrought at a distance much easier rather than harder to believe in. Scientists have been working for a long time now on what is called Extra-sensory Perception – ESP[2] the gaining of perception in ways which are different from those of the ordinary

[1]Alan Richardson, *The Miracle Stories of the Gospels*, pp. 78, 79.

[2]It is obviously impossible to treat this subject at any length here. For further information the reader is referred to two fascinating books by J. B. Rhine – *New Frontiers of the Mind* and *The Reach of the Mind*. There will be few who can read these books and say that ESP does not exist. All the illustrations that I have used have been taken from these books.

senses. One of the classic instances is given by the great German philosopher Kant in his book on Emanuel Swedenborg. When Swedenborg was in Gotenborg in 1759, he described a fire occurring in Stockholm 300 miles away. He gave an account of the fire to the city authorities, naming the owner of the house that was burned, and stating when the fire was put out. Subsequent messages proved him right in every detail.

Dr. Rhine carried out thousands of experiments to show that we can become aware of things other than through the senses. Very frequently a pack of twenty-five cards marked with selected symbols was used. A person was asked to name the cards without seeing them. One subject who was experimented with was a student called Hubert Pearce. On the first five thousand trials – a trial being a run through the whole pack of cards – he averaged ten right out of twenty-five, when the laws of chance would say that four correct could be expected. On one occasion, under conditions of special concentration, he named the whole twenty-five cards correctly. The odds against this extraordinary feat being pure chance are 298,023,223,876,953,125 to 1.

An experimenter called Brugman selected two subjects. He put the sender of the messages in an upstair room and the receiver below. Between the rooms there was an opening covered by two layers of plate glass with an airspace between to make the sending of any messages based on sound quite impossible. Through the glass panel the sender looked down at the hands of the receiver. In front of the receiver was a table with forty-eight squares. The receiver was blindfolded. Between him and the squared table was a thick curtain. He held a pointer which passed through the curtain on to the table. The sender had to will the receiver to move the pointer to a certain square. According to the laws of chance the receiver should have been right in four out of one hundred and eighty results. He was in fact right in sixty. It is difficult to avoid the conclusion that the mind was actually influencing the receiver.

It is a definite fact that a French experimenter, Dr. Janet, was able to hypnotize chosen subjects at a distance. In eighteen out of twenty-five trials Dr. Janet succeeded in putting the subject into a trance at the time attempted and he was partially successful in four other cases.

If a man's mind can influence another man's mind at a distance – and the proof seems to be there that it can – how much more must it have been so in the case of Jesus? We need have no qualms about the miracles which Jesus wrought at a distance.

CHAPTER EIGHTEEN

THE MIRACLES OF THE FOURTH GOSPEL

(i) The Satisfaction of Men's Hunger

The Feeding of the Five Thousand

AFTER this Jesus went to the other side of the Sea of Galilee, which is the Sea of Tiberias. And a multitude followed him, because they saw the signs which he did on those who were diseased. Jesus went up into the hills, and there sat down with his disciples. Now the Passover, the feast of the Jews, was at hand. Lifting up his eyes, then, and seeing that a multitude was coming to him, Jesus said to Philip, "How are we to buy bread, so that these people may eat?" This he said to test him, for he himself knew what he would do. Philip answered him, "Two hundred denarii would not buy enough bread for each of them to get a little." One of his disciples, Andrew, Simon Peter's brother, said to him, "There is a lad here who has five barley loaves and two fish; but what are they among so many?" Jesus said, "Make the people sit down." Now there was much grass in the place; so the men sat down, in number about five thousand. Jesus then took the loaves, and when he had given thanks, he distributed them to those who were seated; so also the fish, as much as they wanted. And when they had eaten their fill, he told his disciples, "Gather up the fragments left over, that nothing may be lost." So they gathered them up and filled twelve baskets with fragments from the barley loaves, left by those who had eaten. When the people saw the sign which he had done, they said, "This is indeed the prophet who is to come into the world!"

(John 6 : 1-14; cp. Matthew 14 : 15-21; Mark 6 : 35-44; Luke 9 : 12-17.)

The Fourth Gospel has a different feel about it from the other three. One of the things which stand out as different is the fact that in it we often find long discourses put into the mouth of Jesus. There are no parables in the Fourth Gospel and few of the vivid, epigrammatic sayings of which the other gospels are full. There is a good reason for this difference.

The Fourth Gospel was the last to be written, many years after the other three. Mark was written about A.D. 60; Matthew about A.D. 85; and Luke about the same time as Matthew; but the Fourth Gospel was not written until some time about A.D. 100. We actually possess certain accounts of how it was written. Clement of Alexandria, a great Christian scholar who lived about A.D. 200, says: "John, perceiving that the bodily facts about our Saviour were sufficiently detailed (in the other three gospels) and *on the exhortation of his familiar friends* and *urged by the Holy Spirit* wrote a spiritual gospel." The first list of New Testament books that the Church ever made is called *The Muratorian Canon*. It gives a list of the books and a short description of each. Its date is about A.D. 170. Of the Fourth Gospel it says: "John was *urged by his fellow-disciples* to write; he asked them to fast for three days and *to await guidance*. That same night Andrew reported that it was revealed to him that John should relate everything but *subject to the revision of the rest*."

Both these accounts of the writing of the Fourth Gospel stress two things; first, that in a special sense the Fourth Gospel was the work of the Holy Spirit and second, that, although it was the work of one man, it was nevertheless produced amidst a circle of friends. What happened must have been this. By the year A.D. 100 John was a very old man. More than seventy years had passed since Jesus died on the Cross, and throughout all these years John had been thinking about Jesus and living in his presence. Year by year the Holy Spirit had been leading him to see more and more the meaning of the things which Jesus had said and done. So John's friends said to him: "You are old now, and the time is short. Before you go from this life will you not write down the things you remember about Jesus?" So John began on the task, not alone, but with his friends talking it all over with him as he went along.

The Fourth Gospel is the result of seventy years thinking and remembering under the guidance of the Holy Spirit. Wordsworth defined poetry as "emotion recollected in tranquillity." That is what the Fourth Gospel is. W. M. Macgregor has a sermon entitled, "What Jesus becomes to a man who has known him long." That is a perfect description of the Fourth Gospel. John is not so interested in what Jesus said as what Jesus meant; and sometimes as we read the gospel we are not quite sure when we are listening to the actual words of Jesus and when we are listening to their meaning as unfolded by years of thinking under the guidance of the Holy Spirit to John's heart and mind. What the Fourth Gospel gives us is not so much a simple account of what Jesus did as the significance of his actions and his words.

That is particularly true of the miracles. John saw the miracles not only as things that Jesus *did* but as things that he *still does*. That is why in *John* they are almost always followed by a long discourse. In these discourses John is saying to us: "This is what Jesus meant for all time and for all eternity, this is what he meant for *you*, when he did this thing." So the miracle of the Feeding of the Five Thousand (John 6 : 1-14) is followed by a discourse in which Jesus talks about himself as the living bread which satisfies the longings of the heart and the soul. John is saying: "This is not simply the story of how Jesus fed five thousand people on a day in Galilee; this is the story of how Jesus, at all times and in all places, can satisfy the unsatisfied longings of men's hearts." The story of Jesus healing the man born blind (John 9) tells us, not only that one day in Jerusalem he gave sight to a man who had never seen, but that, at all times and in all places, he is the Light of the World, opening the eyes of men to truth and to God. When John tells of the raising of Lazarus (John 11), into the story come the words of Jesus: "I am the resurrection and the life." John is saying that this is not just the story of the bringing back to life of one man who was dead; it is the story which tells that to all men in all ages and in all places, Jesus brings victory over death. John's aim is not so much to tell us what Jesus *did*, but to tell us what Jesus can do for *us* now.

The hungry crowd

Let us now look at the story of the Feeding of the Five Thousand. The Sea of Galilee is quite small, only 13 miles long and, at its widest, 8 miles across. To have some quiet time for himself and his disciples, Jesus had crossed over to the other side. But the people followed him in their crowds. In those days people did not work to the clock as they must do in an industrial civilization. They did not start at 9 in the morning and finish at 5.30 in the evening. Most of them were their own masters, maybe farming a croft, or owning a fishing boat, or sharing a little business with their friends and relations. There was no reason why they should not drop their work and go away after Jesus if they felt that they must. So they followed him. Some would sail across the lake; some would walk round its northern end; in their thousands they came and they found him.

For a long time he taught them, and then it was time to go home. But the people were tired and hungry and some at least had a long trudge home ahead of them. Jesus said: "We must give them a meal." Philip's immediate reaction was that it was completely hopeless to think of that. There were no shops and even if there had been where was the money to come from? Philip said that it would take what the Authorised Version calls *two hundred pennyworth* of bread to feed a crowd like that. The word that the Authorised Version translates *penny* is the Greek and Latin word *denarius* which was a silver coin worth about 4p. and the normal day's wage for a working man. Philip was saying: "Why, it would take far more than half a year's wages to feed a crowd like this. It's out of the question."

But Andrew was standing by and he had seen a lad in the crowd. Maybe he knew the lad; at any rate, he had *five barley loaves and two fish*. We are not to think of him as having five loaves of bread. Not even a healthy boy's appetite could manage to deal with that! The 'loaves' were rather like little sandwich rolls. The fish were little salt fish the size of sardines, to act as a relish for eating the dry bread. Very likely the boy had set out for a picnic, had seen the crowds, and, as a boy might, had joined them, neither knowing nor caring where they were going.

Now his picnic meal was going to be used in a way that he had never dreamed of. Most likely Andrew made the suggestion about the boy and his lunch shyly and with embarrassment. It seemed so utterly inadequate. But Jesus took it and with it he fed five thousand hungry people, and in such a way that there was enough and to spare.

The means of the miracle

Many people have made many suggestions as to how this miracle was worked. Many are content to believe that Jesus literally multiplied the loaves and the fish so that they became many; but God gave us minds to use and, if we feel that we must have some further explanation, there are two which merit thought.

(i) It has been suggested that this was not so much a meal as a sacrament. When we sit at the table of our Lord, all that we receive is a morsel of bread and a sip of wine; and yet we rise from that table wondrously strengthened, because somehow we have received the life that Jesus alone can give. At the Lord's table it is not a big meal that we receive; it is a spiritual meal. It has been suggested that that is what happened in this case; all that the people received was the merest crumb of food, and yet somehow it brought strength to their souls.

(ii) It has been suggested that what happened was this. Many in the crowd had brought something to eat, knowing that they would be away from home all day. But many had nothing, having made a sudden decision to accompany the crowd. Those who had food were unwilling to produce it for the simple and human reason that they wished to keep it all to themselves and planned to eat it once they got away from the crowd. Then Jesus produced the five little rolls and the two little fish. "This is all I have got," he said, "but let's share it." Thereupon everyone produced what he had, and when all was pooled there was more than enough.

If we take it that way, this would be a miracle where the influence of Jesus changed a crowd of selfish people to a crowd of people willing to share what they had. If we take it that way, it is a miracle of the birth of love in men's hearts and the awakening of fellowship in their souls.

When we face this question honestly and when we remember how the whole Jewish attitude to any incident is to ask, not what happened but what the story means, many may well wish to take the latter explanation, particularly when we remember Jesus's temptation to change stones into bread (Matt. 4 : 3, 4; Luke 4 : 3, 4). The tempter said: "Give them bread and they will follow you," and Jesus said, "No; the real bread of life is the word of

God." It is hard to think of Jesus actually doing what in the hour of temptation he had seen to be the wrong thing to do, and it may be that we will find a solution by seeing in this incident the miracle of the awakening of love in men's hearts. However that may be, one thing is certain – something so memorable happened that this is the only miracle of which all four gospels tell. The meal with Jesus in the lonely place was something which men never forgot.

Caring for men's bodies

Before we begin to think of the eternal meaning of this miracle, let us look at certain things of which it reminds us. *It tells us that Jesus cared for men's bodies.* He was concerned that this crowd of people were tired and hungry. Sometimes people present Christianity in such a way that it would appear that all that matters is a man's soul. In a sense that is true, but it is never a reason for forgetting that people have bodies and that it is our duty to do all we can to help them with their material needs.

When General Booth began the work of the Salvation Army in London, he gave the people hot meals. Some criticized him for that and said it was no part of the duty of a man who was out to win souls for Christ. Booth answered: "How can you warm a man's heart with the love of Christ when his feet are perishing with cold?"

Dr. E. Douglas Bebb tells a story of D. L. Moody. "One afternoon during Moody's great mission in Chicago, the missioner was missing, nor could he be found, although search was made in every conceivable place. At length it was reported that he had been seen in the negro quarters, and after further search he was discovered at the top of a wretched tenement house in a miserable street. A coloured woman was very ill in bed and Moody was sitting on the only chair in that rather dreadful room with her black baby on one knee while reading to her from the Bible. The people from the mission remonstrated with him for using up his strength in this fashion, and added: 'Besides, any one of our people could do this work.' 'Yes,' replied Moody, 'that is quite true, any of them could do it, but none of them do'."[1] Moody, the man who was filled with a passion for men's souls, saw his duty to men's bodies too, and saw it more quickly than lesser men.

This has something to say to us. It says to us that a servant of God is not only someone who spends his life trying to save men's souls; he is also someone who spends his life trying to help men's bodies. Paul Tournier reminds us of this. " 'Sickness and healing are acts of grace,' writes Dr. Pouyanne. 'The doctor is an instrument of God's patience,' writes Pastor Alain Perrot. 'Medicine is a dispensation of the grace of God, who in his goodness takes pity on men and provides remedies for the evil consequences of their sin,' writes Dr. Schlemner. Calvin described medicine as a gift from God."[2] The man who heals men's bodies and the person who tend the sick and the aged and the child are all doing God's work. The person who invents a more fruiful kind of grain or a way of making the land more fertile, and the person who helps to grow food for men are doing God's work. The person who makes clothes, boots and shoes to keep men warm and healthy is doing God's work. Anyone engaged in any trade which brings health and strength to men is doing God's work. Jesus Christ cared for men's bodies and those who help him so to care are doing his work.

More, this presents us with a challenge. If this is true, it means that every one of us can do work for Jesus. So long as we think of it in terms of preaching and teaching and praying, work is limited to comparatively few; but when we see that Jesus cares for men's bodies, it means that anything that we can do by way of practical help for others is work for him.

A famous preacher tells of an old shoemaker that he knew. The preacher when he was young was poor and had a hard struggle to get through college. He was given constant encouragement and help by the old shoemaker. When the lad had finished his course and was about to be ordained, the old shoemaker said to him: "Will you do me a favour?" "If I can, I will," said the young man. "Well," said the old shoemaker, "I want you to do this. When I

[1] E. Douglas Bebb, *God does intervene*, p. 124.
[2] Paul Tournier, *A Doctor's Case Book in the Light of the Bible*, p. 215.

was young I wanted to be a preacher, but things did not work out that way. You have been given the task I was never able to do. I want you to let me make your shoes – for nothing – and then when you are in your pulpit, I will think of you standing in the shoes I made, preaching the gospel in the way I never got the chance to do."

We need never say that we have no chance to do something for Jesus. Every day brings us the opportunity to bring practical help to someone; to take it is to help Jesus. To refuse it is to hinder him.

Bringing what we have
Further, this miracle teaches us that *our duty is to bring to Jesus Christ what we have*. He can take it, such as it is, and use it for his purposes. The boy's picnic lunch did not look much. Barley bread was actually the poorest bread of all, the food of those who were very poor. Yet this boy's gift was the means whereby Jesus worked his miracle. Jesus never asks us for what we do not have; he wants the gifts we have. It has been said that God does not so much want extraordinary people as people who can do ordinary things extraordinarily well.

The ancient Stoics had a wonderful idea. They believed that in every living creature, however humble, there was a part of God; and they believed that every living creature, however humble, had an essential part to play in the plan of God. People used to say to the Stoic: "You can't really mean that God is in earth-worms and dung-beetles, for instance?" The Stoic answered: "Why not? Cannot an earth-worm serve God? Do you suppose that it is only a general who is a good soldier? Cannot the lowest private or camp attendant fight his best and give his life for the cause? Happy are you if you are serving God and carrying out the great purpose as truly as an earth-worm."[1]

It is hard to get rid of the idea that only those who are doing what look like great things are really serving God. But the plain fact is that the so-called great things could not be done at all unless behind them were all kinds of people doing the things that no one ever sees.

[1]cp. Gilbert Murray, *Stoic, Christian and Humanist*, p. 104.

During the last war the air-crews of the Royal Air Force were rightly considered the most heroic of men; but the fact is that it required almost fifty men on the ground – fitters and mechanics and riggers and all kinds of craftsmen – to get one man into the air. Think how a great surgeon needs the electrician who ensures that the necessary power is available to light and service the operating theatre. Think how the captain on the bridge of a liner is dependent on the unseen members of the crew at their stations below decks.

Whatever gifts we have, Jesus needs them and can use them.

The Bread of Life

Now we come to the real reason why John related this miracle – to tell us that Jesus is the Bread of Life. He did not want us to think only of Jesus feeding five thousand people on a hillside overlooking the Sea of Galilee. He wanted us to see that Jesus can satisfy the deepest hunger in our hearts and souls.

There was a thing that happened to the poet Shelley, just before he died so young and so tragically. In the dead of night he became conscious of another presence in his room. He saw a figure, wrapped in a flowing mantle and with the head and face completely covered. As it passed him, the wrappings were dropped and the figure spoke one sentence: "Art thou satisfied?" As Shelley looked for the moment on the face of the figure, it was his own face that he saw. It was as if his own heart and soul were asking him: "Are you satisfied with the kind of life that you are living and with yourself as you are?" So long as we try to live life alone, deep down in our heart we know that we are not satisfied.

In A. S. M. Hutchison's novel *If Winter comes*, the hero, Mark Sabre, says: "We are all plugging along like mad, because we are all looking for something, You can read it in half the faces you see; some wanting and knowing that they are wanting something; others wanting something but putting up with it, content to be discontented. What is it that they are all looking for, the universal something that is wanting?" Josephine Butler tells of her early days before she came to be a Christian. She tells how she was "goaded by the tyrannous haunting of her own heart." She tells how she went to church and somehow the preaching only "touched the fringes of her soul's deep discontent."

In every one of us there is the discontent, the something missing, so long as we try to live life by ourselves. But Jesus said: "I came that they may have life, and have it abundantly" (John 10 : 10). To put it otherwise, Jesus said: " I came to make life worth living." When we discover that, life is changed. Matthew Arnold has these lines;

> " 'Twas August, and the fierce sun overhead
> Smote on the squalid streets of Bethnal Green,
> And the pale weaver, through his windows seen
> In Spitalfields, look'd thrice dispirited.
>
> I met a preacher there I knew, and said:
> 'Ill and o'erwork'd how fare you in this scene?'
> 'Bravely!' said he; 'for I of late have been
> Much cheer'd with thoughts of Christ, the living bread'."

Because this man knew Jesus, life was different.

The satisfaction Christ brings

How does Jesus make such a difference? He brings us three things. First, *he brings us a standard to reach*. He gives us something to aim at. Suppose we play golf. Suppose our game is just ordinary. Then suppose the Open Championship comes round and we go and see Tony Jacklin and Peter Oosterhuis, and Jack Nicklaus and Gary Player and other great players from overseas. After we have seen them we go back to our own course with a new idea of the game and a new standard to aim at. Suppose we collect stamps. We have a collection but it is a bit mixed up; the stamps have never been properly taken off the paper, are not very well mounted, are not properly arranged; our collection has never been "written up." Then we go to see a stamp display or are allowed to look through a really fine collection. We go back to our own with a far higher idea of what a stamp collection ought to be and with the determination to make ours a little more like it. Jesus gives us a new standard of what life can be like.

Second, *He brings us a new task to do.* So long as we are doing a job simply because it has to be done or to earn so much money, it can be pretty boring. It makes all the difference in the world to discover that even the most ordinary job can be done for Jesus.

> "Life can never be dull again
> When once we've thrown our windows open wide
> And seen the mighty world that lies outside,
> And whispered to ourselves this wondrous thing,
> 'We're wanted for the business of the King!' "[1]

If we are doing anything to make people healthier and happier and better, and see it as being done for Jesus, it makes all the difference. We must always remember that God cannot do things without us. If he wants someone helped or comforted or taught, he has to get someone else to do it. We may be that someone. Once Jesus comes into it, life becomes quite different because everything is done for God.

Third, *he brings us a new presence in which to live.* Jesus is not a figure in a book; he is alive and he is with us all the time. It makes all the difference in the world to discover that all life is lived in his presence.

John tells us how more than nineteen hundred years ago Jesus fed five thousand people on a hillside in Galilee; but he wants us to know that Jesus is the living Bread, who to this day can satisfy all our longings, and who makes life infinitely worth living by giving us a new standard to aim at, a new work to do, and a new presence in which to live.

[1]Quoted Rita S. Snowden, *Through Open Windows*, p. 9.

CHAPTER NINETEEN

THE MIRACLES OF THE FOURTH GOSPEL

(ii) The New Joy

The Wedding Feast at Cana of Galilee

ON the third day there was a marriage at Cana in Galilee, and the mother of Jesus was there; Jesus also was invited to the marriage, with his disciples. When the wine failed, the mother of Jesus said to him, "They have no wine." And Jesus said to her, "O woman, what have you to do with me? My hour has not yet come." His mother said to the servants, "Do whatever he tells you." Now six stone jars were standing there, for the Jewish rites of purification, each holding twenty or thirty gallons. Jesus said to them, "Fill the jars with water." And they filled them up to the brim. He said to them, "Now draw some out, and take it to the steward of the feast." So they took it. When the steward of the feast tasted the water now become wine, and did not know where it came from (though the servants who had drawn the water knew), the steward of the feast called the bridegroom and said to him, "Every man serves the good wine first; and when men have drunk freely, then the poor wine; but you have kept the good wine until now." This, the first of his signs, Jesus did at Cana in Galilee, and manifested his glory; and his disciples believed in him.

(John 2 : 1-11.)

Cana of Galilee was a little village not far from Nazareth. Jerome, the great fifth century scholar who lived for a time in Palestine, says in a letter to his friend Marcella that he actually saw it from Nazareth.[1] It was called Cana of Galilee to distinguish it from another Cana in Coelo-Syria. Today it is identified with a little Arab village called Kefr Kenna; and there are two churches in it. One is a Greek Church where they show travellers two stone urns which some say are two of the very water-pots used in this miracle although it is certain that they are no older than the sixteenth century. The other is a Franciscan Church, built on

[1]Jerome, *Epistle* 46 : 4.

the site of an older church which certainly existed as early as
A.D. 726 and is said to be built on the site of the very house where
the miracle took place.[1]

The occasion of the miracle was a village wedding feast to
which Mary, the mother of Jesus, had been invited. There is no
mention of Joseph. The probable explanation is that by this time
he was dead. The likelihood is that he died young; and that may
well be the reason why Jesus waited in Nazareth until he was
thirty years old. He had to shoulder the task of making a living as
the carpenter of Nazareth for his younger brothers and sisters
before he could go forth to his greater task.

The story shows that in the household where this wedding
took place Mary had a special authority. She knew that the wine
had run out; she must have had a share in the oversight of the
arrangements. She went to Jesus to try to get matters put right.
She clearly had some kind of authority over the servants because
she could instruct them to do what Jesus told them to do. One
of the Coptic apocryphal gospels – that is one of the Egyptian
gospels which did not get into the New Testament – has the
interesting information that Mary was a sister of the bridegroom's
mother.[2] There is an early set of prefaces to the gospels called
The Monarchian Prefaces which say that Mary's sister was
Salome and that the bridegroom was actually John, her son.
If that be so – we cannot tell whether these bits of information
are really historical or not – in this story John is telling of the
wonderful thing which happened at his own wedding.

In any Palestian village a wedding was a great occasion. Virgins
were married on Wednesday. The actual wedding ceremony
took place late at night. After the ceremony the couple were
conveyed to their new home. They walked under a canopy and
by the longest possible route, so that all the village could wish
them well as they passed. They did not go away for a honeymoon
but stayed at home where for a week they kept open house and
there was continual feasting and rejoicing. They wore their
bridal garments and crowns on their heads. They were addressed

[1]H. V. Morton, *In the Steps of the Master*, 178-180.
[2]M. R. James, *The Apocryphal New Testament*, p. 147.

as royalty and treated as such. This week of wedding rejoicing
was the gladdest time in the life of the newly weds and their
friends shared their joy.

At this particular wedding domestic disaster struck. The
wine was in danger of running done. "Without wine," said the
Jewish saying, "there is no joy." It is not that the Jews were a
drunken nation – far from it. In Palestine drunkenness was a
great disgrace. But in ancient times wine was the natural drink
for all social occasions. It may well be that the arrival of Jesus,
not alone, but with the group of disciples who had newly attached
themselves to him, was the main cause of disaster. Jesus had
been expected but his new disciples were probably not. Hospitality in the East was a sacred duty and it was not deemed sufficient
to set before people that which was just enough. Real hospitality,
especially at a wedding feast, demanded a superabundance. If
the supplies had run done at a wedding feast, the family and the
young couple would never have lived down the shame.

In these embarrassing circumstances Mary came to Jesus and
told him of the problem. There is something very suggestive
here. When there was trouble Mary instinctively turned to Jesus.
She knew her son so well. He had been the head of the house and
the support of the family in Nazareth for so many years. Never
had there arisen an emergency that he was not able to cope with.
There is an old legend which tells that, even when Jesus was a
little baby, the people of Nazareth, when they were worried and
upset about things, used to say: "Let us go and look at Mary's
child." And they would go and look at the baby and find the
sunshine and the peace had come back to life. Mary had learned
from years of experience that, when there was trouble, there was
no one like Jesus for putting things to right.

The Authorised Version tends to give a wrong idea of the tone
of the interview between Jesus and Mary. Mary told him that
the wine was running done. As the Authorised Version has it,
Jesus said to her: "Woman, what have I to do with thee?"
That sounds much more harsh and abrupt than it actually was.
The word translated *woman (gunai)* does mean that; but it was
the word by which Odysseus addressed his well-beloved wife

Penelope[1]; and by which Augustus, the Roman Emperor, addressed the beautiful Egyptian queen Cleopatra.[2] It was a word which was often used with the most exquisite courtesy. Later it was to be the word by which Jesus addressed Mary on his cross, when he committed her to the care of the beloved disciple.[3] We would get the flavour of it far better if we translated it *lady*. There is no harshness and no disrespect here. "What have I to do with thee?" also sounds harsh; but it was a common phrase whose impact depended entirely on the tone in which it was said and the circumstances in which it was used. True, it could be said in rebuke, but in a case like this it meant: "Don't worry yourself; leave it all to me." What Jesus said to Mary really was: "Lady mother, don't worry. Leave me to settle this in my own way." One thing is certain – Mary did not consider herself in any way rebuffed. She was quite certain that Jesus would do something – she knew him so well. She went to the servants and told them to do whatever Jesus might tell them to do.

At the door of the house stood six great water pots. The word translated *firkin* in the Authorised Version represents the Hebrew measure called the *bath*; and a *bath* was between eight and nine gallons. Each jar would hold about twenty-five gallons of water. That water was needed for two purposes.

First, the roads of Palestine were unsurfaced. In dry weather they were deep in dust, in wet weather muddy. They were seldom swept or cleaned. The eastern sandal was simply a sole of wood or leather or woven fibre held on to the foot by straps. Inevitably walking on such roads shod with such sandals soiled the feet; and it was the custom for the feet to be washed when a guest entered the house.[4]

Second, the law of Jewish ceremonial washings was very strict. The hands had to be washed in a certain way before a meal was begun; and the really strict Jew repeated the washing between each course of the meal. The right hand was held with

---

[1]Homer, *Odyssey*, 19, 555.
[2]Dio Cassius, *Histories*, 51, 12, 5.
[3]John 19 : 26.
[4]cp. Luke 7 : 44; John 13 : 1-5.

the finger tips pointing upwards and water was poured over it in such a way that it ran right down to the wrist; the same was done with the left hand. The right hand was then held with the finger tips pointing downwards and water was poured over it in such a way that it ran from the wrist down to the tips of the fingers; the same was done with the left hand. Then each hand was further cleansed by being rubbed with the fist of the other.

A plentiful supply of water was therefore necessary if there was a large party. By this stage in the proceedings the water in the jars would be running low. Jesus told the servants to fill them to the brim; and then to draw out the water and take it to the *steward of the feast,* the *architriklinos.* The nearest approach to the *architriklinos* in our western practice is the *head-waiter.* He was responsible for the seating of the guests, the serving of the viands, the smooth running of the meal. All the practical arrangements were in his hands. It was his duty to taste and approve the wine before it was served to the guests. When he tasted the wine which the servants brought he was amazed. He said jestingly: "Most hosts set out the good wine at the beginning of the feast. Then when the palates of the guests become less able to appreciate what they are drinking he puts out his inferior wine, for by that time the guests are not in a state to note the difference; but you have kept the best wine until the end of the feast." And thus a village couple's wedding was saved from disaster.

We have already seen that every story John tells has a deeper meaning, for he is concerned not only with what Jesus did in Palestine but with what he is still doing. But before we come to the deeper meanings of this wonder let us look at the things which lie on the surface, for they too are precious.

Where the wonder happened
1. *This miracle happened at a wedding feast.* Jesus was perfectly at home there. More, he was concerned to see that a wedding feast should be as joyous as it could possibly be. Clearly, Jesus was no killjoy but ready to join in the fun of that village wedding feast.

There are people who think that Christianity takes the fun out of life. They connect Christianity with black clothes and solemn faces and regard happiness with suspicion. Even so great a critic as A. B. Bruce once said that we must conceive of the boy Jesus as a grave and solemn child who seldom smiled. Locke, the great philosopher, called laughter "a sudden glory"; but there is still a type of Christianity which regards laughter as a breach of Christian good manners.

Swinburne, in the *Hymn to Proserpine*, wrote of Jesus:

> "Thou hast conquered, O pale Galilaean; the world
>   has grown grey from Thy breath,"

as if Jesus had taken all the colour and vividness out of life. Ibsen, in his play, makes Julian the pagan emperor of Rome say: "Have you looked at these Christians closely? Hollow eyed, pale-cheeked, flat-breasted all; they brood their lives away, unspurred by ambition: the sun shines for them but they do not see it; the earth offers them its fullness, but they desire it not; all their desire is to renounce and suffer, that they may come to die." The heresy of unhappiness has haunted Christian belief.

When John Ruskin was a child, he was brought up in a home of austere strictness. The one bright spot in his life was his Aunt Bridget of Croydon, a happy, motherly soul whom he loved, starved as he was of real affection. "He owed to his aunt a brief moment of joy in the possession of a gaily clad Punch and Judy which she had bought for him in Soho Bazaar. She showed him how to make the puppets dance, but he never saw it after that first exhibition. His mother, who seems to have regarded all gay or glittering toys as worldly snares to be avoided by the good Evangelical child, told him it was wrong for him to have it and took it away."[1]

W. M. Macgregor quotes with a certain grim scorn the code of rules which John Wesley drafted for his school at Kingswood near Bristol. "Wesley was forty-five years old and ought to have had sense, yet he laid it down that no games were to be

[1] Ada Earland, *Ruskin and his Circle*, pp. 17, 18.

allowed in the school or the grounds, and he sagely adds that 'he who plays when he is a child will play when he is a man'." No holidays were given, and a child, once admitted to the school, stayed there until he left for good. The household, old and young, had to rise at four in the morning, and spend the first hour in private reading and meditation, in prayer and singing, and on Friday they all fasted until three in the afternoon. Such nature-defying foolishness ought at once to have been recognized as such and corrected; but after thirty-five years (in 1783) Wesley still records in his journal – 'The children ought never to play, but they do every day, and even in the school. They run about in the wood, and mix and even fight with the colliers' children . . . They are not religious: they have not the power and hardly the form of it.' One is glad to read of the bairns as running about in the wood and fighting with the little colliers: it is a welcome touch of wholesome nature. But think of a man engaged in the task of leading his fellows to reality and to God, and yet understanding them so badly!"[1] Even Wesley, great man as he was, could not believe that joy and religion could go hand in hand.

There is a charming story in Boswell's life of Johnson. Johnson met a man called Edwards who had been at college with him and whom he had not seen for forty years. They went to Johnson's rooms and talked of many things. Telling of what he had done since they had been to college together Edwards said: "You are a philosopher, Dr. Johnson. I have tried too in my time to be a philosopher; but, I don't know how, cheerfulness was always breaking in."[2] Here was another man infected with the heresy that cheerfulness and the higher things cannot coexist.

In the story of this miracle we see Jesus at a wedding feast. He was not there to cast gloom on the proceedings or to look with austere disapproval on those who were enjoying themselves. He was glad to hear the sound of laughter and to see happy faces, glad to share in the games and the good fellowship. It is time we said goodbye to a religion of gloom. Spurgeon in his *Lectures to my Students* has some pungent things to say. "Sepulchral

[1] W. M. Macgregor, *The Making of a Preacher*, p. 28.
[2] James Boswell, *Life of Dr. Johnson*, entry for 17 April 1778.

tones may fit a man to be an undertaker, but Lazarus is not called out of his grave by hollow moans." "An individual who has no geniality about him had better be an undertaker, and bury the dead, for he will never succeed in influencing the living."

Where the wonder happened

2. This wonderful thing happened in a humble home in a village in Cana of Galilee. It did not happen against the background of great cities and of great crowds but in a home. In the lives of most of us there is a strangely paradoxical attitude to our homes. We would readily admit that they are our most precious possession; and yet the fact remains that most of us are at our worst just there. We behave in our own homes in a way in which we would never behave in any other house. There we are guilty of an irritability, a selfishness, an untidiness, and ungraciousness we would not dare to show in someone else's house. It is the extraordinary fact that the people we hurt most are the people we love most. It is the tragic fact that it is strangers who see us at our best and those who love us who see us at our worst. Any man can do the big thing against the background of the big occasion. Jesus gave his best within a home; and there is no better proof that he *always* did so than Mary's perfect confidence in her son when things went wrong.

Why the wonder happened

3. This wonder happened to save a humble Galilaean family from humiliation. Jesus used his power to save them from shame. There were people present who no doubt would have taken a malicious pleasure in telling how the wine went done. But all Jesus wanted to do was help. We often wish that we had some opportunity to serve God. The occasions lie ready to our hands. In helping others in their misfortune and their need we serve God. We can use someone's misfortune as the material for a cruel jest or a malicious story; or we can use it as an occasion to stretch out the hand of help. We know what Jesus did – and we should do the same.

The deeper meaning

But there is far more to this story than meets the eye. As usual John was not trying to tell the story of something which Jesus did only once; he was trying to teach us about something which Jesus is still doing.

Every detail in this story has an inner meaning. First, we note that there were *six* waterpots. The Jews regarded *seven* as the number that is perfect and complete. *Six*, on the other hand, is essentially imperfect and incomplete. The *six* water-pots stand for the incompleteness and inadequacy of the Jewish law; into the imperfection of the old law Jesus poured the perfection of the new way. Without Jesus life is essentially incomplete.

The superabundant grace

There is one detail in this story which is proof that it is not to be taken with unimaginative literalness. We know that there were six waterpots; we have already seen that each held about twenty-five gallons of water. If we take this literally it means that Jesus produced about one hundred and fifty gallons of wine! That would be material, not for the happy joy of a wedding feast, but for the most drunken of orgies. No one can possibly take that literally. John meant that the grace and joy which Jesus supplies are inexhaustible. He meant that no matter how deeply we draw on Jesus for power to live the kind of life we ought to live, we cannot exhaust his grace.

The new exhilaration

So we come to the essential thing John wished to teach in this story, that whenever Jesus comes into our lives there enters a quality which is like turning water into wine.

The trouble about life is that we get bored with it. Things get stale. Work becomes a weariness. Pleasure loses its thrill. There is a vague dissatisfaction about everything. But when Jesus enters our lives there comes a new exhilaration.

It is just this that people are always looking for. W. M. Macgregor tells of an old woman whom once he knew: "Nearly sixty years ago I knew a crusty, ill-tempered old woman who lived alone in one very dismal room, with no apparent means of support but her parish allowance and occasional charity. Her neighbours resented her caustic tongue, so her solitude was seldom invaded, but at vague intervals she started on a pilgrimage among old acquaintances, from each of whom she exacted a contribution of at least one penny, and on the proceeds of the tour she got satisfactorily drunk. The deliberation of what she did gave it an ugly look, and she was appealed to and denounced as peculiarly a sinner, but only once, as I was told, did she retort – 'Wad ye grudge me my one chance o' getting clean out o' "The Pans" wi' a sup of whisky?' "[1] She wanted something that would give her wretched life some momentary escape. Everyone sometimes gets this feeling of being weary of it. There are times when, as Andrew Carnegie said in spite of all his wealth, "Nothing tastes." It is only in Jesus's company and friendship that life becomes really satisfying.

George Wade Robinson wrote:

> "Heaven above is softer blue,
>   Earth around is sweeter green;
> Something lives in every hue,
>   Christless eyes have never seen:
> Birds with gladder songs o'erflow,
>   Flowers with deeper beauties shine,
> Since I know, as now I know,
>   I am his, and he is mine."

John Masefield in *Saul Kane* tells how a drunken reprobate became a changed man. Jesus had come into his life and Saul Kane said:

> "O glory of the lighted mind
>   How dead I'd been, how dumb, how blind.
> The station brook, to my new eyes,
> Was bubbling out of Paradise,
> The waters rushing from the rain
> Were singing, 'Christ is risen again.'
> I thought all earthly creatures knelt

[1] W. M. Macgregor, *The Making of a Preacher*, p. 25.

From rapture of the joy I felt.
The narrow station wall's brick ledge,
The wild hop withering in the hedge,
The lights in Huntsman's upper storey
Were parts of an eternal glory."

The world became a new world when Jesus came into it.

Dr. Grenfell was a great Christian adventurer who did much for the people of Labrador. He came to the John Hopkins' Hospital in America to look for a head nurse willing to go back to Labrador with him. This is the offer he made: "If you want to have the time of your life, come with me and run a hospital next summer for the orphans of the Northland. There will not be a cent of money in it for you, and you will have to pay your own expenses. But I'll guarantee that you will feel a love for life you have never before experienced. *It's having the time of anyone's life to be in the service of Christ.*" A nurse closed with the offer and accepted the adventure. When she got back to America after her experience in Labrador, she wrote: "I never knew before that life was good for anything but what one could get out of it. Now I know that the real fun lies in seeing how much one can put into life for others." To put it in modern language – never did she get such a kick out of life as when she allowed Jesus in; new exhilaration came.

One of her pupils once said of Alice Freeman Palmer, the great American teacher: "She made me feel as if I had been bathed in sunshine." A Boston newspaper once printed this great tribute to Philips Brooks, great preacher and great soul: "It was a dull, rainy day, when things looked dark and lowering; then Philips Brooks came down through Newspaper Row – and all was bright." That is what Jesus can do; when he enters into life it is as if water turned to wine.

NOTE ON THE VINE AND WINE IN PALESTINE

There is little doubt that the story of the turning of water into wine at Cana of Galilee will raise the question of the use of wine and strong drink. For that reason it will be useful to know the facts about the growing of the vine and the use of wine in Palestine in biblical times.[1] The vine at that time was the most commonly cultivated of all trees. In Egypt grape kernels have been found in mummy cases which date as far back as 2000 B.C.

The cultivation of the vine

The vine is not commonly grown in the rich lowland ground but on hillsides with a southern aspect. Before it can be planted the ground must be completely cleared of all brushwood and root weeds, for the vine will not stand any rival. It likes rocky ground in which it can send its roots deep down into pockets of rich soil to find moisture and nourishment. But the loose stones have to be cleared; and these are heaped into ridges over which the vine is afterwards trained to climb. These stone ridges are to be found today even in the Negev in the south which is now mainly a desert. And in Moab, where there have been no vines for centuries, there are parts where these ridges are still so prominent that the Arabs call them the way of the vine, although in modern times vines have never been seen there.

The hedge

Only vineyards were hedged around. Corn fields and olive yards were left open. But in the vineyard the hedge was an essential feature. The usual way of making it was as follows. A ditch was dug three or four feet wide and two or three feet deep. The earth was piled on the inner side of the ditch. Into the piled earth posts were fixed; then the posts were interlaced with twisted branches. In the ditch itself water collected and briars grew quickly. The briars in the ditch and the interlaced branches

[1]The information in this note has been gathered from the following sources. J. Hastings, *Dictionary of Christ and the Gospels*, vol. ii, article "Wine" by W. Ewing. J. Hastings, *Dictionary of the Bible*, vol. ii, article on "Food," section on "Wine," by A. Macalister. F. R. and C. R. Conder, *Handbook to the Bible*, pp. 191, 192. A. C. Bouqet, *Everyday Life in New Testament Times*, pp. 77, 78. H. B. Tristram, *Eastern Customs in Bible Lands*, pp. 136-142. H. J. Van-Lennep, *Bible Lands and Customs*, pp. 110-120.

between the posts made an almost impenetrable barrier. Sometimes the hedge was even more solid. A mould was made in wood like a box from which two opposite sides were missing. The mould was set on the ground in such a way that the open sides were top and bottom. The earth from the ditch was then packed into the mould and trampled down; then the mould was removed and there remained a solid wall of earth. Another section was placed on the top of this. The whole was then topped with twigs from the vine prunings mixed with mud and clay. The result was a very solid barrier.

The culture of the vine

The vine requires extremely severe pruning. It is always cut back until there remains nothing but a gnarled stump. Certain vines were known to be as much as three hundred years old and the stumps were like trees. For a rod to come from the stem of Jesse was by no means an unnatural picture, for the most ancient vines year by year put out new branches. When in the springtime the green branches came, every branch which had only leaves and no fruit was ruthlessly pruned out so that more strength might go to the fruit-bearing branches. There were various ways of training the vines. As we have seen, sometimes they were trained to trail over the stone ridges. Sometimes the trunk was allowed to grow to a height of six feet or so and then the branches were trained out laterally against a wall. Sometimes the vines were trained against trellises. In the simplest way, the vines were allowed to trail along the ground, and the fruiting branches were upheld on forked sticks.

The tower

The vineyard was a prey to marauders. There were robbers who would steal the grapes. There were foxes and jackals and wild boars who could devastate the vineyard. The hedge was a protection. But all vineyards had a tower. In the smaller ones, it was merely a wickerwork structure, sometimes with two storeys in which the watchman stayed. In the larger vineyards the tower was more elaborate, stone-built and square shaped. It rose to forty feet high and on the top there was a larger square, divided into rooms and with windows all round from which the watchmen watched. Near the harvest time an all-night watch was kept, and during the night continual noise was made to scare away the thieving foxes and jackals.

The winepress

There were four ways in which the grapes were used. (i) They were eaten in their natural state. (ii) They were laid out to dry until they became raisins which were then compressed into cakes. Abigail gave David a hundred such cakes of raisins (1 Samuel 25: 18). (iii) The juice was boiled until it became a syrup which was used as a kind of artificial honey. Jacob sent some of that kind of honey down into Egypt (Genesis 43: 11). (iv) But by far the most of the grapes were used for making wine.

For that purpose a winepress was needed. The winepress was always in the vineyard because the grapes lost their quality when they were carried. The winepress was constructed like this. First, a trough was hewed out in the limestone rock. If there was no rock, the earth was dug out, the sides were carefully lined with stone and then securely cemented. The grapes were put into this trough and trampled with the feet until the juice was pressed out. This was done with singing and shouting. The feet and the garments became stained with the juice which was called "the blood of the vine". Close to this trough on a little lower level, connected to it by holes perforated in the rock, there was another trough into which the grape juice ran. Generally the juice was allowed to lie in that tank for about four days until the process of fermentation had set it. The wine was stored in two ways, either in earthen jars or in skins. For storage ox skins were used, and some of them held as much as sixty gallons. Only new skins would do, for, as the wine fermented, it gave off gases, and, unless the skin had a certain elasticity, would burst. Skins could never be used twice. For ordinary purposes the wine was drawn off into the skins of smaller animals. These smaller skins are what are described as *bottles* in the Bible.

The use of wine

In biblical times the question of total abstinence did not arise. True, the priest when on duty must abstain from wine (Leviticus 10: 9), and so must the man who took the Nazarite vow (Numbers 6: 3). But all ordinary people drank wine, and it was always fermented wine. We have only to think of the inadequate water supply and of the obvious dangers from drinking contaminated water, to see that wine-drinking was a necessity in the ancient world. Wine was the natural drink.

In biblical times it was considered an excellent thing. It was wine which cheered both God and man (Judges 9: 13). Wine is given by God to make glad the heart of man (Psalm 104: 15). It was with wine that Melchizedek greeted Abraham (Genesis 14: 18). In the restoration of Israel she will plant her vineyards and drink her wine (Amos 9: 14). Strong drink is to be given to those who are ready to perish and wine to those in bitter distress (Proverbs 31: 6). That is not to say that the people in biblical times were drunkards – far from it. Drunkenness was abominated. *Proverbs* speaks of the disaster which comes to the man who looks on the wine when it is red (Proverbs 23: 29-35). Wine is a mocker; strong drink a brawler (Proverbs 20: 1). There are the terrible stories of what happened through drunkenness to Noah (Genesis 9: 18-27); to Lot (Genesis 19: 30-38); to Nabal (1 Samuel 25: 36-38); to Ammon (2 Samuel 13: 28, 29). But in Old Testament times the question of total abstinence had simply not arisen. Wine was a divine gift; it was over-indulgence which was the sin.

In the New Testament the situation is still the same. Wine is the ordinary drink. Paul can even advise Timothy to drink it for his health's sake (1 Timothy 5: 23). Once again the dangers are stressed (Ephesians 5: 18; 1 Timothy 3: 8; Titus 2: 3); but there is no prohibition of wine. Its use is natural and universally accepted.

The result of all this is that we cannot settle the Christian attitude by the quotation of texts. For every text on one side another can be cited on the opposite side. This is one of the questions which have to be settled, not by any citation of texts but by the spirit of the Christian position; and that position is undoubtedly to be found in the practical mind of Paul. It is summed up in his argument in Romans 14: 20, 21. Paul is talking about what the Christian, especially the strong brother, may do. The conclusion is: "Do not, for the sake of food, destroy the work of God. . . . It is right not to eat meat or drink wine or do anything that makes your brother stumble." The total abstainer can quote texts to suit his purpose. The man who drinks wine can quote texts to suit his purpose. No one will argue in favour of over-indulgence. But what every man must face is the fundamental question: Can I, as a Christian, demand a pleasure which may well be the ruin of my weaker brother? There may be two answers to that question. But only a man's examined conscience can decide which answer *he* must give.

CHAPTER TWENTY

THE MIRACLES OF THE FOURTH GOSPEL

(iii) Cured after thirty-eight Years

The Man at the Pool

AFTER this there was a feast of the Jews, and Jesus went up to Jerusalem. Now there is in Jerusalem by the Sheep Gate a pool, in Hebrew called Bethzatha, which has five porticoes. In these lay a multitude of invalids, blind, lame, paralyzed. One man was there, who had been ill for thirty-eight years. When Jesus saw him and knew that he had been lying there a long time, he said to him, "Do you want to be healed?" The sick man answered him, "Sir, I have no man to put me into the pool when the water is troubled, and while I am going another steps down before me." Jesus said to him, "Rise, take up your pallet, and walk." And at once the man was healed, and he took up his pallet and walked.   (John 5 : 1-9.)

There were three Jewish Feasts called "Feasts of Obligation." To them every adult male Jew who lived within twenty miles of Jerusalem was bound to come. They were the Feast of Pentecost, the Feast of the Passover and the Feast of Tabernacles. It was probably to the Feast of Pentecost that Jesus had come to Jerusalem at this time. There is no word of his disciples being with him; perhaps on this occasion he had come alone.

As Jesus walked through the city he came to a certain pool. Just where this pool was is uncertain. It may have been near either the Sheep Market or the Sheep Gate.[1] Even its name is uncertain. The Authorised Version calls it the Pool of Bethesda, and Bethesda could mean the House of Mercy. But the better manuscripts of the New Testament call it the Pool of Bethzatha, which might mean the House of Figs. Josephus tells us that Bethzatha was the name of that district of Jerusalem which lay north of the Temple. In Greek the pool is called a *kolumbethra*, which comes from the verb

[1] cp. Nehemiah 3 : 1; 12 : 39.

kolumban, to dive. This was no little shallow pool; it must have been as big and as deep as a swimming-pool. Round it were colonnades with five arches above them which gave shelter from the weather. The colonnades were crowded with all kinds of sick people who had come there on the chance of being healed.

The troubling of the water

In Moffatt's translation verse 4 is put in square brackets; and in the Revised Standard Version it is omitted. The reason is that it is not part of the original text. It is an explanation which was inserted later; but it gives us what people believed in the time of Jesus. Every now and again the pool bubbled up. There must have been a subterranean spring beneath it which every now and then sent out a gush of water. People believed that the bubbling up was caused by an angel and that the person who succeeded in being first into the pool after the water was disturbed would be cured from any disease from which he happened to be suffering. Such a belief may seem strange to us, but it was the kind of thing which ancient people commonly believed, not only in Palestine, but all over the world; and which primitive people believe today.

The people of Hierapolis believed that a goddess called Atargatis and her son had plunged into a sacred pool near their temple; the goddess and her son had died, but their life had been transferred to the waters and gave them special power. There was another pool in Aphaca into which the goddess Astarte was said to have descended in the form of a fiery star which had fallen from the top of Mount Lebanon.[1] It may easily have been that at some time some meteorite had fallen into the pool, and ever after people regarded the waters as impregnated with the divine presence and power. In the Middle Ages it was believed that he who bathed in springtime in the waters of the Euphrates would be free of sickness for one whole year.[2] This belief in the miraculous power of rivers and springs and pools and wells was widespread.[3] Hesiod says that

[1] W. Robertson Smith, *The Religion of the Semites*, p. 159.
[2] W. Robertson Smith, *The Religion of the Semites*, p. 167.
[3] The four following references are given by Sir J. G. Frazer, *Folk-lore in the Old Testament*, vol. ii, pp. 412-423.

when a man is about to ford a river, he should look at the running water, pray and wash his hands; for he who wades through a stream with unwashed hands incurs the wrath of the gods.[1] When the Persian armies of Xerxes reached the River Strymon in Thrace, their wise men sacrificed white horses and carried out other ceremonies before the army crossed the stream.[2] Lucullus the Roman general sacrificed a bull to the Euphrates before he crossed it.[3] In ancient Peru the people would, when they came to a river bank, scoop up a handful of water and drink it, praying to the god of the river to allow them to cross or to give them fish, and they threw maize into the stream as an offering to the god. In the old days in Wales before people would cross water after dark they would spit three times on the ground to avert the wrath of the god of the river. In South-East Africa if a person is drowned in a river the wise men say: "He was called by the spirits." In Central Africa the Baganda will not even try to rescue a man carried away by the current of a river, for they believe that the river spirit has taken him and will take them too if they try to interfere. Primitive peoples not only try to propitiate the spirits in the water; they try to overcome them. Among the Santals in India a bridegroom is given a ceremonial bath before his wedding; when the water is brought from the tank one woman shoots an arrow into it and another beats it with a sword to drive out the evil spirit. When Xerxes, the Persian king, invaded Europe he built a bridge across the Hellespont. The sea carried the bridge away. Xerxes ordered the sea to be given three hundred lashes with the whip.[4] In the temple at Hierapolis in Asia Minor there was a cleft in the rock which was supposed to lead straight to waters beneath the earth. Twice a year, with great solemnity, water from the Euphrates was poured into the cleft to prevent the demon of the well from coming out and injuring men.[5]

It is easy to see how the people of Jerusalem could believe that this pool which bubbled every now and then was disturbed by an

[1]Hesiod, *Works and Days*, 737-741.   [2]Herodotus 7 : 113.
[3]Plutarch, *Life of Lucullus*, 24.
[4]Herodotus 7 : 35.
[5]W. Robertson Smith, *The Religion of the Semites*, pp. 181, 182.

angel. In fact, at this time in their history the Jews believed in millions of angels. They thought of God as so high and so holy that he was entirely separate from the world. It was the angels who, so to speak, presided over the world and kept it going. There were two hundred angels who controlled the movements of the stars. There was an angel who controlled the succession of the years and months and days. There was an angel who was over the sea. There were angels of the frost, the dew, the rain, the snow, the hail, the thunder and the lightning.[1] In Revelation we read of an angel who was over the waters.[2]

In the time of Jesus every Jew would have an elaborate belief in angels and their activities. It is interesting to note that Jesus did not tell the man at the pool that the belief about the moving of the waters was only a superstition. He was too eager to help to spend time in argument. Frank C. Laubach, tnat great missionary servant of Christ, writes: "It would be better for us to throw away ninety-nine per cent. of our learning and of our tangled philosophy and stick to just one simple thing for our daily life – to keep asking God, 'Who needs me next, Father?' "[3] It is much more important to help people than to enter into an argument to prove them wrong; and, in any event, it is only practical help given in love which will ever convince men of the reality and the worth of Christianity. Here, as always, Jesus is our great example.

The helpless man

No doubt around the pool there would be spectators, waiting and watching for the wonderful moment of the troubling of the waters. No doubt Jesus began talking to some of them; and a most pathetic case was pointed out to him. There was a man who had been there as long as anyone could remember. There are three things we have to note about him.

First, his illness was chronic. For thirty-eight long years he had been well-nigh helpless. Here is a great thing. It does not matter

[1]For an account of the Jewish beliefs in angels see A. Edersheim, *The Life and Times of Jesus the Messiah*, vol. ii, Appendix xiii, pp. 748-755.
[2]Revelation 16 : 5.
[3]Frank C. Laubach, *Channels of Spiritual Life*, p. 164.

how deep-seated a trouble may be or how incurable it may seem, Jesus can cure it. Suppose there is a habit which has got such a grip of us that it seems impossible to break it, Jesus can enable us to break it. Suppose there is some indulgence which has such a fascination over us that we cannot stop it, Jesus can help us to stop it. Suppose there is some fear that has haunted us until it has become a complex, Jesus can enable us to conquer it.

Second, this man had no friends. He must have had some people who carried him and his bed to the pool every day. But long since they must have become weary of him and lost interest in his case. Perhaps at the beginning some of them had waited to help him into the water when it was disturbed; but long since they had taken to dumping him down at the side of the pool and leaving him. His friends had to all intents and purposes abandoned him. Boswell, in the early days of his discipleship, expressed surprise to find Johnson harbouring a man of whom he heard had a very bad character. "He is poor and honest," Goldsmith replied, "which is recommendation enough to Johnson. He is now become miserable and that insures the protection of Johnson."[1] To be friendless was to have a claim on Johnson's friendship. Jesus was like that. People who mattered to no one else mattered to him. In Jesus the friendless ever found a friend.

Third, the most significant thing about this man is that somehow he had never totally lost hope. After thirty-eight years of waiting beside the pool he was still waiting. By all the probabilities he should have abandoned hope long ago but somehow hope would not die. Once we give up hope, certainly nothing will happen; so long as we hope on, the door is always open for a miracle to happen.

The piercing question
So Jesus saw this man, this chronic invalid, this man who had waited so long, this man who had somehow preserved a glimmer of hope; and he began by asking him a piercing question: "Do you want to be well again?" That question is not nearly so irrelevant and unnecessary as we might think. Any psychologist will

[1]Quoted in Robert Lynd, *Dr. Johnson and Company*, p 138.

tell us that many people are ill for no other reason than that they want to be.

Leslie Weatherhead quotes a case like that. There was a girl named Kathleen G. She was about twenty, young and healthy, and a typist in a village garage. She became engaged to the curate of the village and was radiantly happy. A good part of her happiness came from the fact that she was no longer going to be in a menial and unimportant job; she was going to be someone of importance and standing in the neighbourhood. The curate broke off the engagement. From that day Kathleen developed certain symptoms. She refused to eat. She would even put food into her mouth and then put it out into her handkerchief or serviette, hide it away and destroy it later. She became pale, thin, and anaemic All that the doctor could say to her parents was: "You must make her eat." She was taken to a specialist and all he could say was that she must be forced to eat. In desperation her parents brought her to Leslie Weatherhead to see if he could treat her by psychological methods. By this time she weighed only five stone three pounds and looked like a famine victim. All she could say was that she knew she ought to eat but an inward power was forbidding her to do so. Under psychological treatment her trouble became clear. Subconsciously she wanted to starve to death. To be ill was to have prominence and not to sink back into the obscurity of being a typist in a village garage. To be ill and die was to have her revenge on the curate; if she died, he would feel responsible for her death. She was ill for no other reason than that she wanted to be ill. She could not be cured for no other reason that that she did not want to be made well. Fortunately psychological treatment was able to reveal the truth to her and to cure her.[1]

We can often see this kind of thing happening very simply. On the morning before some engagement we do not wish to fulfil, we develop a headache or a cold. It is our unconscious mind which produces the condition. We are ill for no other reason than that we want to be. Illness can be an escape. It can make us the centre

[1] Quoted together with other similar cases in Leslie D. Weatherhead *Psychology, Religion and Healing*, pp. 354-361.

of the picture – bringing sympathy and attention that otherwise we would not have received. Many people have escaped into invalidism. To be well the first essential is to want to be well.

To achieve anything, the first essential is to desire it. Jesus's question to the man was by no means superfluous. It went straight to the heart of the matter. It is the same with being good. The first question Jesus asks us is: "Do you really want to give up the bad habits which have you in their grip? Do you really want to be changed?" If in all honesty we have to answer: "Thank you very much. I am quite content as I am," not even Jesus can change us. Jesus put to the helpless man the question which really matters, when he asked him: "Do you want to be well?"

Jesus's command and our effort

The man's answer was totally honest. He pointed out that, as things were, he had no chance of getting to the pool in time; he had no one to rush him down to the water. He wanted to be cured but he did not see how it was to be done. Jesus looked at him. "Get up," he said. "Take up your bed and walk." Here was the crucial test. If the man's reaction had been to say: "You are asking me to do the very thing I can't do. It is impossible," he would never have been cured. Instead, he made a great effort to do as Jesus said, and to his astonishment found himself upon his feet and, after all these years, able to walk again.

Again and again we see Jesus working in this way. It was his habit to urge men to make the effort which would co-operate with his power. He said in effect: "Help yourself and I will help you." He encouraged them to make an effort more strenuous than they had ever made before; and then his grace came in to help – and the miracle happened. With Jesus to back our effort the impossible becomes possible.

It has been suggested that this story is not so much the account of an actual event as an allegory. An allegory is a story in which every event has an inner meaning. The two most famous allegories are Spenser's *Faerie Queene* and Bunyan's *Pilgrim's Progress*. It has been suggested that in this story the helpless man stands for the people of Israel. The thirty-eight years stands for the thirty-eight years during which the people wandered in the wilderness (Deut. 2 : 14). The five porches stand for the five books of the Law. The Law could tell a man what was wrong with his life and show him his sin, but it could never help him to mend himself or cure his sin. The Law, like the porches, was the shelter of people who were ill and knew it, who were morally helpless and could do nothing about it. The pool stands for the waters of baptism through which a man enters a new life with a new goodness and a new power, leaving his sins behind him.

It may be that these things can be read into this story; but it is neither right nor natural to do so, as if it was the story of something which never happened. This is much too like an eye-witness account for that. We are better to take it as a real-life story of a miracle which Jesus worked for a helpless man, who had never lost hope and who was prepared to make the effort which Jesus demanded.

CHAPTER TWENTY-ONE

THE MIRACLES OF THE FOURTH GOSPEL

(iv) Now I see

The Man Born Blind

As Jesus passed by, he saw a man blind from his birth. And his disciples asked him, "Rabbi, who sinned, this man or his parents, that he was born blind?" Jesus answered, "It was not that this man sinned, or his parents, but that the works of God might be made manifest in him. We must work the works of him who sent me, while it is day; night comes, when no one can work. As long as I am in the world, I am the light of the world." As he said this, he spat on the ground and made clay of the spittle and anointed the man's eyes with the clay, saying to him, "Go, wash in the pool of Siloam" (which means Sent). So he went and washed and came back seeing.

(John 9 : 1-7.)

Sin and Suffering

This story is unique among the miracle stories of the gospels in that it is the only case where the sufferer is said to have been afflicted since birth. In *Acts* the man who was healed at the Beautiful Gate of the Temple[1] and the man who was cured at Lystra[2] were both afflicted from birth; but of the gospel miracles this is the only one where the sufferer had never been well. The likelihood is that this miracle also happened at the Temple gates, for it was there that beggars came to beg.

When Jesus and his disciples passed this blind man, the disciples asked Jesus: "Is this man blind because he sinned or because his parents sinned?" Of one thing Jewish thinkers were sure – that where there was suffering there had been sin.[3] Eliphaz

[1]Acts 3 : 2.   [2]Acts 14 : 8.
[3]For a fuller discussion of the connection of sin and suffering see G. F. Moore, *Judaism*, vol. ii, 248-256.

said to Job: "who that was innocent ever perished?"[1] The Psalmist said mournfully: "My wounds grow foul and fester because of my foolishness."[2] "Some because of their iniquities," he said, "suffered affliction"[3] In the terrible killing times of the Maccabean struggle, one of the suffering Jewish heroes said: "We are suffering on account of our sins."[4] Two of the most terrible passages in the Old Testament give a ghastly detailed picture of what is to happen to the nation that is disloyal to God.[5] The Talmud lays it down: "The sick arises not from his sickness, until his sins be forgiven."[6] The Rabbis laid it down: "All God's dealings with men are measure for measure."[7] It was even held that particular sins produced particular diseases. Leprosy came to a man because of seven grave sins – slander, homicide, false-swearing, licentiousness, haughtiness, robbery, stinginess. Diseases which cut off the breath came upon the slanderer. "Where the sin began," they said, "the retribution sets in." So Samson was blinded because he used his eyes lustfully. Absalom was hanged by his hair because he was inordinately proud of it. It was nevertheless held that such suffering was not merely retributive, but that God always meant it to cure a man and to lead him back to himself. For that reason Rabbi Akiba said: "Precious are chastisements." And it was pointed out that King Manasseh's sufferings drew him back to God when all other things had failed to do so.[8] The whole Book of Job is a protest against this rigid doctrine that suffering is inevitably the result of sin.

Sin before birth

The consequence of this unbreakable connection between sin and suffering was one rather fantastic doctrine. Certain of the

---

[1]Job 4 : 7.   [2]Psalm 38 : 5.   [3]Psalm 107 : 17.
[4]2 Maccabees 7 : 8.
[5]Leviticus 26 : 14-39; Deuteronomy 28 : 15-68.
[6]Quoted in his commentary on *John*, by J. H. Bernard, vol, i, p. 234.
[7]This and the following Rabbinic quotations are taken from the material given by G. F. Moore in the section of his *Judaism* already cited.
[8]2 Chronicles 33 : 10-13.

Jews believed that it was possible for a person to sin *before* his birth. They explained this in two ways.

(i). They took it quite literally. They actually believed that a man could sin when he was still an unformed child in his mother's womb. For instance, some teachers said that if a woman carrying a child worshipped in a heathen temple, the unborn child was guilty of idolatry.[1] There is an imaginary discussion between Antoninus and Rabbi Judah the Patriarch. Antoninus asks: "From what time does the evil influence bear sway over a man, from the formation of the embryo in the womb or from the moment of birth?" The Rabbi first answered: "From the formation of the embryo." Antoninus objected to this view and convinced Judah by his arguments, for Judah had to admit that, if the evil influence began with the formation of the embryo, then the child would kick in the womb and break his way out. Judah found a text to justify his revised opinion. Genesis 4: 7 reads: "Sin is crouching at the door," and he took this to mean that sin awaits man at the door of the womb, as soon as he is born.[2] The Jews considered it a real possibility that a man might begin sinning before he was born.

(ii). The other way they arrived at the conception of pre-natal sin was from the belief in the pre-existence of the soul. This was really a belief which Plato had taught and which many of the later Jews had taken over. They believed that all souls had already existed in the Garden of Eden before the creation of the world or were in the seventh heaven or were in a "certain chamber" awaiting entry into a body. In the *Secrets of Enoch,* one of the Jewish apocryphal books, the writer hears it said to him: "Sit and write all the souls of mankind, however many of them are born, and the places prepared to them to eternity; for all souls are prepared to eternity, before the formation of the world."[3] Originally the belief had been that all souls were good

[1] Quoted by C. K. Barrett, *The Gospel according to St. John,* p. 295.
[2] Quoted by G. F. Moore, *Judaism,* vol. i, p. 481.
[3] R. H. Charles, *The Apocrypha and Pseudepigrapha of the Old Testament,* vol. ii, p. 444. The passage is *The Secrets of Enoch* 23 : 4, 5. Charles's note describes the Jewish belief and its origins.

and that it was contact with the body which defiled them. But in the time of Jesus certain Jews had begun to believe that the pre-existing souls were already good or bad. The writer of the *Book of Wisdom* says: "Now I was a child good by nature and a good soul fell to my lot."[1]

We can see at once that if the Jews had these strange ideas in their minds, they could believe that this man's blindness was caused by his own sin, even though he had been blind since his birth. According to their way of thinking, he could have sinned even before he was born.

The sins of the fathers

But the disciples suggested another possibility. Perhaps it was not this man himself who had sinned but his parents. This is one of the key-notes of Jewish thought. All through the Old Testament runs the grim certainty that the parents' sins are visited on the children. "I, the Lord your God, am a jealous God, visiting the iniquity of the fathers upon the children to the third and the fourth generation."[2] Of the wicked man the Psalmist says: "May the iniquity of his fathers be remembered before the Lord; and let not the sin of his mother be blotted out."[3] Isaiah talks about the iniquities of the people and the iniquities of their fathers, and goes on to say: "I will repay into their bosom their iniquities."[4] "Our fathers sinned and are no more; and we bear their iniquities."[5] This is the almost universal view of the Old Testament. But there were two prophets who insisted on personal responsibility and refused to blame the disasters of Israel on the sins of the fathers. Jeremiah said: "In those days they shall no longer say, The fathers have eaten sour grapes, and the children's teeth are set on edge. But every one shall die for his own sin; each man who eats sour grapes, his teeth shall be set on edge."[6] Ezekiel is even more forceful. "What do you mean by repeating this proverb concerning the land of Israel, The fathers have eaten sour grapes, and the

[1]Wisdom 8 : 19.
[2]Exodus 20 : 5; 34 : 7; Numbers 14 : 18.   [3]Psalm 109 : 14.
[4]Isaiah 65 : 6, 7.   [5]Lamentations 5 : 7.   [6]Jeremiah 31 : 29, 30.

children's teeth are set on edge? . . . The soul that sins, it shall die."[1] But the words of Jeremiah and of Ezekiel are protests against the almost universally held doctrine that the sins of the fathers were visited upon the children.

Jesus's answer was that this man's blindness was due neither to his sin nor to the sin of his parents; it was so that God's works should be made plain in him. Here we are face to face with one of the apparent difficulties in the view that the Fourth Gospel has of the miracles of Jesus. In almost every case they are performed to demonstrate his own glory and the glory of God, or to convince men of his supreme greatness. The miracle of the turning of the water into wine at Cana of Galilee ends: "This, the first of his signs, Jesus did at Cana in Galilee, and manifested his glory; and his disciples believed in him."[2] The miracle of the feeding of the five thousand ends: "when the people saw the sign which he had done, they said, 'This is indeed the prophet who is to come into the world!'."[3] When the disciples asked Jesus about the sickness of Lazarus, he answered that it was "for the glory of God, so that the Son of God may be glorified by means of it."[4]

At first sight it looks as if sickness and pain and trouble had come upon people simply to give God a chance to show his glory and this seems oddly inhuman, like a surgeon allowing a patient to become far more seriously ill than necessary in order to demonstrate the excellence of his surgical technique. What makes this more difficult, on the face of it, is that in the other three gospels what moves Jesus to perform his miracles is sheer pity for the sufferer. When the leper came to Jesus, he was "moved with pity."[5] When Jesus saw the hungry, tired crowd he "had compassion on them."[6] When he saw the bewildered crowds he "had compassion for them" because they were like sheep without a shepherd.[7] When the two blind men came to

---

[1]Ezekiel 18 : 2-4.
[2]John 2 : 11.   [3]John 6 : 14.
[4]John 11 : 4.   [5]Mark 1 : 41.
[6]Mark 6 : 34.
[7]Matthew 9 : 36; 14 : 14.

him, he "had compassion" on them and touched their eyes.[1]
When he saw the sorrowing widow of Nain who had lost her
only son, he "had compassion" on her and he raised the son
and – in that phrase of infinite pity – "he gave him to his
mother."[2]

There is no real contradiction here. The two things are different
ways of expressing the same truth. The truth is that God's pity
is God's splendour. Every miracle showed God's power, but in
every case that power was moved by love. When the other
three gospels attribute the miracles of Jesus to his compassion
and the Fourth says that they were designed to show God's
glory, they mean the same thing; for the glory of God is his
compassion.

Demonstrating the glory of God

There is a sense in which all suffering can be used to demonstrate
the glory of God. By the way in which he bears suffering the
Christian can demonstrate what God can do for him.

One of the most famous martyrdoms in history was that of
Polycarp, bishop of Smyrna. He was an old man of over eighty.
He was seized and given the chance of abandoning his loyalty
to Christ or being burned at the stake. He stood firm. "Eighty and
six years have I served Christ," he said, "and he has never done
me wrong. How can I blaspheme my King, who saved me?"
They were about to burn him to death; and they intended to
nail him to the stake so that he could not escape. "Leave me,"
he said. "God will grant me to endure the fire without the
security you seek from the nails." And, as he died, he prayed:
"O Lord God Almighty . . . I thank thee that thou hast judged
me worthy of this hour."[3] By the way in which he bore his
suffering Polycarp demonstrated the glory of God.

There was a boy called William Henry Jackson. When he
was three he became blind. Anyone might say that that was
the end of all possibility of a career; but it was not. He trained

[1]Matthew 20 : 34.   [2]Luke 7 : 13.
[3]There is a full account of the martyrdom of Polycarp in H. B.
Workman, *Persecution in the Early Church*, pp. 307-310.

as a priest. Anyone might say that a blind priest would seek a safe parish in his own country; but he did not. He went as a missionary to Burma. All alone – a blind man – he would set out by bullock-cart or on foot. A blind man cannot see snakes but that did not trouble Father Jackson. Native bridges are sometimes made of a single bamboo but somehow he crossed them. Blindness was common in Burma and was believed to be due to sin; and so blind people were outcasts for whom there was nothing to do but beg. Father Jackson put off his European clothes and dressed like a native. In a town called Kemmendine he gathered round him a group of blind boys. He taught them to type and weave and make furniture, for he could do all these things himself. He wanted them to be able to read. So he invented a braille script in Burmese. He then began to print braille books. He hammered the braille signs in flattened out kerosene tins, and rolled off paper copies by putting the punched tin sheets and paper through a second-hand mangle. The "Big Father" his boys called him; and he told them about their Father in Heaven. He died in Kemmendine in 1931. By the way in which he conquered his affliction, William Henry Jackson demonstrated the glory of God.[1]

It does not need to be as dramatic as that. By the way in which we cheerfully bear an illness or uncomplainingly accept a disappointment or by the spirit in which we accept a defeat, we too can demonstrate the glory of God.

Further, we can demonstrate the glory of God, not only by the way in which we react to our own sufferings, but by the way in which we react to the sufferings of others. Albert Schweitzer was one of the most brilliant students in Germany. He was outstanding in philosophy. He was one of the greatest of all organists, and in particular played Bach as no one else could play him. But at the back of his mind there was a feeling that would not be stilled. "As far back as I can remember, the thought of all the misery in the world has been a constant source of pain to me. . . . The sight of a limping horse which a man

[1]The story of William Henry Jackson is told in Maud M. Higham, *Torches for Teachers*, pp. 218-220.

was dragging along behind him to the slaughter-house in Colmar whilst another belaboured it with a stick haunted me for weeks. It became steadily clearer to me that I had not the moral right to take my happy youth, my good health and my ability to work as a matter of course. . . . We must all take our share of the misery which weighs so heavily upon the world."

So Albert Schweitzer decided to give everything up and to study night and day to be a doctor and go out to Lambarene in Africa to bring medical skill to native Africans who had never known it. He tells how a poor, suffering native was brought to his hospital. "Pain is a more terrible lord of mankind than even death himself." Schweitzer laid his hand upon his head and said: "Don't be afraid. In an hour's time you will be put to sleep and you will feel no more pain when you wake up." The operation is finished; Schweitzer waits beside the man; he wakes up, stares around, and suddenly says again and again and again: "I have no more pain! I have no more pain!" "His hand feels for mine and will not let it go."

By the way in which Schweitzer reacted to the need of suffering humanity he demonstrated the glory of God.[1]

Again it does not need to be as dramatic as that. Most people are selfish and do not care very much what happens to others so long as they themselves are comfortable and care-free. If we help where help is needed and try to make life better and happier for others, we too demonstrate the glory of God.

Jesus works the cure

So Jesus cured this man. The method of cure was that Jesus first spat on the ground and made clay.[2] He then sent the man to wash in the Pool of Siloam. In this anointing of the man's eyes with clay some of the early fathers discovered a most interesting parallel. In the creation story God formed man out of the dust of the earth.[3] Irenaeus said that here Jesus is showing himself in

[1]The quotations are taken from Oskar Kraus, *Albert Schweitzer, his Life and his Philosophy*, pp. 10, 17, 26.

[2]For the use of spittle to heal in the ancient world, see chapter 9, pp. 65-72.

[3]Genesis 2 : 7.

his creating power. Originally God formed man out of clay; so Jesus created this man's eyes out of clay and showed himself as the creator and the re-creator of man.[1]

The Pool of Siloam

Jesus sent the man to wash in the Pool of Siloam, and John interprets *Siloam* as meaning *Sent*. The Pool of Siloam was the result of one of the great engineering feats of the ancient world. Jerusalem was dependent for its water-supply on the Virgin's Fountain or the spring Gihon, outside the city wall in the Kidron Valley. It had been expanded into a stone basin and thirty-three steps cut in the rock so that people might the more easily descend and draw water. The danger was that this spring was outside the city wall and completely exposed so that in the event of a siege it would have been easy to deny the people of Jerusalem its use and so compel the city to surrender.

About the year 700 B.C. Hezekiah realized that Sennacherib of Assyria intended to attack Jerusalem and so he determined to construct a conduit or tunnel through the solid rock by which the water of the spring might be brought into the city.[2] His engineers had to cut through 366 yards of solid rock. For some reason they pursued a devious course – it has been conjectured that it was to avoid the tombs of the kings, but it may simply have been that they were following a natural fissure in the rock – and the actual length of the tunnel is 583 yards. The tunnel is still there and visitors often wade through it, carrying torches to guide their way. In places it is only 2 feet wide; and its height varies from 6 to 14 feet. It was obviously constructed in a hurry. The rough marks of the axes are still there. Sometimes it deviates for a foot or two and then comes back to its proper course. It was begun from both ends at once and the engineers met in the middle. In A.D. 1880 the inscription originally cut to commemorate its completion was accidentally discovered by two small boys who were wading in the pool. It dates to 701 B.C. and reads: "The

[1] Irenaeus, *Against the Heretics*, 5, 15, 2. Quoted by E. C. Hoskyns and F. N. Davey, *The Fourth Gospel*, p. 354.
[2] 2 Chronicles 32 : 2-8, 30; Isaiah 22 : 9-11; 2 Kings 20 : 20.

boring through is completed. Now this is the story of the boring through. While the workmen were still lifting pick to pick, each towards his neighbour, and while three cubits remained to be cut through, each heard the voice of the other who called his neighbour, since there was a crevice in the rock on the right side. And the day of the boring through the stone-cutters struck, each to meet his fellow, pick to pick; and there flowed the waters to the pool for a thousand and two hundred cubits, and a hundred cubits was the height of the rock above the heads of the stone-cutters."

This was indeed an almost incredible engineering feat of the ancient world. Hezekiah sealed up the opening of the Virgin's Fountain in the Kidron Valley so that no enemy would be able to interfere with it. And the place where the conduit ended in Jerusalem was the Pool of Siloam. The commoner Hebrew for the word is *Shiloah*, which comes from the verb *shalach*, to *send*; and the pool was so called because the water had been *sent* into it by the conduit. The pool itself was 71 feet from north to south and 75 feet from east to west. Probably in the time of Herod it was surrounded by a covered colonnade 12 feet wide and $22\frac{1}{2}$ feet high. It was to this famous pool, which every one in Jerusalem knew and used, that the man was sent to wash his eyes.[1] Having done so, he returned able to see.

A series of reactions

One of the most interesting studies in this story is that of the reactions of the people involved. This is a masterpiece of character drawing; there is no New Testament story in which the people come so vividly to life.

(i). First there is *Jesus*. The great point about him in this story is that with complete deliberation he broke the Sabbath Law in order to help this man;[2] and did so three times over.

[1] There are good articles on Siloam in J. Hastings, *Dictionary of the Bible*, vol. iv, p. 515, and in Harper's *Dictionary of the Bible*. There is a vivid description of the tunnel in H. V. Morton, *In the Steps of the Master*, pp. 69–72. Mr. Morton actually walked from one end of the tunnel to the other.

[2] For a full account of the Sabbath Law see chapter 12, pp. 87–95.

(*a*) To heal on the Sabbath Day was to work. True, help could be given if life was in actual danger; but any steps taken could only see to it that the patient grew no worse; it was forbidden to take steps to make him better, for that would have been to work. For instance, a man might not suck his fingers through his teeth if they pained him on the Sabbath Day. A dislocated or sprained hand or foot might be washed, but cold water might not be poured over it.[1] Jesus had healed this man who was in no imminent danger of his life; therefore he had broken the Law. (*b*) Jesus had made clay. By doing that he had technically kneaded the clay and kneading was one of the thirty-nine "fathers of work" which the Law expressly forbade.[2] (*c*) In the Rabbinic expansion of the Law one of the things expressly forbidden was to put fasting spittle on the eyes on the Sabbath Day.[3] Fasting spittle was an accepted remedy and no remedy might be used. Jesus deliberately broke the Law to heal the blind man.

To Jesus people were always more important than rules and regulations. For instance, he would have completely failed to comprehend the mind of the man who refused to help because the appeal came to him outside his statutory working hours or because the act of helping lay outside his division of labour. For Jesus the only valid law was that which ordered that help should be given. For him – and it should be so for us – nothing could take priority over human need.

(ii). There were the *Pharisees*. To them it was nothing that a man had had his sight restored; all that mattered was that a trifling Sabbath law had been broken. They cared for regulations more than they cared for people. To support their position and their authority, they were reduced to three things. First, they resorted to *abuse*.[4] Second, they resorted to *insult*.[5] Third, they resorted to *threats*.[6] When a man's position can be supported only by abuse and insult and threats, it is a poor position.

[1]H. Danby, *The Mishnah, Tractate Shabbath*, 14 : 4; 22 : 6; pp. 113, 119.

[2]H. Danby, *The Mishnah, Tractate Shabbath*, 7 : 2; p. 106.

[3]The regulation is quoted by C. K. Barrett, *The Gospel according to St. John*, p. 296.

[4]John 9 : 28.   [5]John 9 : 34.   [6]John 9 : 34.

(iii). There were the man's *parents*. They, too, were brought into the argument. The Pharisees in savage cross-examination demanded if the blind man was really their son, if he really had been blind and if they knew who had cured him. The parents were unwilling to give any answer at all. They claimed that the man was legally old enough to be a witness on his own behalf. At the age of thirteen a Jewish boy became old enough to be a witness. The fear of the parents was that they might be excommunicated, because the Pharisees had decided that anyone who admitted that he believed Jesus to be the Messiah should be put out of the synagogue. The word used *for being put out of the synagogue* literally means *unsynagogued*.[1]

Excommunication[2] was a serious matter for a Jew. It had various forms. The lightest was known as *Neziphah*. If pronounced by the elders it lasted for seven days; if it was pronounced by the President of the Sanhedrin it lasted for thirty days. In later times it sometimes lasted for only one day. *Neziphah* literally means an *inveighing* or a *rebuke*, and this form of excommunication may well have been something like discipline before a Scottish Kirk Session, followed by a public rebuke. The second and more severe form of excommunication was called *Niddui*, which comes from a verb which means *to thrust* or *cast out*. It lasted for thirty days. If it was ineffective, it was prolonged for another thirty days, and might be then followed by a still more severe sentence. When a person had had sentence of *Niddui* passed on him, he must sit on the ground and conduct himself like one in deep mourning. He must allow his beard and hair to grow untrimmed; and he must not bathe or anoint himself. He was not admitted to any assembly of ten men or to public prayer; but he might either teach or be taught by an individual person. He was treated as a leper and people might not go nearer to him than four cubits, that is six feet. If he died

---

[1] John 9 : 22.
[2] The facts about Excommunication are to be found in E. Schürer, *A History of the Jewish People in the Time of Jesus Christ*, 2, 59-62; and in A. Edersheim, *The Life and Times of Jesus the Messiah*, vol. ii, pp. 183, 184.

there must be no ordinary funeral; stones were flung at his coffin; and any mourning for him was forbidden. The most severe sentence of all was the *Cherem* or ban. This lasted for an indefinite time. When sentence of *Cherem* was passed on him, a man was reckoned as dead. He was not allowed to study with others, not even with one individual. No intercourse whatever was to be held with him; he was not even to be told or shown the right way. He was entitled to buy the necessities of life, but no one might eat or drink in his company.

The people who were the original readers of the Fourth Gospel would well know what all this meant. The Fourth Gospel was not written until about A.D. 100. By that time the cleavage between Jews and Christians was complete and the Christian Jew was automatically excommunicated. At the synagogue service there were eighteen benedictions. These were prayers which were always used. By the time the Fourth Gospel was written there was one called "The heretic benediction," which probably ran: "For the renegades let there be no hope, and may the arrogant kingdom soon be rooted out in our days, and the Nazarenes and the heretics perish in a moment, and be blotted out from the book of life and with the righteous may they not be inscribed. Blessed art Thou, O Lord, who humblest the arrogant."[1] It can be well understood that even a Christian Jew would hear a curse like that with an involuntary shiver of horror. The Jews who became Christians and who read the Fourth Gospel would well know how the parents of the blind man felt.

These parents were just ordinary people who would not take a risk. They feared human authority too much to go the whole way with Jesus Christ.

(iv). There was the *man himself*. There is no figure in the New Testament who stands out more clearly. We see him as a fearless, independent, brusque character. He has more than a touch of mocking humour and he is not in the least overawed by authority. His most characteristic statement is his affirmation that he knows only one thing about Jesus—he may or may not be a sinner, but

[1] Quoted in this form by C. K. Barrett, *The Gospel according to St. John*, p. 300.

he made him able to see, and no one in all history had ever given sight to a man who had been *born* blind. The blind man could not say who Jesus was; but he was determined to say what Jesus had done for him. He might have no ideas about the person of Jesus; but he had very definite ideas about the power of Jesus.

He is the great proof that it is far more important to know Jesus than to know about him. We do not need to be theologians in order to be Christians. Sooner or later we have to think out our faith. But too many people start the wrong way round. We cannot think until we have something to think about; the real beginning of every Christian life must be the experience of what Christ can do.

The great progression

There is one other most interesting thing in this story: it is fascinating to trace how the man's idea of Jesus expands.

(i) He begins by calling Jesus a *man*.[1] Whatever else we say about Jesus he was a man among men. As Mark Antony said of Caesar:

> "His life was gentle, and the elements
> So mix'd in him that Nature might stand up
> And say to all the world, 'This was a man!' "[2]

If ever a gallery of heroes of the world should be assembled, Jesus must be there. If ever an anthology of beautiful lives should be made, his must find a place. If ever a collection of masterpieces of literature should be collected, his parables must be included. Simply as a man Jesus ranks at the top of human greatness.

(ii) He goes on to call Jesus a *prophet*.[3] A prophet is a man who brings God's word and thoughts to men. No one did that like Jesus. Even the non-Christian would admit that Jesus speaks with a wisdom far surpassing that of any other man; and that, if the principles he laid down were accepted, the world's personal, social, economic, political, national and international problems

[1] John 9 : 11.　　[2] Shakespeare, *Julius Caesar* 5, 4, 67-71.
[3] John 9 : 17.

would be solved. If ever any man deserved the name of prophet, Jesus does.

(iii) Then comes the climax. After the man had been cast out, Jesus sought him out; he never leaves any man to fight his battles or to bear the consequences of his loyalty alone. He spoke to the man and he suddenly discovered that Jesus was the Son of God.[1] No one quite knows just what that means and to the end of the day men will go on trying to explain it. But this is clear—human categories are not adequate to describe Jesus. Men did not call him the Son of God because they chose to, but because they had to. It is told that once Napoleon was in a group of sceptical people. They dismissed Jesus as one of the world's greatest men. "Gentlemen," said Napoleon, "I know men, and Jesus Christ is more than a man."

[1] John 9 : 35-38.

CHAPTER TWENTY-TWO

THE MIRACLES OF THE FOURTH GOSPEL

(v) The Resurrection and the Life

The Raising of Lazarus

Now a certain man was ill, Lazarus of Bethany, the village of Mary and her sister Martha. It was Mary who anointed the Lord with ointment and wiped his feet with her hair, whose brother Lazarus was ill. So the sisters sent to Jesus, saying, "Lord, he whom you love is ill." But when Jesus heard it he said, "This illness is not unto death; it is for the glory of God, so that the Son of God may be glorified by means of it." Now Jesus loved Martha and her sister and Lazarus. So when he heard that he was ill, he stayed two days longer in the place where he was. Then after this he said to the disciples, "Let us go into Judea again." The disciples said to him, "Rabbi, the Jews were but now seeking to stone you, and are you going there again?" Jesus answered, "Are there not twelve hours in the day? If any one walks in the day he does not stumble, because he sees the light of this world. But if any one walks in the night, he stumbles, because the light is not in him." Thus he spoke, and then he said to them, "Our friend Lazarus has fallen asleep, but I go to awake him out of sleep." The disciples said to him, "Lord, if he has fallen asleep, he will recover." Now Jesus had spoken of his death, but they thought that he meant taking rest in sleep. Then Jesus told them plainly, "Lazarus is dead; and for your sake I am glad that I was not there, so that you may believe. But let us go to him." Thomas, called the Twin, said to his fellow disciples, "Let us also go, that we may die with him."

Now when Jesus came, he found that Lazarus had already been in the tomb four days. Bethany was near Jerusalem, about four miles off, and many of the Jews had come to Martha and Mary to console them concerning their brother. When Martha heard that Jesus was coming, she went and met him, while Mary sat in the house. Martha said to Jesus, "Lord, if you had been here, my brother would not have died. And even now I know that whatever you ask from God, God will give you." Jesus said to her, "Your brother will rise again." Martha said to him, "I know that he will rise again in the resurrection at the last day." Jesus said to her, "I am the resurrection and the life; he who believes in me, though he die, yet shall he live, and whoever lives and believes in me shall never die. Do you believe this?" She said to him, "Yes, Lord; I believe that you are the Christ, the Son of God, he who is coming into the world."

When she had said this, she went and called her sister Mary, saying quietly, "The Teacher is here and is calling for you." And when she heard it, she rose quickly and went to him. Now Jesus had not yet come to the village, but was still in the place where Martha had met him. When the Jews who were with her in the house, consoling her, saw Mary rise quickly and go out, they followed her, supposing that she was going to the tomb to weep there. Then Mary, when she came where Jesus was and saw him, fell at his feet, saying to him, "Lord, if you had been here, my brother would not have died." When Jesus saw her weeping, and the Jews who came with her also weeping, he was deeply moved in spirit and troubled; and he said, "Where have you laid him?" They said to him, "Lord, come and see." Jesus wept. So the Jews said, "See how he loved him!" But some of them said, "Could not he who opened the eyes of the blind man have kept this man from dying?"

Then Jesus, deeply moved again, came to the tomb; it was a cave, and a stone lay upon it. Jesus said, "Take away the stone." Martha, the sister of the dead man, said to him, "Lord, by this time there will be an odour, for he has been dead four days." Jesus said to her, "Did I not tell you that if you would believe you would see the glory of God?" So they took away the stone. And Jesus lifted up his eyes and said, "Father, I thank thee that thou has heard me. I knew that thou hearest me always, but I have said this on account of the people standing by, that they may believe that thou didst send me." When he had said this, he cried with a loud voice, "Lazarus, come out." The dead man came out, his hands and feet bound with bandages, and his face wrapped with a cloth. Jesus said to them, "Unbind him, and let him go." (John 11 : 1-44.)

Things had become so dangerous for Jesus, and the situation so serious, that he was compelled to retire from Jerusalem and take temporary refuge on the far side of the Jordan. The Jewish authorities were so enraged against him that they had attempted to stone him to death.[1] While he was there, news came to him that Lazarus was ill. One of the most precious things in life is to have somewhere to go where the tensions are relaxed and we can be at peace; to have a circle into which we can go and open our minds and hearts

[1]John 8 : 59; 10 : 40.

and know that we will neither be laughed at nor mis-understood. Jesus had just such a place in the home of Martha and Mary and Lazarus at Bethany;[1] and it was doubly sweet and valuable to one who had nowhere which he could call home.[2]

We might have expected that Jesus would leave post-haste for Bethany; but he did not and remained two days longer where he was. To many this delay is bewildering. It has been suggested that Jesus remained where he was so that when he arrived in Bethany Lazarus would have been dead for four days and the miracle he intended to perform would therefore be all the more amazing and impressive. But we can hardly believe that Jesus would deliberately arrange matters in such a way that Martha and Mary would have to endure two more days of bitter anguish in order that he might obtain more glory.

The fact that Jesus remained where he was for two further days after he received the message is part of John's picture of him, one of whose characteristics is that Jesus is always self-determined. John always shows us Jesus taking his own decisions in his own good time.

There are two outstanding examples of that. At the marriage feast in Cana of Galilee, John shows us Mary coming to Jesus and telling him of the domestic disaster which threatened when the wine was going done; and then he shows us Jesus very courteously but very definitely telling Mary that he would deal with the matter in his own way. To put it more crudely, he told her not to interfere.[3] As John tells the story, Jesus acted, not because someone persuaded him to act, but because he chose to do so. The other instance is when his brothers sought to dare him into going to Jerusalem. He quietly but firmly rejected their demands; and later, in his own good time, he went up to Jerusalem.[4] Here too, John is showing us Jesus acting under no compulsion or persuasion but solely as he himself chose to act. Behind all this is the great truth that it is wrong to try to persuade Jesus into doing things in our way and in our time. We must not seek to bend Jesus to our will; we must submit to his will.

[1]Luke 10 : 38-42.   [2]Luke 9 : 58.
[3]John 2 : 3-7.   [4]John 7 : 1-10.

Jesus sets out for Bethany

When Jesus told his disciples about the news which had come to him, at first they misunderstood. Here again we come upon a regular habit of John. Over and over again when he reports a conversation of Jesus, the conversation follows a definite pattern. It begins with a quite simple saying of Jesus; that saying is misunderstood; and then follows the explanation. That is the pattern when Jesus talks to Nicodemus about being born again[1] and when he talks to the woman at the well about the living water.[2]

He began by telling his disciples that the illness of Lazarus would not prove fatal. He then went on to say that Lazarus was asleep and that he was going to waken him from his sleep. The disciples were puzzled. They well knew that sleep was the best of all cures and they could not understand why Jesus should wish to waken Lazarus. But often in the Bible sleep is used for the sleep of death. At the end of the story of Stephen's martyrdom it is said that he fell asleep.[3] Paul speaks of those who sleep in Jesus.[4] Jesus told the disciples plainly that Lazarus was dead.

He went on to say a surprising thing. He said that this illness was designed for God's glory and for his. Time and time again John's statements have two meanings, one which lies on the surface and a far more significant one which lies below the surface. So is it here. First, there is the obvious meaning that the raising of Lazarus from the dead would bring glory to Jesus by its very wonder. But in the Fourth Gospel the *glory* of Christ and the *Cross* of Christ are inextricably intertwined. John tells us that the Spirit had not yet come because Jesus was not yet *glorified*, that is to say, because he had not yet died upon his Cross.[5] He shows us the Greeks coming to Jesus and Jesus saying to them: "The hour has come for the Son of Man to be glorified."[6] He meant that the hour of the Cross had come.

When Jesus said that the illness of Lazarus was designed for his glory, he meant that it was going to lead to his Cross, as indeed it did, for, as John saw the chain of events, it was the raising of

[1]John 3 : 3-8.   [2]John 4 : 10-15.
[3]Acts 7 : 60.   [4]1 Thessalonians 4 : 13.
[5]John 7 : 39.   [6]John 12 : 23.

Lazarus which finally decided the Jewish authorities that action must be taken to eliminate Jesus.[1] When Jesus went to the help of his friends in Bethany, he knew that in the realest sense he was going to die for his friends. The disciples knew it, too. They regarded a journey to Jerusalem as the surest way to commit suicide. They might well have hung back and refused to go had not Thomas, that gallant pessimist, given a lead.

Here is John writing below the surface of the very reason why Jesus came into the world – to help men, even if that help meant his death. There is a story of the life-boat service. There was a terrible storm. A ship was driven on to the rocks and the life-boat was called out. As it was being manned a younger member of the crew was plainly afraid. He looked at the raging sea and said to one of the older members of the crew: "If we put out into that sea, we will never get back alive." The older man, with all the tradition of the life-boat service behind him, answered quietly: "Son, we've got to go out; but we haven't got to come back." Jesus knew that to go to Judaea and to Bethany to help that home was certainly to die; and without hesitation he went. It can often happen that in some sudden moment of crisis a man may do an heroic thing, almost without realizing what he is doing; but the highest heroism is clearly to see the consequences and still to go on.

Miracle at Bethany

So Jesus set out for Bethany. When news came to the sorrowing household that he was near at hand, Martha ran to meet him. She was always the one who leaped to action; and Mary was always the one who quietly waited. Her first words to Jesus were of mingled reproach and faith. "If you had been here," she said, "my brother would not have died," Beneath the surface she would have liked to say: "Why didn't you come at once?" But Martha's regret is swallowed up in her faith. "I know," she said, "that even now God will do anything for which you ask him." Jesus told Martha that her brother would rise again; she agreed that at the general resurrection he would rise. Then Jesus made his great claim: "I am the resurrection and the life; he who believes in me, though

[1] John 11 : 47-54.

he die, yet shall he live, and who ever lives and believes in me shall never die."[1]

Then Martha went back to tell her sister that Jesus had arrived. She wanted to do so without telling other people so that Mary could have a few moments alone with him. The house would be crowded with people, for the Jews believed that visits of sympathy to the mourner were the highest duty a man could perform.[2] When the condoling visitors saw Mary leave the house they followed her, for they thought that she had gone to weep at the tomb of Lazarus. It was the custom for the mourners to go to the tomb to weep there every day for a week after the funeral. Jesus was led to the tomb where Lazarus was laid. Tombs in Palestine were either natural caves or caves hollowed out in the rock, usually about six feet long and nine feet wide and ten feet high. Such tombs usually held eight bodies, laid on shelves in the rock; there were usually three shelves on each side and two on the wall facing the entrance. There was no door, but a groove in the ground ran along the front of the cave. In the groove was set a great stone like a cart wheel and the stone could be rolled across the opening of the cave to form a door which no single person could move.

Jesus asked that the stone should be removed. To Martha this seemed a needlessly harrowing experience. She could think only that Jesus wished last look at his friend Lazarus; and she could not think that to look on an already putrefying body could be any possible consolation. In the climate of Palestine decay was quick. Martha pointed out that Lazarus had already lain in the tomb for four days. The point is that the spirits of departed people were supposed to hover over the tomb for four days after death. Then they departed, because by that time the face of the dead person was so decayed that recognition was impossible. It was Martha's belief that Lazarus was dead beyond recall.

When the body was laid in the tomb it was clothed in a simple linen garment which was sometimes very beautifully called

[1]John 11 : 25, 26.

[2]For an account of death and burial customs, see A. Edersheim, *Sketches of Jewish Social Life,* chapter 10, *In Death and after Death,* pp. 161-181.

"the travelling dress." The hands and feet were wrapped in long strips like bandages and the head was enclosed in a napkin. There was a time when the Jews showed every possible extravagance in the clothes in which the corpse was clothed. People were buried in the finest robes; the tombs were filled with costly gifts and possessions. The ostentatious luxury of burial clothes and gifts had become an almost intolerable burden; but no one wished to stop it because no one wished to be inferior to his neighbour in apparent respect for the dead. The custom was ultimately stopped by the example of Rabbi Gamaliel the Second who gave orders that he was to be buried in a simple linen robe; and to this day at a Jewish funeral a cup is drunk in his memory.

Jesus stood before the open tomb; with a great voice he commanded Lazarus to come forth; and at his command the man who had been dead staggered out in the enveloping grave clothes.

An insoluble problem

Such is the story of the raising of Lazarus. Now, whether we like it or not, we have to face the fact that it presents us with more problems than any other miracle of Jesus.

(i) It is astonishing that the other three gospels never even mention this miracle. If they had known about it, it seems incredible that they would have omitted it. And it is difficult to see how they could have failed to know about it, if the raising of Lazarus was an actual historical happening. One attempt at explanation has been offered. As we know, Mark is the earliest gospel and the other gospel writers base their story on it. We also know that it is based on the information which Peter supplied. It so happens that here is no mention of Peter in John 5 or in John 7-12. It is suggested that during that period he was not with Jesus, and that therefore he was not present when Lazarus was raised. In support of this is pointed out that it was Thomas, and not Peter, as one might expect, who was the spokesman of the disciples.[1] But even if Peter was not there, surely there were others who would know the story; if the raising of Lazarus is to be

[1] J. H. Bernard, *St. John*, vol. i, p. clxxxiii.

regarded as an actual historical happening, the silence of the other three gospel writers is very difficult to explain.

(ii) According to the Fourth Gospel it was this miracle which precipitated the crucifixion of Jesus.[1] Because of it the Jewish authorities came to the decision that Jesus could no longer be allowed to go on. The other three gospels indicate that the decisive event was the Cleansing of the Temple. It seems amazing that they should apparently deliberately omit the event which above all others led to the Cross. On the other hand Bernard makes an interesting point.[2] How can the Triumphal Entry[3] be explained without some such event as the raising of Lazarus. The raising of Lazarus to rouse the people's enthusiasm and make Jesus known throughout the country? Even allowing for that, it is difficult to understand how the other three gospel writers could have omitted the event which led directly to Jesus's death, if they had known about it. And it is impossible to understand how they could not have known about it, if it was an actual historical happening.

(iii) The miracle itself is difficult. The other three gospels have accounts of two miracles which involved the raising of persons from the dead, the daughter of Jairus and the son of the widow at Nain.[4] The difference is that in these two cases death had taken place only hours before and it may well be that they were cases of a coma which looked like death. Burial took place almost immediately after death in Palestine owing to the climatic conditions. We know from the evidence of the tombs that as a result it was not unusual for people to be buried alive. It is by no means impossible that these were miracles of diagnosis rather than cure, in which Jesus rescued two young people from what would have been a most terrible death. Of these J. H. Bernard goes so far as to say: "Those who reject all miracles need find no difficulty in them."[5] It is a very different thing when the person

[1]John 11 : 47-54.
[2]J. H. Bernard, *St. John,* vol. i, pp. clxxxiii, clxxxiv.
[3]Mark 11 : 8, 9.
[4]Mark 5 : 21-43; Matthew 9 : 18-26; Luke 8 : 40-56; Luke 7 : 11-16.
[5]J. H. Bernard, St. John, vol. i, p. clxxxiv.

raised had been dead for four days and the body was already putrefying in the tomb. Further, it is neither too curious nor yet irrelevant to ask what the effect of all this was on Lazarus. Early legends say that he lived for another thirty years, and one declares that he never smiled again.[1] If ever life was a problem for a man, it must have been a problem for Lazarus.

The most serious difficulties meet us when we try to find out whether or not the raising of Lazarus was an actual historical event. G. H. C. Macgregor writes: "In view of the silence of the Synoptists it is evidently impossible to accept the narrative as strictly historical. It is inconceivable that the greatest of all recorded miracles, performed during the last critical week, and in the presence of crowds of people, should have been simply omitted by the first three evangelists."[2] E. F. Scott writes: "We cannot with any show of probability find room for it in any intelligible scheme of the life of Christ. It is inconceivable that a miracle of such magnitude, performed in the one week of our Lord's life of which we have a full record, and in presence of crowds of people in a suburb of Jerusalem – a miracle, moreover, which was the immediate cause, according to John, of the crucifixion – should have been simply passed over by the other evangelists. We are almost compelled to the conclusion that the narrative is, in the main, symbolical."[3]

Various explanations have been put forward.

(i) It has been suggested that Lazarus was in a trance. The whole tone of the story makes this unlikely and certainly John did not mean us to believe that.

(ii) Renan suggested that the raising to life was a deliberate fraud arranged by Martha and Mary, with the connivance of Jesus.[4] Simply to state that suggestion is to refute it. Nothing could be more impossible, and even Renan himself later departed from his own grotesque theory.

---

[1] Quoted in J. H. Bernard, St. John, vol. ii, p. 401.
[2] G. H. C. Macgregor, *The Gospel of John*, p. 253.
[3] E. F. Scott, *The Fourth Gospel*, p. 45.
[4] Quoted by J. H. Bernard, *St. John*, vol. i p. clxxxiv, footnote.

(iii) It is suggested that the story is to be read as an allegory. Loisy suggests the following interpretation: "Martha who first meets Jesus symbolizes the first Christian group of converted Jews, and Mary the believing recruits from among the Gentiles, the two groups, united in Jesus, realizing through him the resurrection of humanity, of the man their brother, who lay dead in the tomb for four days, perhaps the four thousand years which preceded the coming of Christ."[1] The trouble about an explanation like that is that it reads neither possible nor true. When a man reads *The Pilgrim's Progress,* the allegory unfolds intelligibly before him, but no one reading John's story would ever dream that this inner meaning was in it.

(iv) It is suggested that the story is really a kind of teaching amplification of the parable of Dives and Lazarus in Luke 16 : 19-31. In that parable the rich man in his agony in hell asks that someone should be sent from the other world to warn his five brothers of the fate which awaited them. His plea is that if someone rose from the dead to tell them, they would surely take warning. Abraham's answer was: "If they do not hear Moses and the prophets, neither will they be convinced if some one should rise from the dead."[2] It is suggested that this story amplifies that parable and turns it into a dramatic story.[3] This is by no means impossible. The date of the Fourth Gospel is about A.D. 100, and as the years went by this is the kind of process which might have taken place.

(v) It has been suggested that the story is a dramatic way of saying that "Jesus in his obedience to and dependence on the Father has the authority to give life to whom he will."[4] If that be so, it is a vividly constructed illustration of an earlier saying of Jesus: "For as the Father raises the dead and gives them life, so also the Son gives life to whom he will."[5]

[1]Quoted by G. H. C. Macgregor, *The Gospel of John*, p. 254.
[2]Luke 16 : 31.
[3]For a statement of this view, cp. J. Warschauer, *The Historical Life of Christ*, p. 119.
[4]C. K. Barrett, *The Gospel according to St. John*, p. 322.
[5]John 5 : 21.

The central truth

None of these suggested explanations is fully satisfactory. We must start from certain basic positions.

(i) It cannot really be doubted that the story goes back to something factual. The detail is so vivid.

(ii) But it also cannot really be doubted that the story is not meant to be taken literally. There can be no doubt that it centres in the great saying of Jesus: "I am the Resurrection and the Life: he who believes in me though he die, yet shall he live; and whoever lives and believes in me shall never die."[1] Just before Jesus says that, there is a kind of atmosphere of tingling expectation; and after it the story marches triumphantly to its conclusion. It seems clear that it was for the sake of that saying that the story was preserved,

We now take another step. Clearly *that saying of Jesus cannot be taken literally*. It is not true that in terms of physical life the man who believes in Jesus will never die. If the rest of the story is taken as literally true, this statement becomes irrelevant; it is not even illustrated by the story in that sense. *But* if it be taken *spiritually*, the saying of Jesus is wonderfully true. For the man who believes in Christ there is no such thing as death but only death-defying eternal life. Physical death is no longer a terror to such a man; and spiritual death is conquered.

This story is meant to teach that Jesus Christ can raise a man from the death which sin brings and that he can give him the life which goes beyond death. Is it possible that Lazarus had committed some terrible sin which shattered the home in Bethany, had done something which made his name stink like a corpse, so that he was dead to shame and to honour and the hearts of his sisters were broken; and that Jesus came and raised him from sin, filled him with a new life and gave him back to the family who thought they had lost their brother for ever? Is it possible that here we have the greatest conversion story in the New Testament?

When Jesus said: "I am the Resurrection and the Life," the primary thing he meant was that he is able to rescue men from

[1] John 11 : 25, 26.

the deadly power of sin. It was just this resurrecting power that the ancient world was searching for.

There never was an age so conscious of what Epictetus called its "weakness and insufficiency in necessary things."[1] Seneca, thinking of himself and of his fellow men, could write: "Look at the city of Rome and the crowds unceasingly pouring down its broad streets – what a solitude, what a wilderness it would be, were none left but those whom a strict judge would acquit. We have all sinned, some in greater measure, some in less, some in purpose, some by accident, some by the fault of others; we have not stood bravely enough by our good resolutions; despite our will and resistance we have lost our innocence. Nor is it only that we have acted amiss; *we shall do so to the end.*"[2] Persius wrote: "Let the guilty see virtue, and pine that *they have lost her for ever.*"[3] Seneca described the half-hearted, hopeless search for virtue. "He thinks he wishes reason. He has fallen out with luxury, but he will soon make friends with her. But he says he is offended with his own life! I do not deny it; who is not? *Men love their vices and hate them at the same time.*"[4] Epictetus said grimly that the philosopher's school had become an infirmary, not for the glad, but for the sorry.[5] Seneca, in a burst of self-revulsion, could call himself a *homo non tolerabilis*, a man not to be tolerated.[6]

Again and again and again this note of despair sounded out. It was not that men did not know that they were bad; it was simply that they regarded it as hopeless that they should ever be any better. For all the power they had to conquer themselves they were as dead men. It is curious how even the metaphor of death occurs. Persius speaks of "filthy Natta *benumbed* by vice."[7] "When a man is hardened like a stone," demands Epictetus, "how shall we be able to deal with him by argument? What are we to do with what can only be called mortification, necrosis, death of the soul?"[8]

[1]Epictetus, *Discourses* 2 : 11.

[2]Seneca, *Ad Clem.* 1 : 6. This and the majority of the other translations in this section are by T. R. Glover, and are taken from various chapters in *The Conflict of Religions in the Early Roman Empire.*

[3]Persius, *Satires* 3 : 38.   [4]Seneca, *Epistles* 112 : 3.
[5]Epictetus, *Discourses* 3 : 23.   [6]Seneca, *Epistles* 57 : 3.
[7]Persius, *Satires* 3 : 31.   [8]Epictetus, *Discourses* 1 : 5.

The ancient world had lost the moral battle, and it knew it. It was in the power of sin; and it was in despair. It could think the highest thoughts and set out the highest ideals but it had no power to work them out in reality.

On the other hand the Christian witnessed with a singing joy to the power of Christianity to make bad men good. Corinth was one of the worst cities in the ancient world, and yet one of Paul's most triumphant passages comes from the letter to his friends there. "Do you not know that the unrighteous will not inherit the kingdom of God? Do not be deceived; neither the immoral, nor idolators, nor adulterers, nor homosexuals, nor thieves, nor the greedy, nor drunkards, nor revilers, nor robbers will inherit the kingdom of God. *And such were some of you.*"[1] Men who had been dead were made alive. "Who," demands Paul, "will deliver me from this deadly body?" And triumphantly he answers: "Jesus Christ."[2] It is abundantly, demonstrably, historically true that Jesus Christ was to men the Resurrection and the Life from the power of sin.

That resurrecting power still goes on. One of the great modern examples was Tockichi Ishii. Ishii was a Japanese criminal with an unparalleled record of bestial crime. He had murdered men, women and children. At last he was caught. In prison, he was like a caged tiger. He was visited by two Canadian women who tried to speak to him through the bars; but he simply glowered at them like a wild beast. They left a Bible with him; he began to read and could not stop. He read on and on, coming eventually to the story of the crucifixion. It was the words: "Father, forgive them, they know not what they do," which broke him. "I stopped," he said. "I was stabbed to the heart as if pierced with a five-inch nail. Shall I call it the love of Christ? Shall I call it his compassion? I do not know what to call it. I only know that I believed and my hardness of heart was changed." Later when the gaoler came to lead him to the scaffold, he found not the surly brute that he had expected to find, but a radiant man, for Tockichi

[1] 1 Corinthians 6 : 9-11.
[2] Romans 7 : 25.

Ishii, the murderer, had been born again.[1] Jesus is still the Resurrection and the Life.

It need not be as dramatic as that. When Jesus enters into a life the selfish person becomes filled with the desire to serve, the moody and the irritable person becomes sweet and kind, the bad habits are broken, the self-indulgences are conquered, the person who was difficult becomes easy to live with. That resurrecting power is still available to those who will accept Jesus as Saviour, Master and Lord. It might well be said that this story is a commentary on his saying: "I came that they may have life, and have it abundantly."[2]

Life after death

But in another sense Jesus is the Resurrection and the Life. He gives to men the certainty of the life beyond. Christianity came into a world which was longing for some assurance that death was not the end.

For some it was a hope. "I surrendered myself," said Seneca, "to that great hope."[3] "For my part," said Plutarch, "I will never let go the continuance of the soul."[4] But the very way in which these men speak of this life beyond shows that for them it was no certainty but only a haunting hope.

For some, death was the complete and inevitable end, with nothingness to follow. When Catullus, "the tenderest of Roman poets," as Tennyson called him, wrote to his Lesbia, he pled for her kisses because the endless night was on the way.

> "Lesbia mine, let's live and love!
> Give no doit for tattle of
> Crabbed old censorious men;
> Suns may set and rise again,
> But when our short day takes flight
> Sleep we must one endless night."

[1]This story is taken from A. M. Chirgwin, *The Bible in Modern Evangelism*, pp. 65, 66. The story of Tockichi Ishii is told by Caroline Macdonald, *A Gentleman in Prison*.
[2]John 10 : 10.   [3]Seneca, *Epistles* 102 : 2.
[4]Plutarch, *De. ser. Num. Vind.* 17, 560, B-D.

For some it was a great "perhaps". When Tacitus was finishing his great tribute to Agricola, he wrote at the end of it: "If there be any habitation for the spirits of the just; if, as wise men will have it, the soul that is great perishes not with the body, may you rest in peace . . . Whatever we have loved in Agricola, whatever we have admired, abides and will abide, in the hearts of men, in the procession of the ages, in the records of history. Many of the ancients has Forgetfulness engulfed as though neither fame nor name was theirs: Agricola, whose story here is told, will outlive death, to be our children's heritage." Tacitus could be certain of an immortality of name and fame; but when it came to a personal immortality, all he could say was: "If it is so."[1]

The strangest of all attitudes to death in the ancient world was that of Epicurus; and there were many Epicureans. He held that the supreme evil in life was fear; and that the greatest fear was the fear of death. In his view there were many who "through fear of death were all their life-time subject to bondage," as the writer to the Hebrews put it so memorably.[2] So Epicurus set himself to abolish that fear. He did so by formulating his atomic theory. He said that everything in this world was formed by a fortuitous conglomeration of atoms. In the beginning there was nothing but atoms falling through the void of space like rain. They had the power to swerve. When they swerved, they knocked into each other and became little groups; and out of these haphazard conglomerations of atoms everything was formed. Epicurus went on to say that it was so with the soul; it too was simply a chance conglomeration of atoms; and when a man died all that happened was that the atoms dispersed and he ceased to be. "Atoms thou art, and to atoms thou shalt return." In his view the idea of a life after death was something from which a man had to be set free.

Into this doubting world Jesus came with the certainty of the life beyond. "Because I live, you will live also."[3] The great difference was in the conception of God that Jesus brought to men. So long as God was a blind tyrant, there was no reason why he should not wipe them out as a man sweeps a fly from a window-

---

[1]Tactius, *Agricola* 46.   [2]Hebrews 2 : 15.
[3]John 14 : 19.

pane. So long as he was an austere judge, men were bound to look on the idea of immortality with dread. But Jesus came to tell of a God whose name was Father and whose nature was love; life after death became a certainty and something, not to be dreaded, but to be desired, for it meant being for ever at home in the Father's house.

The eternal power

So then this story tells us of the power of Jesus Christ to raise men from the death of sin and to give them a life which nothing can destroy. This is not the story of the raising of a corpse in A.D. 30; it is the story of something which Jesus Christ can do today.

Robert McAfee Brown, an American professor, tells a story.[1] He was chaplain on a troopship in which 1,500 marines were returning from Japan to America for discharge. To his surprise and delight a group of them came and asked him to do Bible study with them on the voyage home. Towards the end of the trip they were studying this chapter of *John*. Professor Brown was thinking: "What are these men making of this 'I am the Resurrection and the life. . . .'? The question is not 'Was a corpse reanimated in A.D. 30?' but, 'Are these words true in A.D. 1946?'" At the end of the study a young marine came to him. He said something like this. "Padre, everything in that story we have been studying today points to me. I've been in hell for the last six months; and since I have heard this chapter I am just getting free." He went on to explain. He had gone into the Marines straight from College. He had been sent overseas to Japan. He had been bored and had gone out to find amusement; and he had got into trouble, bad trouble. No one else knew about it – *but God knew*. He had a terrible feeling of guilt; he felt his life was ruined; he felt he could never again face his family, even if they did not know the wretched story. "I've been a dead man," he said. "But after reading this chapter I'm alive again. This Resurrection and Life that Jesus was talking about is the real thing here and now."

That is precisely what this story teaches; that young marine had clearly seen its real meaning. John meant to tell us far more

[1] Robert McAfee Brown, *The Bible speaks to you*, chapter 1.

than the story of the raising of a dead man whose name was Lazarus more than 1900 years ago. He meant to tell us that Jesus is still the power today who can raise us to new life and make us new people.

CHAPTER TWENTY-THREE

The Miracles of the Old Testament

The mind of the poet

It is not only in the New Testament that we find accounts of miraculous happenings; we find them frequently in the Old Testament also. There are two differences between the miracles in the Old and New Testaments.

First, the New Testament miracles, at least those in the gospels, are *the miracles of Jesus*. Because Jesus was who he was it becomes easy to believe in his miracles. We do not believe in his uniqueness because of them; we believe in them because of his uniqueness. The Old Testament miracles have not got the person and personality of Jesus behind them to accredit them.

Second, many of the Old Testament stories are very ancient. Some of them go back not only into ancient history but to a time before history can be said properly to have begun at all. And obviously what appears a miracle to a man of primitive knowledge will not necessarily appear so to a man who has learned more about the wonder of the world.

In a very real sense increasing knowledge is the key to an increasing understanding of the miracles. So when we read the Old Testament we will always have to remember that we are moving amidst men who knew far less of this world than we do; and who knew far less of God than is given to those who know Jesus Christ.

We must begin with a very simple realization. *A great deal of the Old Testament is poetry, and poetry is destroyed when it is taken literally*. Let us take an actual example. Joshua 10 : 12-14 tells how the sun stood still:

"Then spoke Joshua to the Lord in the day when the Lord gave the Amorites over to the men of Israel; and he said in the sight of Israel, "Sun stand thou still at Gibeon, and thou Moon in the valley of Ajalon." And the sun stood still, and the moon stayed, until the nation took vengeance on their enemies. Is this not written in the Book of Jashar? The sun stayed in the midst of heaven, and did not hasten to go down for about a whole day. There has been no day like it before or since, when the Lord hearkened to the voice of a man; for the Lord fought for Israel."

If it be insisted that this story be taken literally we are beset with difficulties. There is the simple fact that the sun does not move in any event and that the only way to produce an effect of the sun standing would nave been for the earth to stop revolving on its axis, which would have been in the most literal sense the end of the world. Further, there is a moral difficulty. If the story be literal, it means that God suspended the normal working of the machinery of the universe in order that a mass slaughter of his enemies could be carried out. When we have discovered the character of God in Jesus Christ, that becomes something at which the mind shudders with horror.

What then are we to say? First, we must note that the story comes from *The Book of Jasher*. *The Book of Jasher* goes back to a still more primitive time than *Joshua* with a still more childlike way of speaking and thinking about life and its events.

The plain fact is that this is poetry and is meant to be understood as such. In poetry we speak as Dorothy Frances Gurney spoke:

> "The kiss of the sun for pardon,
>   The song of the birds for mirth,
> One is nearer God's heart in a garden
>   Than anywhere else on earth."

No one for one moment thinks of the sun stooping down literally to kiss anyone. Poetry has its own language and that language becomes ridiculous when taken literally. Tennyson writes in *Ulysses*:

> "The long day wanes; the slow moon climbs; the deep
>   Moans round with many voices."

No one is literally minded enough to complain that that particular day was no longer than any other day or that particular moon was no slower than any other moon or that in fact the sea has not got a voice, let alone many voices. We know what Tennyson means; but we make no attempt to take the words with unimaginative literalness. We constantly use such expressions even in ordinary speech. We say of a happy evening: "I never knew an evening to pass more quickly," but in fact it took exactly the same time to pass as any other evening. We say of some specially thrilling time: "The hour went past in a flash." We say of some specially moving moment: "Time stood still." We say of some boring performance: "It was the longest hour I ever spent in my life."

We do not in life insist on a crude literalism and it is hard to see why we should do so with the poetry of the Bible. What happened in this particular incident is surely that Joshua, confronted with the opportunity of total victory and conscious of the shortness of time to take advantage of it, said: "Would that this day were long enough for victory to be won." And it was. Afterwards, when the battle was being refought round the camp-fire, the story-teller said: "And somehow that day was stretched by God until all that was necessary for victory was done." The poet has his own way of speaking; we wrong him when we take him with cold literalness.

Many Old Testament wonder stories are properly understood only in this way. There are the occasions when Elisha by his insight and wisdom frustrated the purposes of the Syrian king. The king discovered that Elisha was at Dothan and surrounded the town with the intention of capturing the prophet.

> "When the servant of the man of God rose early in the morning and went out, behold, an army with horses and chariots was round about the city. And the servant said, "Alas, my master! What shall we do?" He said, "Fear not, for those who are with us are more than those who are with them." Then Elisha prayed, and said, "O Lord, I pray thee, open his eyes that he may see." So the Lord opened the eyes of the young man, and he saw; and behold, the moun-

tain was full of horses and chariots of fire round about Elisha (2 Kings 6 : 13-18).

This is a pictorial way of putting an experience which has come to many a man. There is the famous story of Shackleton's sledge journey across the snow and ice of the Antarctic with his two friends. One of them, called Worsley, came to him afterwards and said: "Boss, all the time we were pulling these sledges across the ice, somehow I felt that there were not three of us, but four." When Mahomet and a single friend were surrounded by hordes of their enemies, the friend was much afraid. "There are only two of us, " he said, "and there are hundreds of them." "There are not two of us," said Mahomet, "there are three, and the third is God." When St. Theresa was about to build a convent all the money she had was half a crown. Someone said to her: "Not even St. Theresa can do much with half a crown." "True," she said, "but Theresa and half a crown and God can do anything." The Christian has invisible resources. John Buchan once described an atheist as a man "who has no invisible means of support." The Christian is the opposite of that and there are times when the invisible supporters become so real that the eye of faith can see them.

Let us take another example. 2 Kings 2 : 11 has a thrilling picture of the end of Elijah. He was with Elisha, his chosen successor, and the story goes on:

> "And as they still went on, and talked, behold, a chariot of fire and horses of fire, separated the two of them; and Elijah went up by a whirlwind into heaven."

Let us set beside that the death-scene of Mr. Valiant-for-truth in *The Pilgrim's Progress*:

> "After this it was noised abroad that Mr. *Valiant-for-truth* was taken with a summons, by the same *Post* as the other; and had this for a Token that the Summons was true, *That his pitcher was broken at the Fountain*. When he understood it, he called for his Friends and told them of it. Then, said he, 'I am going to my Fathers, and tho with great Difficulty

I am got hither, yet now I do not repent me of all the Trouble I have been at to arrive where I am. My *sword,* I give to him that shall succeed me in my Pilgrimage, and my *Courage* and *Skill,* to him that can get it. My *Marks* and *Scarrs* I carry with me, to be a witness for me that I have fought his *Battels,* who now will be my Rewarder.' When the Day that he must go hence, was come, many accompanied him to the River side, into which, as he went, he said, '*Death, where is thy Sting?*' And as he went down deeper, he said, '*Grave, where is thy Victory?*' So he passed over, and the Trumpets sounded for him on the other side."

That is one of the most magnificent pieces of English prose ever written and, also, one of the greatest descriptions of the death of a man of faith; and there is hardly one expression in it which can be taken literally, least of all that some heavenly orchestra played some celestial fanfare to welcome Mr. Valiant-for-truth. The Elijah passage is to be read in exactly the same way, as meaning that for the man of God death is a sudden glory, that he goes out, not to the unknown dark, but to the splendour of God, that death is not the snapping of the cord of life and thrusting into oblivion but rather the summons of God to a man's soul.

If we read a story like that of Elijah with an insistent literalism, we lose by far the greater part of its value; it becomes a description of an incident which happened once and will never happen again, a detached and irrelevant wonder. But if we read it as poetry enshrining divine truth, it becomes not simply the description of the death of Elijah; it becomes the description of the triumphant passing which comes to any man of faith *and which can come to us.* To remember that much of the Old Testament is poetry makes it, not an inferior book, but a far greater book, for time and again it is seen to describe, not what happened to isolated wonder-figures in the past, but what can happen to us through faith.

Stories which are parables

Certain stories both in the Old and in the New Testament are to be read as parables far more than as historical records. The Jewish Rabbis had teaching methods which may seem strange to us but without a correct understanding of them no one can hope really to understand the Bible. C. J. Ball sums up the Rabbinic method in this way:

> "We have to bear in mind a fact familiar enough to students of the Talmudic and Midrashic literature. . . the inveterate tendency of Jewish teachers to convey their doctrine, not in the form of abstract discourse, but in a mode appealing directly to the imagination, and seeking to arouse the interest and sympathy of the man rather than the philosopher. The Rabbi embodies his lesson in a story, whether parable or allegory or seeming historical narrative; and the last thing he or his disciples would think of is to ask whether the selected persons, events and circumstances which so vividly suggest the doctrine are in themselves real or fictitious. The doctrine is everything; the mode of presentation has no independent value. To make the story the first consideration, and the doctrine it was intended to convey an after-thought as we, with our dry Western literalness, are predisposed to do, is to reverse the Jewish order of thinking, and to do unconscious injustice to the authors of many edifying narratives of antiquity."[1]

It can be put in another way – the Jewish teachers were more interested in truth than fact; their first question was not, Did this story actually happen? but, What is it designed to teach? To them it was the most natural thing in the world that the story should be constructed to convey eternal truth, which, in fact, is exactly what John Bunyan did in *The Pilgrim's Progress* and what Jesus did in every parable he uttered. We must therefore always look first, not for historical fact, but for eternal truth; and we shall be the more likely to penetrate to the truth if we can find the historical circumstances in which the story was composed, for then we shall better understand the aim of the writer in composing it.

[1] Quoted in W. O. E. Oesterley and G. H. Box, *The Religion and Worship of the Synagogue*, pp. 77, 78. The *Talmud* may be described as the commentary on the law; and the *Midrash* was the homiletic treatment of scripture.

There are two wonder-books in the Old Testament which have to be read in the light of this principle. In other words, it is not their history, but their doctrine, which is of prime importance.

The first is *The Book of Jonah.* In the light of the Rabbinic principle, we can see that the last thing any devout Jew would ask would be whether or not it was literally true that Jonah was swallowed by a whale and then later disgorged to preach to Nineveh. He would ask, What is the lesson that this book is designed to teach? The purpose of *The Book of Jonah* is clear. *It is the only purely missionary book in the Old Testament;* for that very reason, it is one of the very greatest. The Jewish attitude to the Gentiles was clear and unmistakable. The Jews were the chosen people. The ordinary, narrow, nationalistic outlook was that God loved only Israel of all the nations that he had made and had no use for the Gentiles, who existed at best to become servants of the Jews and at worst to be exterminated by the wrath of God.

The whole point of *The Book of Jonah* is that *it was to the people of Nineveh Jonah preached and that he did so compelled by God and against his will.* It was destruction that he went to preach,[1] and when the people of Nineveh repented from their sins he was bitterly disappointed. He had come to gloat over the destruction of Nineveh and felt himself cheated.[2] The mercy of God was a new revelation to Jonah and one which he was very unwilling to accept.[3] *Jonah* is not the story of a man swallowed by a whale but the book of a prophet who made the staggering discovery that the man of God must be a missionary. It is not a wonder story for children but the story of one of the greatest revelations in all history – the revelation that God loves all men.

Now let us read the story in that light. Jonah stands for the people of Israel. They were given the task of bringing the nations to God; but they never even realized their task and fled from it. Jonah was sent to Nineveh but took ship to Tarshish. That is to say, he was sent to the country east of Asia Minor but went to Spain.[4] Israel refused her task of evangelizing the nations and God stepped in by means of the exile. The exile compelled the

[1]Jonah 3 : 4.   [2]Jonah 4 : 1-3.   [3]Jonah 4 : 11.
[4]Jonah 1 : 3.

Jews to take their faith into the world. Jonah being swallowed by the whale represents the nation of Israel being swallowed up by the exile and the exile taking them where they were unwilling to go. Even when God had so stepped in, to the very end Jonah was angry at the mercy of God.[1] The nation would not accept its God-given task.

When we read the story of Jonah in that way, what a leap of the human mind it becomes! It is the writing of one of the very few Jews who ever grasped the width of the mercy of God. *Jonah* is not an historical narrative and was never meant to be. No devout Jew would ever read it that way. He would say, what does this book teach? If we read *Jonah* literally it is a wonder story and nothing more. If we read it as a parable written to show men the infinite width of the mercy of God, it becomes the most Christian book in the Old Testament. It is no longer the miracle of a man swallowed by a whale: it is the miracle of the revelation of God's love.

The second wonder-book in the Old Testament is Daniel. The Book of Daniel is to be read, not as a history book, but as a tremendous word of encouragement to a people who were up against it as hardly any people have ever been. The setting of the story which Daniel tells is in the sixth century B.C.; but it is easy to see that the book itself was written long after that, because its language is not classical Hebrew but Aramaic, which did not even come into being until hundreds of years after the sixth century.

The background of Daniel is this. In 175 B.C. there came to the throne of Syria a king called Antiochus Epiphanes who had a passion for all things Greek. He was one of the very few men who ever made a deliberate attempt to wipe a religion out of existence. He made up his mind that he would introduce Greek ways and Greek customs into Palestine and that once and for all he would overthrow what he called "the superstition of the Jews." Some Jews were willing and eager to co-operate with him in his attempt to introduce the Greek way of life; but most were firm in their faith The crisis came in the year 170 B.C. when Antiochus invaded Egypt. When he was on the very borders of Egypt, the Romans

[1] Jonah 4 : 9.

forbade him to go farther. He was bitterly humiliated but he did not dare defy the Roman power. So he turned homewards to Syria. His way led through Palestine; and his anger was directed against the stubborn Jews. In his fury he attacked Jerusalem. It was said that in his attack 80,000 Jews perished; and an equal number were sold into slavery. From the Temple treasury he took 1,800 talents (a talent is £240). But the reign of terror was just beginning. Antiochus erected a great image of Olympian Zeus in the very court of the Temple. He offered swine's flesh on the great altar of the burnt-offering. He set up brothels in the very Temple courts. He made possession of a copy of the law a crime punishable by death. He who circumcised his child was liable to immediate execution. Never in history was there such a savage attempt to wipe out a nation's faith.

There are two famous stories from Jewish history in these killing times. There was an aged priest called Eleazar whom Antiochus's men sought to compel to eat swine's flesh and thereby deny the Jewish law. The old man answered: "No, not if you pluck out my eyes and consume my bowels in the fire." They bound him and scourged him until "his flesh was torn off by the whips and he streamed down with blood and his flanks were laid open with wounds." They deliberately kicked him as he lay prostrate in agony on the ground. Even the soldiers were moved to pity and suggested to him that they should bring him other meat and that he should pretend it was swine's flesh. He refused and in the end was burned to death.[1]

The other story is that of the seven brothers. They were brought before Antiochus's men and given the choice of death by torture or of forsaking their beloved law. Their aged mother was with them. The first was scourged and then broken on the wheel; the second had the skin torn from his head and then his flesh lacerated by men wearing gauntlets spiked with iron; the third was twisted on the wrack and then flayed alive; the fourth had his tongue cut out; the fifth was fastened to a catapult and torn limb from limb; the sixth was burned and tortured with sharp burning spits; the seventh was roasted in a gigantic frying pan; and all the

[1] 4 Maccabees 5 and 6.

while their mother watched urging them not to give in (4 Macc. 8-13). As the historian said of his people in those days: "They chose to die and they died " (1 Macc. 1 : 63).

These were the killing times and they lasted until Judas Maccabaeus and his brothers led the revolt which regained their liberty. It may well be said that that was the most crucial time in all history. It was a deliberate attempt to wipe out the Jewish religion. If it had succeeded, *Christianity could not have come*. The fate of the world was in the balance and only the unbreakable loyalty of the Jews to God made the future coming of Christianity possible. *It was just in these days that Daniel was written*. It was a summons to be true. It is not simply the story of Daniel in the lions' den nor of Shadrach, Meshach and Abed-nego in the burning fiery furnace. It is a man of God writing to a stricken people: "Hold fast to your faith. When a cruelty like the blood-lust of lions is savaging you, when an affliction like a burning fiery furnace is searing you, God is with you and, if you hold on, he will see you safely through." Any devout Jewish teacher reading Daniel would not say, Is this a literal account of historical events? but What does this book teach me? The answer leaps out, God is with you and he can bring you safely through.

Nature or God

The main cause of the wonder stories in the Old Testament is the simple fact that the Hebrews saw the hand of God in every-thing. It has been put in this way – *the Hebrews knew nothing of secondary causes*. If the rain falls or the thunder sounds, we explain these things by changes in wind and temperature and cloud formation and electrical disturbance and so on. But the Hebrew said: "God sent the rain; God sent the thunder."

In a book entitled *God does intervene* Dr. E. Douglas Bebb writes: "Not only is there a God, and not only is there a God who is concerned with our affairs, but that God is one whose concern for us makes him intervene frequently."[1] The Hebrew believed that with the greatest literalness. It is significant to note that in Hebrew there is no word for *nature*; the Hebrew did not think

[1] E. Douglas Bebb, *God does intervene*, p. 7.

of nature or natural law; he thought of God. Where we think in terms of natural and scientific causes, the Hebrew sees the direct action of God.

There is one passage of Old Testament history where we can actually trace in detail this Hebrew way of mind at work. One of the most amazing deliverances which ever came to any city was that of Jerusalem from the army of Sennacherib. He had encamped around Jerusalem; the fate of the city seemed sealed; and then one morning the people of Jerusalem awoke to find Sennacherib and his armies gone. The Old Testament tells the story in simplicity and in vividness:

> "And that night the angel of the Lord went forth, and slew a hundred and eighty-five thousand in the camp of the Assyrians; and when men arose early in the morning, behold, these were all dead bodies. Then Sennacherib king of Assyria departed, and went home, and dwelt at Nineveh."[1]

This destruction of the army of Sennacherib got itself woven into ancient history. It was something so notable that it occurs not only in the Bible but in secular historians too. It occurs in Egyptian history and Herodotus, the Greek historian, records the Egyptian version. The people were in terror at the coming of Sennacherib and Sethos, the priest, went and prayed to his god about it. The god told him to be of good courage because, he said, "Myself will send you a champion." The story goes on that one night a multitude of field mice swarmed over the Assyrians and devoured their quivers and their bows and the handles of their shields so that they fled unarmed and many fell. Herodotus goes on to tell that in the Temple of Hephaestus there is a statue of the king with a mouse in his hand and the inscription: "Look on me and fear the gods."[2]

The Hebrew tells the story of the angel of the Lord; the Egyptian tells the story of the attack of the mice. But the story is not finished. Josephus repeats the version given by a certain Berosus who wrote the history of Chaldaea. Berosus says that

[1] 2 Kings 19 : 35, 36.   [2] Herodotus 2 : 141.

God sent "a pestilential distemper" on Sennacherib's army. The king was in great dread and terrible agony at this calamity. "And being in great fear for his whole army, he fled with the rest of his forces to his own kingdom."[1] Here we have the solution. In the ancient world mice were correctly associated with plague. *Sminthos* is the Greek for a mouse and *Apollo Smintheos* was the god of plague. What really happened was that a violent outbreak of bubonic plague decimated the army of Sennacherib and compelled his rapid and panic-stricken retreat.

Here we have three ways of telling the same story. Modern science says that plague decimated the army of Sennacherib. Greek ancient history says that mice were responsible for the disaster. The Hebrew historian says, "God did it." That was always the Hebrew method. To the Hebrew what we would often call a natural event was a direct act of God. *And surely the Hebrew was every bit as right as we are.* James Drawbell, journalist, thinking of some of the wonderful deliverances of the Second World War, and especially of Dunkirk, said: "A miracle is the will of God expressed in events." The Hebrews were continually seeing the will of God in events. The fact that we know how the events happened, whereas the Hebrews with their limited knowledge did not, does not make these things any less the will of God. What it does mean is that God was not acting as it were from outside the world but using the processes and the laws of the world for his purposes.

Let us take this key to certain other great events. The trench in the world's surface, which runs right down the Jordan valley, through the Dead Sea and the Red Sea and down the Nile Valley into Africa, is one of the great faults in the earth. It is ultimately a volcanic area and all the phenomena connected with volcanoes and faults in the earth's surface are liable to happen.[2] We look at two of the plagues in Egypt in the light of this fact.

One is described like this: "All the water that was in the Nile turned to blood. And the fish in the Nile died . . . so that the Egypt-

[1]Josephus, *The Antiquities of the Jews,* 10, 1, 5.
[2]For many of the facts which follow I am indebted to *The Call of Israel,* by W. J. Phythian-Adams, pp. 137-172.

ians could not drink water from the Nile."[1] One of the most terrible of all volcanic eruptions was that of Mount Pelée which destroyed St. Pierre on 6th May, 1902, and killed 30,000 people. On the day before the eruption a terrible torrent of boiling mud was evacuated from one of the lakes on the mountain and swept down to the shore. At the same time torrential rains turned all the streams on that side of the island into muddy cataracts of black and poisonous water. "Great quantities of dead fish were observed later floating at the mouths of these rivers and the smell of the sulphur hung overpoweringly over all." That describes exactly what happened in Egypt. In the upper waters of the Nile something like this happened. The waters were poisoned; the fish died; the river stank; and men could not drink.

The other is the plague of thick darkness.[2] It was a darkness which could be felt. In the eruption of Vesuvius in 1906 the third phase was that of the dark ash and it lasted for a fortnight. Black gas clouds charged with volcanic ash covered the city. "An impenetrable pall of darkness covered Naples and the surrounding country." A hundred thousand people left the city in terror on this dreadful night. In April, 1932, eight volcanoes in the Andes erupted and spread a pall of darkness over the southern half of South America. Again it is the same thing as happened in Egypt. Modern science calls it volcanic action; the Hebrew called it God.

One of the unforgettable incidents in the history of Israel is the crossing of the Red Sea. No one knows exactly where that crossing took place. The matter is complicated by the fact that the sea involved is not the *Red* Sea but the *Reed* Sea (*Yamsuph*), as Moffatt correctly translates it. Major C. S. Jarvis, who was military governor of Palestine and knew the whole territory intimately for years, wrote a fascinating book called *Yesterday and Today in Sinai*. In it he expounds a theory which may well be true.[3] If the Israelites went north and turned along the coast they would come to Lake Barawil which is really an immense mud pan. It is separated from the Mediterranean Sea by a narrow spit of

[1]Exodus 7 : 20, 21.   [2]Exodus 10 : 21, 23.
[3]C. S. Jarvis, *Yesterday and To-day in Sinai*, pp. 175-185.

sand which varies from one hundred to three hundred yards wide. In modern times it is used as a mullet fishery and is a real lake because channels have been dug through this spit. To walk across it is exactly to feel that there is a wall of water on the right hand and on the left. It may well have been that the Israelites started across this spit of sand. The Egyptians came after them and sought to save time by crossing the mud pan. First they got bogged down as many a man has done in modern times. "The Lord clogged their chariot wheels so that they drove heavily."[1] Moses in his song of triumph actually says that the earth as well as the sea swallowed them up.[2] By the time the Israelites had safely crossed the spit, the wind blew; the waves rose and broke through the sandy spit; the waters poured into the mud pan and it became a lake; and the Egyptians, already bogged down in that sea of mud, were drowned to a man. That exactly fits the picture of *Exodus*. God was in the storm, as the Hebrews saw it, and they were right.

The Exodus story goes on to tell of the coming of the quails which the people ate.[3] And the story is repeated in greater detail in Numbers.[4] That in fact was a regular phenomenon in that part of the world. C. S. Jarvis tells how the quails migrate northwards and reach the Mediterranean sea-coast absolutely exhausted. "The Israelites fed on the quails that came in from the sea in a cloud and settled near the camp. This is a sight that may be seen today at almost any part of the Mediterranean coast during the autumn migration. In the months of September and October, shortly after dawn on almost any day, one may see a cloud of quail coming in from the sea so completely exhausted that they pitch on the seashore and stagger into the nearest scrub for cover. It is quite easy when the birds are in this condition to catch them by hand, and in a year when the migration is good it would be quite possible for a host as numerous as the Israelites to eat their fill."[5] Modern science would call this bird migration; the Hebrew called it God.

[1] Exodus 14 : 25.   [2] Exodus 15 : 10, 12.   [3] Exodus 16 : 13.
[4] Numbers 11 : 31-33.
[5] C. S. Jarvis, *Yesterday and To-day in Sinai*, p. 170 cp. Louis Golding, *In the Steps of Moses the Lawgiver*, p. 222 for a similar account.

With the quails came the manna.[1] There is manna in that part
of the world to this day. It is found beneath a certain kind of
tamarisk tree. Louis Golding quotes Burckhardt's description
of it:

"In the month of June it drops from the thorns of the tamarisk
upon the fallen twigs, leaves and thorns, which always cover
the ground beneath that tree in its natural state; the manna
is collected before sunrise, when it is coagulated, but it
dissolves as soon as the sun shines upon it. The Arabs clear
away the leaves, dust, etc., which adhere to it, boil it, strain
it through a coarse piece of cloth, and put it into leathern skins
...The manna is found only in years when copious rains have
fallen; sometimes it is not produced at all."[2]

For a long time this manna substance was known and used, but
no one knew where it came from although it was always found
under the tamarisk tree. But its origin was discovered by Dr.
Bodenheimer of Jerusalem University. It is excreted by a little
insect called *Trabutina mannipara*. It is excreted in little clear
beads the consistency of syrup. In a few days they crystallize and
turn milky white. They are originally deposited on the twigs and
the leaves and then fall to the ground. Sometimes spider's nets
woven in the lower branches glisten with pinpoints of manna
like little jewels. Dr. Bodenheimer actually gave some to Louis
Golding to taste and it was honey sweet.[3] The modern naturalist
will tell us what manna is. The Hebrews found it in their wander-
ings; it saved them from starvation; and they said – rightly –
"This is the gift of God."

The Book of Joshua tells of the drying up of the River Jordan
and its crossing by the Israelites. The drying up of Jordan actually
happens. It happened as recently as 1927, and there are recorded
instances at various times from 1267 onwards. It happens most
commonly at Damieh, sixteen miles north of Jericho, and is

[1]Exodus 16 : 14, 15.
[2]Louis Golding, *In the Steps of Moses the Lawgiver*, p. 225.
[3]Louis Golding, *In the Steps of Moses the Lawgiver*, pp. 230, 231
cp. C. S. Jarvis, *Yesterday and To-day in Sinai*, p. 169.

usually due to earthquake tremors. We have already seen that the Jordan valley is part of the great fault in the surface of the earth. Professor Garstang records the 1927 occasion. "A section of the cliff, which here rises to a height of 150 feet, fell bodily across the river and completely dammed it, so that no water flowed down the river bed for twenty-one and a half hours. . . . During this time, it is asserted by several living witnesses that they crossed and re-crossed the bed of the river freely on foot."[1] The Israelites must have been searching for a way to cross the impassable river; and suddenly the river dried up before them. To them there was no question of earthquake tremors; this was the work of God.

All through the history of Israel, especially in its early days, we see the Israelites looking at some event and saying with grateful admiration: "This is God." Nowadays we are able to explain the secondary causes which brought these things about. But that does not for one moment mean that they are any the less the work of God. So far from making them less wonderful it makes them more wonderful, for it means that God is continually using the natural processes of this world for his purposes. It was not that the Israelites were wrong; it is that we are blind. Often we have discovered the physical and secondary causes only to lose sight of God. "It is recorded of Shackleton's last expedition to the Antarctic that one day, from their camp upon the ice-floe which had been their shelter since the loss of their ship Endeavour, they saw two huge ice-bergs, each a million tons in weight, bearing down upon them from different directions. Nothing, it appeared, could save them; these ice-bergs were crashing their way throught the ice-floe, working destruction. Then, quite suddenly, they changed course and passed the camp at a safe distance. Shackleton asked, 'Was it some freak or eddy of the current or was it a greater Power?'"[2] The defeat of the Spanish Armada changed the face of history. That defeat was caused not only by Drake but by the winds of the heavens; and today there stands on Plymouth Hoe a monument with the inscription: "He blew with his winds and

[1] Quoted by W. J. Phythian-Adams, *The Call of Israel*, p. 138.
[2] Quoted by John Mauchline, *God's People Israel*, p. 33.

they were scattered." In anything we can see only the product of natural causes or we can see God.

In the Second World War many British troops were delivered at Dunkirk when all seemed lost. Assisting that deliverance were a concealing mist and phenomenally high tides. An Old Testament prophet would have written the story somewhat like this:

> "And the hosts of the enemy prevailed against the armies of Israel and drove them to the coasts of the sea. They pressed sore upon them and the people were hemmed in and in great distress. So from the sea there came the ships of the deliverers. And God sent a mist to cover his people; and God made the waters to rise upon the sea-shore that there might be a way to the ships. And the angel of the Lord stood behind the people that the enemy might not come upon them and destroy them. And so the Lord delivered his people and brought them through the waters to safety."

Essentially it was the Hebrew who was right and we who are wrong. The Hebrew saw miracles everywhere, because he lived in a world that was full of God and of the action of God. We see miracles nowhere because we think that we know the explanation of everything. But not all our knowledge has eliminated God and there are still miracles for those who have eyes to see. During the Battle of Britain, Hugh Dowding was in charge of Fighter Command. After the battle was won, he said: "The English are a queer people; they pray for a miracle, and when they get one they don't recognize it."

ADDITIONAL NOTE TO CHAPTER TWENTY-THREE

IN the body of the preceding chapter we have been seeing how again and again the Hebrew saw the hand of God in the happenings of nature. As further possible illustrations of this we may note the following. Two writers relate incidents which may well have something to do with the bush which burned and was not consumed (Exodus 3 : 1-3). In regions where there is or has been volcanic action, flames are often emitted from rifts in the ground. A photograph published in *The Sphere* on August 12th, 1933, shows a happening from the Copsa region in Transylvania. It shows an enormous column of flame, 900 feet high, leaping out from the earth in the middle of a grass covered orchard, while two women are unconcernedly at work a few hundred yards away. The fire issued from a large vent in the ground and was due to the inflammable gases coming from the crater of an extinct volcano.[1]

LOUIS GOLDING tells of something that he actually saw when travelling in the very area where Moses saw the burning bush: "I am at this point compelled to quote the apparition of a Burning Bush which was so exact a rendering of the strange and lovely marvel described in the Bible, that I quite literally was afraid to trust my eyes. The apparition lasted several seconds, and though I was aware of its exact rationale while it endured, I still said to myself it was mirage or inward fantasy. The thing happened 'in the back of the wilderness' in one of the wadis under the flank of Sinai. It was the evening of a hot and windy day. As we approached the arena where two or three wadis debouched, the winds met, and, joining forces, became a cyclone, a tall pillar of air violently rotating on its axis, its whole length defined by the sand it sucked up from the dry wadi bed. In the centre of this arena was a large thorny acacia, the only tree which grows in these regions. The sun had for some moments been hidden behind a long bank of cloud. It remained hidden until the cyclone reached the acacia. Then in the moment the cyclone possessed itself of the tree, the sun hurled its rays obliquely upon their embrace. The whole tree went up in flame. The smoke of it soared in golden gusts. Every thorn was a spit of fire. It continued so for several seconds. It seemed as if the cyclone were impaled on the sharp spikes of the branches. It turned and thrust and turned again. The bush burned with fire and was not consumed. Then at last the cyclone freed itself, and went hurtling along one of the wadis. The tree was no more than a thorny acacia again, arid and lonely in the centre of the hills."[2]

In the story of the Burning Bush we may have a wonderful example of that of which Mrs. Browning wrote so beautifully in *Aurora Leigh*:

> "Earth's crammed with heaven,
> And every common bush afire with God;
> But only he who sees, takes off his shoes,
> The rest sit round it and pick blackberries."

We may well believe that Moses, just because he was Moses, found God in a natural and amazing loveliness. It was because he took his shoes from off his feet in reverence that the bush lit like fire in the desert left him face to face with God. It may well be that here we

[1]Quoted in W. J. Phythian-Adams, *The Call of Israel*, p. 144.
[2]Louis Golding, *In the Footsteps of Moses the Lawgiver*, pp. 99, 100

have an instance of that awareness of which **Joseph Mary Plunkett**
wrote:

> "I see His blood upon the rose,
> And in the stars the glory of his eyes;
> His body gleams amid the eternal snows,
> His tears fall from the skies.
>
> I see his face in every flower;
> The thunder and the singing of the birds
> Are but his voice; and, carven by his power,
> Rocks are his written words.
>
> All pathways by his feet are worn;
> His strong heart stirs the ever-beating sea;
> His crown of thorns is twined in every thorn,
> His Cross is every tree."

The man who is "far ben" lives in a God-filled world. A common bush,
flaming in the strange power of some vivid light, would surely bring
him to his knees before God.

We have already seen that the Hebrews had no word for *nature*; they
did not think of nature, they thought of God. But it may well be
that the experience of Moses was in essence the experience which
Wordsworth enshrined so perfectly in *Lines composed a few miles
above Tintern Abbey*:

> "I have learned
> To look on nature, not as in the hour
> Of thoughtless youth: ....
> ....
> .... And I have felt ....
> A presence that disturbs me with the joy
> Of elevated thoughts; a sense sublime
> Of something far more deeply interfused,
> Whose dwelling is the light of setting suns,
> And the round ocean and the living air,
> And the blue sky, and in the mind of man."

If we lived as close to God as Moses did, we, too, might find in ordinary
things, lit by the light of God, the Burning Bush afire with him and
his voice speaking to us from it.

C. S. JARVIS had an experience which is a commentary on the passage
that tells how water came from the rock when Moses struck it.[1]
The Numbers passage begins: "Take the rod, and assemble the

[1]Numbers 20: 7-12.

[2]Louis Golding, *In the Steps of Moses the Lawgiver*, p. 244.

congregation." Louis Golding suggests that it is by no means impossible that Moses was a water-diviner.[2] That would certainly be a special gift given to him by God. Jarvis tells how he actually saw the very thing that Moses did happen before his own eyes. "Some of the Sinai camel corps had halted in a wadi and were digging in the loose gravel accumulated at one of the rocky sides to obtain water that was slowly trickling through the limestone rock. The men were working slowly, and the Bash Shawish, the Colour-sergeant, said: 'Give it to me,' and, seizing a shovel from one of the men, he began to dig with great vigour, which is the way with N.C.O.'s the world over when they wish to show their men what they can do, and have, incidentally, no intention of carrying on for more than two minutes. One of his lusty blows hit the rock, when the polished hard face that forms on weathered lime-stone cracked and fell away, exposing the soft porous rock beneath, and out of the porous rock came a great gush of clear water. It is regrettable that these Sudanese Camel Corps men, who are well up in the doings of all the prophets and who are not particularly devout, hailed their N.C.O. with shouts of 'What ho, the Prophet Moses!' "[1] Jarvis goes on to suggest that Moses, "an extraordinarily knowledgeable man," may well have discovered this phenomenon in the days when he wandered in the desert as the keeper of the flocks of Jethro. Let us put it in another way. It may well be that God had *given Moses the gift* of finding water and had *taught* him the secret of the lime-stone rock. The man who lives with God will never lack for the wonders of God all around him.

[1]C. S. Jarvis, *Yesterday and To-day in Sinai*, pp. 174, 175.

CHAPTER TWENTY-FOUR

Healing in the Early Church

The New Testament leaves us in no doubt that Jesus committed the ministry of healing into the hands of his apostles. When the Twelve were chosen, he gave them power over unclean spirits. They went out to preach that men should repent; " and they cast out many demons and anointed with oil many that were sick, and healed them."[1] When the Seventy returned from their mission, their report was: "Even the devils are subject to us in your name."[2] In the ending of Mark as it now stands, the prophecy of Jesus about his disciples is: "They will lay their hands on the sick and they will recover."[3] When Paul is enumerating the various gifts which Christians are able to lay at the service of the church, he includes "gifts of healing" and "miracles."[4]

As the history of the early church is unfolded to us in the Book of Acts we see this gift of healing in action. "Signs and wonders" are more than once referred to as typical of the life of the apostolic church.[5] The apostolic figures are shown as healing the sick. Peter healed the lame man at the gate of the Temple; it is said that even his shadow had healing power; he is shown healing Aeneas and raising Tabitha.[6] Stephen is said to have worked wonders and miracles.[7] In Samaria the evangelist Philip exercised a notable healing ministry.[8] Ananias by laying on of hands restored Paul's sight after the dazzling vision on the Damascus Road.[9] Paul claims as a matter of common knowledge that he had been able to work miraculous healings.[10] From the letter of James we learn that it was routine custom to take those who were sick to the elders of the church for anointing with oil.[11] Healing was an integral part of the activity of the early church.

[1] Mark 6 : 7, 12, 13; Matthew 10 : 1; Luke 9 : 1.
[2] Luke 10 : 17.   [3] Mark 16 : 18.   [4] 1 Corinthians 12 : 9, 10, 28.
[5] Acts 2 : 43; 5 : 12.   [6] Acts 3 : 6; 5 : 15; 9 : 34-40.
[7] Acts 6 : 8.   [8] Acts 8 : 6, 7.   [9] Acts 9 : 17.
[10] Romans 15 : 19; 2 Corinthians 12 : 12; Galatians 3 : 5.
[11] James 5 : 14.

After the apostles

It is clear that this gift of healing did not pass out of the church for many years. About the middle of the second century Justin wrote an Apology for the Christian faith in which he says that numberless demoniacs have been healed by Christians, when all other exorcists were helpless and all drugs and incantations unavailing.[1] Irenaeus, writing in defence of the Christian faith a little later, insists that those who are the disciples of Christ still have the power to work miracles. "Some do certainly and truly drive out devils, so that those who have thus been cleansed from evil spirits, often both believe and join themselves to the Church. . . . Others still heal the sick by laying their hands upon them, and they are made whole. Yea, moreover, as I have said, the dead even have been raised up, and remained among us for many years."[2] Tertullian, writing midway through the third century, declares that one of the Roman Emperors, Severus, was healed by being anointed by a Christian: "Even Severus himself, the father of Antoninus, was graciously mindful of the Christians; for he sought out the Christian Proculus, surnamed Torpacion, the steward of Euhodias, and, in gratitude for his having once cured him by anointing, he kept him in his palace to the day of his death."[3] Tertullian indeed makes the boldest of all claims. He says that he will not argue for demonstration is far quicker and more unanswerable; let a demoniac be brought in and a Christian exorcist will at once master the demon who possesses him.[4] Even as late as the middle of the fifth century, Augustine can still write: "As for miracles there are some wrought even yet."[5]

These statements are incontrovertible evidence that the early church possessed the gift of healing. Let us remember the circumstances in which they were made. Christianity was under persecution or the threat of persecution. Theophilus of Antioch, who wrote in a time of active persecution, said: "Even to this day

[1] Justin Martyr, *Second Apology* 6; cp. *The Dialogue with Trypho* 85.
[2] Irenaeus, *Against Heresies* 2, 32, 4.
[3] Tertullian, *Ad Scapulam* 4.
[4] Tertullian, *Apology* 23.
[5] Augustine, *The City of God*, 18 : 8.

the demon-possessed are sometimes exorcised in the name of the living and true God."[1] These writers were writing defences of Christianity seeking to persuade the Roman government that Christianity did not deserve such treatment. Every statement in them would be minutely examined; these apologists could not afford to make claims which could be proved untrue quite apart from the fact that being Christians they might be expected to tell the truth. There is no way of getting round their evidence that in the early church healing powers were exercised.

By the end of the second century so integral a part of the life and work of the church was this matter of healing that there was legislation to cover it. One of the earliest books of church administration extant is the *Canons of Hippolytus*. The eighth canon deals with this question. Men who possess the gift of healing are to be ordained as elders, after careful investigation has been made that the gift they possess really does come from God.[2] Such a regulation makes it clear that the ministry of healing was being so widely practised that it lent itself to abuse and had to be controlled.

Another early work, the *Clementine Letters*, lays it down as a regulation: "Let the deacons of the Church move about intelligently and act as eyes for the bishop, carefully enquiring into the actions of every Church member. . . . Let them find out those who are sick in the flesh, and bring such to the notice of the main body who know nothing of them, that they may visit them and supply their wants, as the president may judge fit."[3]

The church and the sick

The more one reads the documents of the early church, the more one sees Christianity in the early days as the gospel of the sick.[4] In the *First Epistle of Clement* the prayer of the church is: "Heal

---

[1]Theophilus, *To Autolycus* 9.

[2]Quoted T. M. Lindsay, *The Church and the Ministry in the Early Centuries*, p. 248.

[3]*The Pseudo-Clementine Letters*, *Ad Jacob*. 12, quoted by A. Harnack, *The Expansion of Christianity*, vol. i, p. 150.

[4]A. Harnack deals most fascinatingly with this whole subject in *The Expansion of Christianity*, vol. i, chapter 2.

the sick . . . raise up the weak, cheer the faint-hearted."[1] Justin Martyr in his *Apology* says that it was the practice of the early church to bring free-will offerings to worship. They were given to the bishop, "who dispenses them to orphans and widows, and any who, from sickness or some other cause, are in want."[2] A very early church instruction runs: "In every congregation at least one widow is to be appointed to take care of sick women; she is to be obliging and sober, she is to report the cases of need to the elders, she is not to be greedy or addicted to drink, in order that she may be able to keep sober for calls to service during the night."[3] The letter of Justin to Zenas and Serenus runs: "The sick are not to be overlooked, nor is anyone to say that he has not been trained to this mode of service. No one is to plead a comfortable life, or the unwonted character of the duty, as a pretext for not being helpful to other people."[4] The sick were a first call on the Christian congregation; and no excuse could be accepted for shirking the duty which the church had to them. Eusebius, in praising the character of Seleucus, said that like a father and a guardian he had shown himself a bishop and patron of orphans and destitute widows, of the poor and of the sick.[5]

When we read the literature of the early church it would almost seem that care for the sick was the test of a Christian. This in fact the heathen noted with astonishment. According to the heathen idea God did not want the sick. He sought only the sound to be his worshippers. The sick and the sinful were the prey of the powers of darkness. Let them recover their health and *then* come to God.[6] Celsus sneered at the Christians precisely because they said that sick and sinful people were dear to God. Julian the Apostate condemned as unintelligible the infamous Galilaeans who give themselves to that kind of people.[7]

[1]*First Clement* 59.
[2]Justin Martyr, *First Apology* 67.
[3]Quoted A. Harnack, vol. i, p. 149.
[4]The letter of Pseudo-Justin to Zenas and Serenus, 17.
[5]Eusebius, *Concerning the Martyrs of Palestine*, 11 : 22.
[6]A. Harnack, vol. i, p. 125.
[7]Both these instances are quoted in L. D. Weatherhead, *Psychology, Religion and Healing*, p. 79.

The Christian care for the sick had brought something quite new into the world.

It was this in fact that attracted people to Christianity. Porphyry, the heathen attacker of Christianity, was convinced that religion was for intelligent people and not for the sufferers of humanity.[1]

Harnack quotes a charming legend. It is naive and impossible, but it shows how many people must have been won by Christianity's healing power. The people of Edessa traced their Christianity back to the time of Jesus and treasured a correspondence which they thought had taken place between him and their king Abgar. Abgar, who was ill, was said to have written to Jesus: "Abgar, ruler of Edessa, to Jesus the excellent Saviour, who has appeared in the country of Jerusalem—greeting. I have heard of you and of your cures, performed without medicine and without herb. For it is said, you make the blind to see and the lame to walk; you cleanse the lepers, you cast out evil spirits and demons, you heal those afflicted with lingering diseases, and you raise the dead. Now. as I have heard all this about you, I have concluded that one of two things must be true; either, you are God, and having descended from Heaven, you do these things, or else you are a son of God, by what you do. I write to you, therefore, to ask you to come and cure the disease from which I am suffering. For I have heard that the Jews murmur against you and devise evil things against you. Now I have a very small, yet an excellent city, which is large enough for both of us." The letter which Jesus was said to have sent back ran: "Blessed are you for having believed in me without seeing me. For it is written concerning me that those who have seen me will not believe in me, while they who have not seen me will believe and be saved. But, as to your request that I should come to you, I must fulfil here all things for which I have been sent, and, after fulfilling them, be taken up again to him who sent me. Yet after I am taken up, I will send you one of my disciples to cure your disease and to give life to you and yours." The legend goes on to say that

[1] Quoted A. Harnack, vol. i, p. 126.

Thaddaeus came to Edessa and cured Abgar.[1] It is an obvious legend but a lovely story; and it shows that one of the greatest of Christian missionary weapons was the power to heal.

The fading power

So then the earliest church was clearly and characteristically a healing church. But the day was soon to come when the church was to regard the healing ministry as belonging to the great days of the past. Eusebius, writing in the fourth century, says: "A great many wonderful works of the Holy Spirit were wrought in the primitive age through the pupils of the apostles, so that whole multidues of people, on first hearing the word, suddenly accepted with the utmost readiness faith in the Creator of the Universe."[2] Augustine, writing in the fifth century, still believes that miracles happen, but they are few and a man should not want them. " 'Why,' say they, 'are these miracles which you declare were wrought, not wrought now?' I might indeed answer that they were necessary ere the world believed, to the end that the world might believe. Who so still seeks for prodigies, that he may believe, is himself a great prodigy, in that, while the world believes, he does not."[3] In the seventh century Chrysostom tells us that the wonder-working power had quite gone.[4]

Many explain this by saying that the power to work these healing miracles was necessary in the early days of the church in order to attract the world to Christianity. That, in effect, is what Eusebius said. David Smith says: "Nor indeed is either the gift or its withdrawal inexplicable. It was a providential dispensation. At its first planting Christianity required special aids, but once it had taken root, these were no longer needed, and it was left to its normal development."[5] Philip Schaff, the Church historian, held the same point of view. "These miracles were outward credentials and seals of the divine mission of the

---

[1]The story is in Eusebius, *The Ecclesiastical History*, 1 : 13.
[2]Eusebius, *The Ecclesiastical History*, 3 : 37.
[3]Augustine, *The City of God*, 22, 8, 1.
[4]Chrysostom, *Sermons on 2 Thessalonians* 4 (at the beginning).
[5]David Smith, *Life and Letters of Paul*, p. 36.

apostles in a time and among a people which required such sensible helps to faith. But as Christianity became established in the world, it could point to its continued moral effects as the best evidence of its truth, and the necessity for outward physical miracles ceased."[1] As someone put it, "The miracles were the bells to call people into the Church."

If this is true, it is a grim thought. It means that the great days are behind us. There was an age in which God was operative in a way in which he was never operative before and never will be again. We who come after are living in the twilight and there are no wonders any more.

Anointing with oil

The extreme instance of this is anointing with oil. We have seen how James took it for granted that a sick person would come to the elders to be anointed for his cure.[2] Until the eighth century anointing was always designed to cure and never a preparation for death. But in A.D. 852 it was laid down that anointing was a preparation against death; and in A.D. 1151 it became Extreme Unction, which is one of the seven Roman Catholic sacraments and is administered at the point of death. In mediaeval times a person who had received Extreme Unction was expected to die. If he recovered he had to live as one dead. He was not allowed to marry nor to alter his will.[3] The wheel had gone full circle. In the early church anointing was for healing; by the time of the Middle Ages it was for death. In the beginning the person anointed was meant not to die; in the end the person anointed had no right to live.

Something extraordinary had happened to the church's ministry of healing.

[1] P. Schaff, *History of the Church, Apostolic Christianity*, A.D. 1-100, vol. ii, p. 439.
[2] James 5 : 14.
[3] Leslie D. Weatherhead, *Psychology, Religion and Healing*, pp. 93, 94. There is a long and learned note on *anointing* in J. B. Mayor, *The Epistle of St. James*. The note is on James 5 : 14, pp. 165-167.

The lost and rediscovered gift

We may well ask why this ministry of healing was lost in the church. It was never entirely lost, for in every age there have been great Christian saints who possessed this gift of healing. But in general the place of the ministry of healing grew progressively less. There were two main reasons.

First, the thrill and expectancy of the first great days had gone. There have been certain great times in history when the world was on tiptoe with expectancy. As Wordsworth wrote of the days of the French Revolution:

> "Bliss was it in that dawn to be alive,
> But to be young was very heaven!"[1]

But it is not possible to live for ever in a *qui vive* of excitement. The routine business of everyday must go on. What happened in the church was that things settled down; men ceased to expect thrilling things; and because men ceased to expect them, they ceased to happen.

Second, the longer the church went on, the more it became an institution. At first the church had practically no organization at all. The apostles went from city to city and from country to country preaching the gospel. The prophets wandered here and there bringing their message from God. In each town and city elders were appointed to oversee the affairs of the Christian community. But the church was still not a great business organization. It was in fact not until midway through the third century that it had any buildings of its own. Till then it was not able to build them. But bit by bit it became an organization. It acquired all sorts of permanent officials, including bishops whose word was law within their sphere of authority. Things were reduced to rules and to regulations.

The more rigid a set-up becomes, the more difficult it is for the man with unusual gifts to find a place within it. A highly organized institution tends to dislike and suspect that which is unusual and cannot be fitted into the pattern. Clearly—as we

---

[1]Wordsworth, *The French Revolution as it Appeared to Enthusiasts,* and *The Prelude,* Bk. xi, line 108.

shall see—healing was a special gift; equally clearly no man can tie healing down to a set of rules and regulations. The plain fact was that there was little room for the exceptional activity within the system of the church; and the more organized the church became the less room there was. So the man with the gift of healing found himself more and more out of place.

The rebirth of the ministry of healing

Of the reality of spiritual healing in the early church there can be no argument. When the Sanhedrin were seeking to deal with the first of the Christians after the healing of the lame man at the gate of the Temple, they were baffled, because all they could in the end say was: "What shall we do with these men? For that a notable sign has been performed through them is manifest to all the inhabitants of Jerusalem; and we cannot deny it."[1] It is possible to deny many a thing but it was impossible to get away from the fact of a man who had been lame and now walked. One of the first of the Christian apologists was Quadratus who wrote soon after A.D. 100. Only fragments of his defence of Christianity are still extant; but the main fragment is of outstanding importance for this subject. He writes: "The works of our Saviour were always present, for they were genuine. I mean those who actually had been cured, those who rose from the dead. They were not only seen in process of being cured and in process of being raised; they were always present. It was not only when our Saviour sojourned here that they were seen, but even after he had left this world, they remained for a considerable time. So that certain of them lived down to our own time."[2] No man defending Christianity to the Roman government could have dared write that unless it was true. The case is not otherwise when Paul writes to the Corinthians and enumerates among the gifts of the church *gifts*

[1]Acts 4 : 16.

[2]This passage of Quadratus is so important that we give full details of where to find it. The fragment itself is in M. J. Routh, *Reliquae Sacrae*, vol, i. p. 75. It is quoted in Eusebius, *The Ecclesiastical History*, 4 : 3. A translation of it is in A. C. M'Giffert's translation of Eusebius in the *Library of the Nicene and Post-Nicene Fathers* p. 175.

of healing.[1] Paul never wrote to a more hostile audience; he could not afford a false statement. It would have been immediately pounced upon and used to discredit him and his whole argument. It is impossible to shake the evidence for healing as part of the ministry of the early church.

The interesting thing is that in recent times this ministry of healing has had a splendid rebirth. In regard to this rebirth three things are to be said.

First, there is no doubt that the gift of healing *is* being exercised in the church today. If evidence is required, a great army of those who have been healed and helped could be assembled as proof.

Second, spiritual healing is not intended to take the place of healing by medical and surgical means; it should co-operate with the doctors' work. The history of medicine is curious. In the early days it was to the holy man that every sufferer automatically came and it is still so among primitive people. A Jew in illness would turn to the Rabbi. In Greece or Rome the sufferer would turn to the Temple of Aesculapius. Harnack records a most interesting fact. It was in 219 B.C. that the first Greek surgeon came to Rome. The Roman government welcomed him by giving him the citizenship and providing him with a shop to carry on his practice. But Pliny tells us: "Owing to the cruelty in cutting and cauterizing, the name of surgeon soon passed into that of butcher, and a disgust was felt for the profession and for all doctors."[2] In a day when anaesthetics were unknown that was a natural reaction. In view of that the sufferer continued to turn to the priest rather than to the doctor. But gradually medicine developed and the physician became a respected and well-loved figure. Eusebius took some words of Hippocrates about the physician and applied them to Jesus: "like some excellent physician, in order to cure the sick, he examines what is repulsive, handles sores and reaps pain himself from the sufferings of others."[3]

But it was not long afterwards that the disaster happened. There came a split between medicine and religion. The church

[1] 1 Corinthians 12 : 9, 10, 28.
[2] A. Harnack, *Expansion of Christianity*, vol. i, p. 128.
[3] *Eusebius, The Ecclesiastical History*, 10, 4, 11.

has always been stubbornly slow to move when she thought that new discoveries of science were interfering with her settled beliefs and ways. Under its influence the Emperor Justinian, in the middle of the sixth century, closed the medical schools of Athens and Alexandria, although in the monasteries the monks still copied the medical manuscripts. The final clash came in the thirteenth century. In 1215 Pope Innocent the Third condemned surgery and all priests who practised it. In 1248 the dissection of the human body was pronounced sacrilegious and the study of anatomy condemned.[1] The tragic breach was complete. Even as late as the nineteenth century Sir James Simpson had to fight against certain sections of the church when he proposed to use chloroform to ease the pain of childbirth. There were those who argued that chloroform was not mentioned in scripture, that Genesis said that women must bring forth children in sorrow, and that Simpson was interfering with the ordinances of God.[2]

Today, however, the healing ministry of the church neither seeks to compete with nor to displace the ministry of ordinary medicine. The church's ministry of healing has two great spheres. It comes in when the resources of medicine have reached their limit to ease the pain and maybe even heal the disease, which have defied human powers. And, even more, it conveys to the patient a frame of mind and heart and spirit which the doctor and the surgeon find a great ally for their work. The age of healing has come again.

Third, when Paul mentions healing he calls it a *charisma*[3] a *gift*. He regards the church as the body of Christ. The body functions well only when each part is doing its work. The parts of the body do not envy each other; they do not try to do each other's work but do their own; and with that they are content. That is Paul's picture of the church. Each man in the church must exercise his own gift and not covet another's nor lay claim to one which he does not possess. Paul in fact comes to the end of this chapter by asking: "Have all the gifts of healing?" and gives answer that

[1] L. D. Weatherhead, *Psychology, Religion and Healing*, p. 96.
[2] Harley Williams, *Masters of Medicine*, p. 98.
[3] 1 Corinthians 12 : 12, 28.

they have not.[1] In this passage he speaks of "varieties of gifts," "varieties of service," "varieties of working."[2] All this is necessarily involved in *charisma*. A *charisma* is something which, by definition, is not acquirable but is given by God. It can be discovered; it can be developed; but it cannot be acquired if it is not already there. Paul uses it for the gift of God's grace;[3] for the gift of God's forgiveness;[4] for the gift that is implanted in a man when he is ordained to the ministry.[5]

This idea of gift dominates every part of life. A man might train and practise for ever and yet never sing like Dietrich Fischer-Deskau, play the violin like Yehudi Menuhin or golf like Jack Nicklaus; he might study for ever and yet be quite unable to write Shakespeare's plays, Milton's epics, Wordsworth's sonnets, Keats's Odes, Shelley's lyrics. Life is built on the basic principle: "To each man his gift." Nothing but trouble can develop when a man refuses to exercise his own gift or seeks to acquire one which is not for him.

In the matter of the church's ministry of healing this is of supreme importance. Not every minister has the gift of healing. A man can discover if he has it only by trying out his own ability, if he feels moved to do so; but he is failing God and his fellow men if he has the gift and refuses to use it. On the other hand, if he tries to use it when he does not possess it, nothing but frustration for himself and harm for others can result. There is no need for regret or self-criticism on a minister's part if he does not possess this gift; there is some other gift that God has given him; let him cheerfully exercise that. No one should feel that there is any failure or inadequacy in the man who does not possess the gift of healing; no man possesses all gifts.

[1] See the whole passage 1 Corinthians 12.
[2] 1 Corinthians 12 : 4-6.
[3] Romans 1 : 11; 1 Corinthians 1 : 7.
[4] Romans 5 : 15, 16; 6 : 23.
[5] 1 Timothy 4 : 14; 2 Timothy 1 : 6.

CHAPTER TWENTY-FIVE

The Virgin Birth

BEFORE we begin to discuss the belief in the Virgin Birth[1] of Jesus, we must note two quite general facts. First, this doctrine states that Jesus was born without the intervention of any human father, not that here the Holy Spirit was specially operative in what was otherwise a normal human birth. Second, there may be some who feel that we have no right to discuss this matter at all and are bound to accept the Virgin Birth without question. It must be noted that this is one of the doctrines which the Church of Scotland has agreed does not enter into the substance of the faith and on which, therefore, a man is free to arrive at his own conclusion. In other words, it may be orthodoxy to retain the full belief in the Virgin Birth but it is not heresy to reject it.

The New Testament evidence

It will be best to begin by setting out the evidence of the New Testament. It has only two places where the Virgin Birth is spoken about. The first is in Matthew.

"Now the birth of Jesus Christ took place in this way. When his mother Mary had been betrothed to Joseph, before they came together she was found to be with child of the Holy Spirit; and her husband Joseph, being a just man and

[1]Should the reader wish fuller discussion of the Virgin Birth than is possible here, he will find excellent material in the following sources. These two books are written in support of the Virgin Birth – J. Gresham Machen, *The Virgin Birth of Christ;* G. H. Box, *The Virgin Birth of Jesus.* The opposite point of view is stated at its strongest, in regard to evaluation of the evidence, by J. M. Thompson, *Miracles in the New Testament,* chapter ix, pages 133-159. In our opinion, the most valuable short discussion of all is in C. K. Barrett, *The Holy Spirit and the Gospel Tradition,* chapter ii, pp. 5-25, *The Conception of Jesus by the Holy Spirit.*

unwilling to put her to shame, resolved to divorce her quietly. But as he considered this, behold, an angel of the Lord appeared to him in a dream, saying, 'Joseph, son of David, do not fear to take Mary your wife, for that which is conceived in her is of the Holy Spirit; she will bear a son, and you shall call his name Jesus, for he will save his people from their sins.' All this took place to fulfil what the Lord had spoken by the prophet; 'Behold, a virgin shall conceive and bear a son, and his name shall be called Emmanuel' (which means, God with us). When Joseph woke from sleep, he did as the angel of the Lord commanded him; he took his wife, but knew her not until she had borne a son; and he called his name Jesus."   (Matthew 1: 18-25)

The relationship between Joseph and Mary as set out in that passage sounds to modern western ears very complicated. In verse 18 Mary is said to be betrothed to Joseph; in verse 19 he is called her husband; and in verse 24 he is said to take her as his wife. There is, however, no real complication. In Palestine there were three stages to a wedding—first, the engagement, second, the betrothal, and third, the marriage. The "engagement" was simply the arrangement of the marriage; and it might take place while the couple were still children and before they had even seen each other. It was normally carried out by the parents, or by professional match-makers. "Betrothal" lasted for a year, was as binding as marriage and could not be broken except by a process of divorce. During the time of betrothal the couple were known as husband and wife. In fact, in the Jewish law we often come across what seems to us a very strange phrase. If during the year of betrothal a girl's betrothed died, she was known as a widow; and the law frequently speaks of a "virgin who is a widow." The marriage proper came at the end of the year of betrothal. This explains why in successive verses Mary could be said to be betrothed to Joseph and that Joseph was her husband; and why the story can then go on to tell that Joseph took Mary as his wife.

One further word of explanation is necessary. Matthew quotes a prophecy in Isaiah 7 : 14 : "Behold a virgin shall conceive and bear a son." In this text there is one of the mysteries of biblical quotation. In the Hebrew of the Isaiah passage the word translated *virgin* is *almah,* which means simply a young women of marriageable age. The Hebrew word for *virgin* is *bethulah.* The Isaiah passage obviously does not refer to any kind of miraculous birth but to a child who is going to be born quite naturally in the near future. In fact no Jewish interpreter ever took the passage any other way. How then did the idea of *virgin* get into it? For some unknown reason, when the Hebrew scriptures were tranlated into Greek in the famous version known as the Septuagint, the translators chose to translate *almah* by the Greek word *parthenos,* which does mean *virgin.* In the Hebrew the text has no necessary connection with *virgin.* But it was very natural that, once the Christian Church came to believe in the Virgin Birth and began to look for Old Testament prophecies foretelling it, they should joyfully accept the words of the Septuagint as one such.

At the same time, apart altogether from his use of Isaiah 7 : 14, Matthew seems to believe unequivocally in the Virgin Birth of Jesus.

Luke's story

The other story of the Virgin Birth is in Luke's gospel.

"In the sixth month the angel Gabriel was sent from God to a city of Galilee named Nazareth, to a virgin betrothed to a man whose name was Joseph, of the house of David; and the virgin's name was Mary. And he came to her and said, "Hail, O favoured one, the Lord is with you!" But she was greatly troubled at the saying, and considered in her mind what sort of greeting this might be. And the angel said to her, "Do not be afraid, Mary, for you have found favour with God. And, behold, you will conceive in your womb and bear a son, and you shall call his name Jesus. He will be great and will be called the Son of the Most High; and the

Lord God will give to him the throne of his father David, and he will reign over the house of Jacob for ever; and of his kingdom there will be no end." And Mary said to the angel, "How can this be, since I have no husband?" And the angel said to her, "The Holy Spirit will come upon you, and the power of the Most High will overshadow you; therefore the child to be born will be called Holy, the Son of God.

And behold, your kinswoman Elizabeth in her old age has also conceived a son; and this is the sixth month with her who was called barren. For with God nothing will be impossible." And Mary said, "Behold, I am the handmaid of the Lord; let it be to me according to your word." And the angel departed from her (Luke 1 : 26-38).

Luke's version is not nearly so definite as that of Matthew. In fact, if we had read Luke's version without knowing the other and without the idea of the Virgin Birth in our minds, we would not necessarily have said that it told of a virgin birth at all. But there can be no doubt that Luke is telling the same story as Matthew, although in a different way. That Matthew tells the story from Joseph's point of view and Luke from Mary's is an explanation which covers the facts.

As we shall see, there is no other evidence for the Virgin Birth of Jesus in the New Testament. Everything is founded on these two passages.

The Virgin Birth in the early church

Of one thing there can be no doubt. By the second century the Virgin Birth had become part of the belief of the church. We cite only three witnesses. Ignatius, bishop of Antioch, who was martyred in Rome early in the second century, writes that we are "fully persuaded as touching our Lord that is he truly of the race of David according to the flesh, but Son of God by the divine will and power, *truly born of a virgin*, and baptized by John that all righteousness might be fulfilled by him, truly nailed up in the flesh for our sakes under Pontius Pilate and Herod the tetrarch."[1]

[1] Ignatius, *The Letter to the Church at Smyrna*, 1 : 1, 2.

And that is by no means the only reference that he makes to the Virgin Birth as being one of the historical events in the life of Jesus. Aristides, one of the earliest of the Christian apologists, wrote his defence of Christianity probably about A.D. 140. He writes: "The Christians, then, reckon the beginning of their religion from Jesus Christ, who is named the Son of God Most High; and it is said that God came down from heaven, and *frcm a Hebrew virgin* took and clad himself with flesh, and in a daughter of man there dwelt the Son of God."[1] Justin Martyr defended Christianity in his writings round about A.D. 170 and in the *Dialogue with Trypho*—Trypho was a Jew whom he was trying to persuade of the truth of Christianity—he describes Jesus as "The First-born of every creature, *who became man by the Virgin,* who suffered and was crucified under Pontius Pilate by your nation, who died, who rose from the dead, and ascended into heaven."[2]

The Virgin Birth was an article of the faith in the early church soon after the beginning of the second century and continued to be so.

The Apostles' Creed

So much was this the case that the statement of this belief became embedded in what we know as the Apostles' Creed: "I believe . . . in Jesus Christ, his only Son, our Lord, who was conceived by the Holy Ghost, *Born of the Virgin Mary.*" As it stands, the Apostles' Creed is a fourth or fifth century summary of the Christian faith.[3] It took its name from a legend passed down to us by Rufinus. He says that while the apostles were still alive, soon after the Ascension of Jesus, "The Lord commanded them to journey to separate countries to preach the word of God. When they were on the point of taking leave of each other, they first settled on a common form for their future preaching, so that they might not find themselves, widely dispersed as they would

[1] Helen B. Harris, *The Newly-recovered Apology of Aristides,* pp. 82, 83.
[2] Justin Martyr, *Dialogue with Trypho,* 85.
[3] For further information see J. N. D. Kelly, *Early Christian Creeds.*

be, delivering divergent messages to the people they were persuading to believe in Christ. So they all assembled in one spot and, being filled with the Holy Spirit, drafted this short summary, as I have explained of their future preaching, each contributing the clause he deemed fitting: and they decreed that it should be handed out as standard teaching to converts."[1] This is obvious legend; but this much is true— the substance of the Apostles' Creed was in fact the confession of faith used by the church at Rome as early as A.D. 150 and required from candidates for baptism.

The value of the doctrine of the Virgin Birth

The doctrine of the Virgin Birth seeks to conserve the real fact that Jesus was God as well as man. As we have said more than once, we are not concerned to prove or disprove the possibility of the Virgin Birth. As Luke put it: "For with God nothing will be impossible" (Luke 1 : 37). It might well be argued that, if in Jesus God made a special entry into the world, it is not difficult to believe that he made that entry in a special way.

The other side of the case

But there is more to be said. One thing is perfectly certain—there is a stratum of New Testament thought which knows nothing of the Virgin Birth.

In the New Testament there are two long genealogies of Jesus (Matt. 1 : 1-17; Luke 3 : 23-38). Their existence is not in itself surprising; the Jews were supremely interested in a man's descent. When Josephus wrote his autobiography, he began by describing his own descent and finishes by saying: "Thus have I set down the genealogy of my family, as I have found it described in the public record."[2] The existence of the genealogies is not

---

[1]Rufinus, *A Commentary on the Apostles' Creed*, 3 (J. N. D. Kelly's translation); for the legend cp. Irenaeus who spoke of "the rule handed down from the Apostles and their disciples" (*Against Heresies* 1 : 2), and Tertullian who spoke of "the rule of truth which descends from Christ, transmitted through His companions" (*Apology* 47 : 10).

[2]Josephus, *The Life of Flavius Josephus* 1.

surprising but both are *pedigrees of Joseph*. The point that the maker of the genealogies was trying to prove was that Jesus was indisputably of the line of David, and he does so by tracing the descent of Joseph. Clearly he regarded Jesus as the son of Joseph. It is futile to argue that Jesus would in any event be *regarded* as the son of Joseph, that he would be, in the regular word, the *putative* son of Joseph. If he was not the *real* son of Joseph, the point of the pedigrees is gone and they do not show that Jesus was the son of David at all. The genealogies come from a line thought which does not know of the Virgin Birth.

Very early the New Testament was translated into different languages. One of the earliest translations was into Syriac, the language of Palestine itself. The Sinaitic-Syriac translation of Matthew 1 : 16 runs: "Joseph, to whom was betrothed Mary the Virgin, begat Jesus, who is called the Christ."[1] We are not at the moment concerned to argue about the truth of that statement but only to show that it must have been made by a man who did not know about the doctrine of the Virgin Birth.

Further, even the gospels which have the story of the Virgin Birth speak about Jesus in such a way as to show that they are drawing information from a line of thought which did not know about the Virgin Birth. After the blessing of Simeon, Luke says: "And his father and his mother marvelled at what was said about him."[2] When he is telling the story of how Jesus remained behind in Jerusalem and Joseph and Mary searched for him, he makes Mary say: "Your father and I have been looking for you anxiously."[3] If the source of that story believed in the Virgin Birth, that would be an almost incredible statement to put into her mouth. When Jesus comes to Nazareth, Luke shows the people as saying: "Is not this Joseph's son?"[4] Matthew has it that they said: "Is not this the carpenter's son?"[5] John tells us how

[1] F. G. Kenyon, *Textual Criticism of the New Testament*, pp. 153, 154.
[2] Luke 2 : 33. The Authorised Version has it that "*Joseph* and His mother marvelled." *Joseph* is the reading of only very inferior manuscripts of the New Testament. The Revised Version correctly translates *His father* as do Moffatt and the American Revised Standard Version, and all modern translations.
[3] Luke 2 : 48.   [4] Luke 4 : 22.   [5] Matthew 13 : 55.

Philip described Jesus as "Jesus of Nazareth, the son of Joseph."[1] When the Jews were discussing the great claims of Jesus, they said: "Is not this Jesus, the son of Joseph, whose father and mother we know?"[2] Mark shows us Jesus's friends, with Mary among them, coming to take him home because they were worried about him and thought that he was going mad.[3] It is surely beyond belief that, if Jesus had been miraculously born, Mary would have had any such thought or would have lent her presence to any such expedition.

Further, Luke shows us the parents of Jesus bringing him to the Temple to go through the ceremony of the ransoming of the first-born.[4] According to Jewish custom, every first-born male creature was sacred to God. In the case of a child, he was bought back from God at the price of five shekels paid to the priests in the Temple.[5] We know the modern form of that ceremony, and it is a form which may well have been used in the time of Jesus. The father brings the child to the synagogue and the service begins with a declaration by him that the child is his first-born son and an acknowledgment of the duty to ransom him back from God. Thereafter the priest asks: "Which wouldst thou rather, give me thy firstborn son, the firstborn of his mother, or redeem him for five shekels, which thou art bound to give according to the law?" The father replies: "I desire rather to redeem my son, and here thou hast the value of his redemption which I am bound to give according to the law." The priest then takes the money and holds it over the head of the child and says: "This instead of that, this is commutation for that, this in remission for that." The service then ends with a blessing.[6] The mind staggers at the thought of Joseph going through that ceremony, and declaring that Jesus was his firstborn son, if the Virgin Birth was a physical fact.

The silence
It is further to be noted that no New Testament writer, other than Matthew or Luke, seems to know about the Virgin Birth.

[1]John 1 : 45. [2]John 6 : 42. [3]Mark 3 : 21, 31-35.
[4]Luke 2 : 22-24. [5]Exodus 13 : 2; Numbers 18 : 16.
[6]W. O. E. Oesterley and G. H. Box, *The Religion and the Worship of the Synagogue*, p. 410.

Mark's gospel shows no knowledge of it. It is sometimes claimed that Mark implies a belief in the Virgin Birth. In Mark's version of Jesus's visit to Nazareth, the people of Nazareth say: "Is not this the carpenter, the son of Mary, the brother of James and Joses and of Judas and Simon?"[1] But the significant thing is that the people of Nazareth are citing that fact as a strong reason for *disbelieving* in Jesus and for questioning his right to speak as he did. They are citing it for the precise reason of showing that he is a very ordinary person, from a very ordinary home and of very common parentage. The reason why they called him Mary's son is probably because by this time Joseph was dead and Jesus had become the head of the carpenter's business and the support of his mother.

John's gospel shows no knowledge of it. The only suggested indication that John believed in the Virgin Birth comes from a variant reading in John 1 : 12, 13 in the accepted text, and it is that of all the best manuscripts, these verses run: "But to all who received him, who believed in his name, he gave power to become children of God; who were born, not of blood nor of the will of the flesh nor of the will of man, but of God." One Latin manuscript, the Codex Veronensis, and certain quotations in Tertullian and Irenaeus, have *was* born instead of *were* born.'[2] That would be a reference to the Virgin Birth but the manuscript evidence is against this reading and it may safely be said that the Fourth Gospel does not refer to the Virgin Birth.

Most surprising of all, Paul shows no sign of knowing about the Virgin Birth. It is sometimes claimed that he gives a hint that he accepts the Virgin Birth when he writes: "But when the time had fully come, God sent forth his Son, *born of woman,* born under the law."[3] But *born of a woman* is the regular biblical phrase for a human being. Job says: "Man that is born of a woman is of few days and full of trouble."[4] Eliphaz says: "What is man that he be clean? or he that is born of a woman that he can be righteous?"[5]

---

[1]Mark 6 : 3.

[2]For the textual evidence see A. Souter, *Notum Testamentum Graece John* 1 : 13.

[3]Galatians 4 : 4.   [4]Job 14 : 1.   [5]Job 15 : 14.

Bildad says: "How then can man be righteous before God? How can he who is born of a woman be clean?"[1] Jesus says of John the Baptist that there is none greater amongst those born of women.[2] When Paul used this phrase, so far from saying that Jesus entered the world in an extraordinary way, he was saying that he came into it in the same way as every human. It would seem that Paul did not know about the Virgin Birth; and certainly he did not teach it. If it be claimed that he did not teach it because it was a dangerous doctrine to teach to heathens who already had their myths of demi-gods, we can only answer that it seems impossible to conceive of Paul keeping silence about any doctrine simply because there was risk involved in preaching it.

The meaning of the Virgin Birth

We have come to see that the only notice of the Virgin Birth in the New Testament is in the birth stories of Matthew and Luke; and that even in these gospels there is a stratum of thought which either does not know about the Virgin Birth or does not take the stories at their face value. If then the Virgin Birth is not to be taken as a *physical* fact, what is the meaning of the story and where did it come from? It has sometimes been claimed that it came through the influence of the kind of stories that the Greeks loved to tell about their heroes. The Greeks, like the Romans, loved to build up legends in which they attributed the birth of their heroes to the action of some God. For instance, they passed down the story that Hercules and Alexander the Great were begotten by Zeus; they said that Pythagoras and Plato and Augustus were begotten by Apollo. But the Greeks very well knew that these were legends and they never took them seriously. The stories which Matthew and Luke tell bear not the slightest resemblance to these Greek tales.

Where, then, will we find an explanation of the stories of the Virgin Birth. It was the first Jewish principle of the interpretation of any story, that a Jew would not ask: "Is this story true in the historical and physical sense of the term?" He would ask every

[1] Job 25 : 4.   [2] Matthew 11 : 11; Luke 7 : 28.

time: "What does this story teach?"[1] Suppose we go to the two stories of the Virgin Birth and ask: "What is the basic truth that these two stories teach? "There can only be one answer—the one truth that leaps out is that the Holy Spirit was uniquely operative in the birth of Jesus. "Mary was found to be with child of the Holy Spirit." "That which is conceived in her is of the Holy Spirit."[2] "The Holy Spirit will come upon you and the power of the Most High will overshadow you."[3] Whoever reads these stories from any point of view must agree that the basic truth enshrined in them is that the birth of Jesus was in a unique sense the work of the Holy Spirit.

The Spirit in Jewish thought

We must remember that these passages are taken from a time before Jesus was born. Therefore, when they speak of the Holy Spirit, they are thinking of the Spirit in *Jewish* terms.

In Jewish thought the Spirit had two great functions. First, *it was through him that the work of creation was done.* In the beginning the Spirit of God moved upon the face of the waters and the chaos became a cosmos.[4] "By the word of the Lord the heavens were made," said the Psalmist, "and all their host by the breath of his mouth."[5] The word for Spirit and the word for breath are the same. "Thou sendest forth thy Spirit, they are created."[6] "The Spirit of God is in my nostrils," said Job, describing the secret of life.[7] "The Spirit of God has made me, and the breath of the Almighty gives me life."[8] This thought continues to appear in the Jewish literature written between the Old and the New Testaments.

> "Let all creation serve thee:
>   For thou spakest and they were made,
>   Thou didst send forth thy Spirit and it builded them,
>   And there is none that shall resist thy voice."[9]

[1] Chapter 23, *The Miracles of the Old Testament*, pp. 234-235.
[2] Matthew 1 : 18, 20.
[3] Luke 1 : 35.
[4] Genesis 1 : 2.   [5] Psalm 33 : 6.   [6] Psalm 104 : 30.
[7] Job 27 : 3.   [8] Job 33 : 4.   [9] Judith 16 : 14

Through all Jewish thought runs the idea of the Spirit as the Creator of God.

Second, it is not only the Spirit who creates; *it is the Spirit who also re-creates*. Ezekiel draws a grim picture of a valley of dry bones, and goes on to tell how the dry bones came alive. And he finishes his picture: "I will put my breath in you and you shall live."[1] Sometimes the Rabbis expressed the same idea: "God said to Israel, 'In this world my Spirit has put wisdom in you, but in the future my Spirit will make you to live again'."[2] The Spirit of God is the power and the presence who can give men life again when the soul is dead.

With these basic Jewish ideas let us go back to the story of the Virgin Birth. It will then say to us: "In the birth of Jesus the power which created the world and the power which alone can re-create the world was uniquely operative." Whatever our point of view all must agree with that.

How, then, did the idea of a *Virgin* Birth get into the matter? It may be that the solution is to be found in the very lovely Jewish belief that no child could be born without the Spirit of God. When a man and a woman came together a child was not always born; when a child *was* born, the Holy Spirit was there. On that subject there were certain beautiful sayings. "Rabbi Simlai said . . . In the past Adam was created from the dust of the ground and Eve was created from Adam. Henceforward it is to be 'in our image and after our likeness'—meaning, man will not be able to come into existence without woman, nor woman without man, nor both without the glory of God." "When husband and wife are worthy the Glory of God is with them." "There are three partners in the production of the human being: The Holy One, blessed be He, the father and the mother."[3] It is then quite possible to believe that the stories of the Virgin Birth are not meant to tell of a supernaturally amazing birth

[1] Ezekiel 37 : 1-14.
[2] Quoted C. K. Barrett, *The Holy Spirit and the Gospel Tradition* p. 21. I owe the substance of this section to Mr. Barrett's work.
[3] Quoted C. K. Barrett, *The Holy Spirit and the Gospel Tradition*, p. 14.

but of an ordinary birth in which the Holy Spirit was operative as he never was before or after in any birth in history. This much is certain—that they were written, not primarily to tell that Jesus was born of a virgin but to tell that he was born of the power of the Holy Spirit.

The difficulty of the doctrine of the Virgin Birth

If we are to take the story of the Virgin Birth physically we are confronted with one great difficulty. It destroys his likeness with men. True, it conserves the fact that he is fully God, but it wrecks the fact that he is fully man. And the thought that Jesus is fully man is one on which the whole New Testament loves to dwell. "God," said Paul, "sent his own Son in the likeness of sinful flesh."[1] Paul talks of how the goodness of the one man Jesus Christ conquered the evil of the one man Adam.[2] The writer of the Pastoral Epistles says: "There is one God and one mediator between God and man, the man Christ Jesus."[3] The writer to the Hebrews says with a kind of thrill in his voice: "Therefore he had to be made like his brethren in every respect."[4]

The New Testament holds triumphantly to the humanity of Jesus. It is a thought which the great early thinkers repeated again and again. "Out of his great love," said Irenaeus, "he became what we are that he might make us what he is."[5] But if the Virgin Birth is physically true that is precisely what Jesus never did; he was different from any man who ever came into the world. The supreme problem of the Virgin Birth is that it belittles the humanity of Jesus; but if we can believe that we may read the story, asking, not: "Is this physically true?" but: "What truth does this teach?" we may find in it a very simple and lovely way of saying that the Spirit of God was supremely operative in the birth of Jesus, even if that birth was a natural and not a supernatural one.

---

[1]Romans 8 : 3.   [2]Romans 5 : 15-17.   [3]I Timothy 2 : 5.
[4]Hebrew 2 : 17.   [5]Irenaeus, *Against Heresies*, 3, 19, 6.

The conclusion

We are allowed to take the view of this matter which our own mind and heart demand. If we believe in the physical Virgin Birth of Christ we conserve the true divinity of our Lord, but his manhood loses something precious. If we choose to believe that this is a lovely story to tell how in a village home in Palestine the Holy Spirit was specially active in the birth of Jesus, there is nothing to prevent our doing so. In either belief we shall find that which will warm our hearts and nourish our faith.

CHAPTER TWENTY-SIX

The Resurrection

We have kept to the end the greatest of all the miracles, the
Resurrection.[1] It would be true to say that the Resurrection is the
greatest single event in human history. Certainly for the church
it is the greatest thing in the world, for, as we shall see, had there
been no Resurrection there would have been no church. For that
very reason the Resurrection is one of the things about which we
must be sure or we lose the central reality of the Christian faith.

Explaining it away
We must begin with the fact of the empty tomb. When the friends
of Jesus went to visit his tomb after the Sabbath was past, they
were carrying out a routine duty; it was the custom to visit the
tombs of the dead every day for a week after the funeral. But when
they got there they found that the tomb was empty.[2]

It is here that certain of the sceptical critics begin explaining
things away. Kirsopp Lake suggested that after the crucifixion the
disciples went back to Galilee. There they had certain hallucinations that Jesus was not dead but had risen. The women mean-
time had gone to the tomb on the day after the Sabbath. Mary
Magdalene had gone very early when it was still grey dark.[3] In
the grey dark she went to the wrong tomb, and very naturally
found it empty. Not knowing where to turn, she met a stranger
who said: "The tomb you are looking for is not this one. Your
friend is not here."[4] Mary in fright took to her heels and ran
back to Jerusalem with a strange story about an empty tomb.

[1]The best short book on the Resurrection is *The Resurrection of Christ*
by A. M. Ramsey (in Fontana).
[2]Luke 24 : 12; John 20 : 1-10.
[3]John 20 : 1.
[4]Matthew 28 : 6; Luke 24 : 6.

This story together with the fancied visions of the disciples in Galilee produced the story of the Resurrection.

It would be extraordinary if belief in the Resurrection arose because a woman mistook a tomb in the dark; it is incredible that the central fact of the Christian faith should be founded on a mistake. We have only to think of the obvious fact that someone was bound to check up on Mary's story to see how little that theory merits belief. We may be quite certain that the tomb was empty, but there have been three other main explanations suggested of that fact.

(a) It has been suggested that Jesus did not really die on the Cross, that in the cool of the tomb he revived from the swoon into which he had fallen, that he succeeded in escaping from the tomb and appeared to his friends again.

Let us think of what that story involves. Jesus was scourged (John 19 : 1). The Roman scourge was a terrible thing. The victim was bent so that his naked back was exposed. The lash was a long leather thong studded at intervals with pieces of bone and lead. It was laid on to the victim's back and literally tore it to pieces. Few men retained consciousness after such an ordeal; many went raving mad under it; and not a few died. On the way to Calvary Jesus staggered under the weight of the Cross and Simon of Cyrene was impressed into the Roman service to carry it for him (Mark 15: 21). The routine of crucifixion was gone through, and finally the spear was thrust into Jesus's side, and out came water and blood, which was the sign of a physically broken heart (John 19 : 34). He was clothed in the grave clothes, and bound in the long linen strips like bandages about his head and feet, strips from which Lazarus had to be freed before he could walk, according to John's story (John 11 : 44). Across the entrance to the tomb was rolled a stone, which the women on their way to the tomb did not know how they were to move (Mark 16 : 3). How could Jesus possibly have survived the lash, the cross, the spear thrust in the side? How, if he had survived, could he have freed himself from the cocoon-like wrappings of the grave-clothes in the tomb? How, if he had freed himself from them, could he possibly have moved the stone which closed the mouth of the tomb? And, if all these things had somehow been done, how could he have appeared to his friends as anything other than a broken figure? We have only to state the difficulties of this theory to show that they make it impossible.

(*b*) It is suggested that what happened was that the Jews actually removed Jesus's body themselves, lest the tomb become a place of pilgrimage. That theory is wrecked by one basic difficulty. The thing the disciples preached in the first days of Christianity was the Resurrection. They never preached a sermon without making it the crown of their argument.[1] If the Jews had really removed the body of Jesus, nothing would have been easier for them than to disprove the Resurrection. They could have published abroad what they had done; they could even have produced the body; they could have destroyed the story of the Resurrection overnight. Again this is a theory that has only to be stated to be disbelieved.

(*c*) It has been suggested that the disciples removed the body and then claimed that Jesus had risen from the dead. Apparently the Jews were afraid that the disciples might do that very thing, for they asked Pilate to post a guard at the tomb to prevent it (Matt. 27 : 62-66). If the disciples did that, it means that they in the end died for a known lie. It is possible that a man might die for a delusion but no man will die for a lie which he himself has produced. Again this is a theory that has only to be stated to be disproved.

The theory of vision and hallucination

It has been claimed that what really happened was that the disciples suffered from hallucinations which gave rise to their belief that Jesus had appeared to them. There are two basic objections to that theory. First, an hallucination comes only to a person who is conditioned to receive it, who is expecting it. But, if one thing is clear from the Resurrection story, it is that the last thing that the disciples expected was that Jesus would rise again. In fact, they regarded the Cross as unmitigated disaster and looked on the

[1]cp. Acts 2 : 24, 32; 3 : 15, 26; 4 : 10, 33; 5 : 30; 10 : 40; 13 : 30, 33, 34; 17 : 31.

death of Jesus as the end of everything. It is psychologically incredible that such men should have an hallucination that Jesus had risen. Second, Jesus's appearances were not confined to individual people. He appeared to the ten, and then later to the eleven (John 20 : 19-29). He appeared to five hundred men at the same time (1 Cor. 15 : 6). It is beyond belief that groups of people like that should all undergo the same hallucination at the same time.

There is one very interesting variant of this theory. Between 1867 and 1872 a great German scholar named Theodor Keim produced a massive life of Jesus. He believed that the Resurrection appearances of Jesus were indeed visions but *visions sent by God*. He likened the appearances to what he called, in a famous phrase, *telegrams from heaven*. At first sight this is a not unattractive theory. God sent the visions to tell the disciples that Jesus was most gloriously spiritually alive and that his presence was always with them. The one trouble is that it does not explain the empty tomb. On that difficulty it breaks down.

The great proof

The fact is that the evidence for the Resurrection is too strong to be broken down. No other theory really explains the facts; and one unanswerable proof of the Resurrection is the existence of the Christian church.

The crucifixion left the disciples in mingled despair and terror. The two whom Jesus met on the Emmaus road said with poignant pathos: "We had hoped that he was the one to redeem Israel."[1] And the inevitable conclusion is: "But we were mistaken and wrong." When Mark tells of the arrest of Jesus in Gethsemane, he says with bleak brevity: "They all forsook him and fled."[2] John draws a picture of the disciples meeting behind locked doors,[3] and the inference is that they were shivering with terror lest it be their turn next. To focus this matter in one person – when Jesus was arrested, Peter was guilty of a terrified denial which sent him weeping bitterly when he realized what he had done.[4] And yet

[1]Luke 24 : 21.   [2]Mark 14 : 50.   [3]John 20 : 19.
[4]Luke 22 : 54-62.

just seven weeks later that same Peter was standing before the Sanhedrin, who could have had him crucified too, and telling them to do their worst.[1] The coward had become the hero. Mr. Fearing had become Mr. Standfast.

For every effect there must be an adequate cause. What changed that hopeless, despairing, terrified group of men into a band who were ready to go out and win the world? What convinced them that what they thought was the end was really the new beginning? There could only have been one cause. Jesus had come back. The change in the disciples is explicable on no other grounds. It is quite clear that, if there had been no Resurrection, the apostolic group would simply have broken up, and each would have gone his own way to try to forget. If there had been no Easter Day we would never have heard of Good Friday. Without the Resurrection the church would never have come into being.

The differences
It has sometimes been objected that there are differences, and even contradictions, among the Resurrection stories. The list of Jesus's appearances after his Resurrection is:–

1. To Mary Magdalene – Mark 16 : 9, 10; John 20 : 11-18.
2. To the women returning home – Matthew 28 : 9.
3. To two disciples on the road to Emmaus – Mark 16 : 12, 13; Luke 24 : 13-35.
4. To Peter – Luke 24 : 34; 1 Corinthians 15 : 5.
5. To ten apostles in the Upper Room – Luke 24 : 36-48; John 20 : 19-23.
6. To eleven apostles in the Upper Room – John 20: 26-29.
7. To the disciples by the lake-side – John 21 : 1-24.
8. To five hundred brethren at once – 1 Corinthians 15 : 6.
9. To James – 1 Corinthians 15 : 7.
10. The Ascension – Luke 24 : 50, 51; Acts 1 : 1-10.

It is quite true that not all the accounts are the same. For instance, some of the appearances are in Jerusalem and some in Galilee. But that is exactly what we would expect. The appearances of Jesus

[1]Acts 4 : 19, 20.

covered a period of seven weeks; inevitably his followers would be sometimes in Jerusalem and sometimes in Galilee.

The typical difference between the stories is found in the different accounts of what happened at the empty tomb. In Mark the messenger who announces that Jesus has risen is a young man.[1] In Luke the message is brought by *two men in dazzling apparel.*[2] In Matthew the messenger is *the angel of the Lord.*[3] In John the message is given by *two angels.*[4]

There is difference here. But there are three things to be said.

First, no two people ever gave precisely the same account of anything, be it a football match, a street accident, a church service or a play. We would have much more cause to doubt the veracity of the Resurrection narratives if they dove-tailed completely in every detail. Such precise correspondence would indicate collusion. The very fact that different witnesses give slightly differing accounts is a guarantee that they are telling the truth.

Second, it is inevitable that, when the story of a wonderful event is handed down from age to age, it tends to become more wonderful in the telling. The core of the story remains the same; its details tend to increase in wonder. That does not affect the truth of the central fact; it simply means that we have to find our way back through the accompanying details to what really happened.

Third, in this particular case, the fact remains that, whoever tells the message, the message itself remains the same; "He has risen."[5]

The slight differences which occur in the narratives of the Resurrection are no barrier to belief.

The Resurrection and the constitution of the world
Let us turn to the great truths which the Resurrection teaches us. The Resurrection teaches us something about God's government of this world. It teaches us three great truths about the constitution of the world.

(i) *It teaches us that in the end goodness is always stronger than evil.* It was the sin of man which nailed Jesus to his Cross. Jesus

[1]Mark 16 : 5.   [2]Luke 24 : 4.   [3]Matthew 28 : 2.   [4]John 20 : 12.
[5]Matthew 28 : 6; Mark 16 : 6; Luke 24 : 6.

was the loveliest figure who ever walked this earth; and if there had been no Resurrection, it would have meant that evil was proved stronger than goodness. But Jesus rose again to prove that in the end goodness is always stonger than evil, no matter how things may appear at any given moment. George Bernard Shaw puts some noble words into the mouth of St. Joan: "Do not think you can frighten me by telling me that I am alone. France is alone; and God is alone; and what is my loneliness before the loneliness of my country and my God. I see now that the loneliness of God is his strength: what would he be if he listened to your jealous little counsels? Well, my loneliness shall be my strength too; it is better to be alone with God; his friendship will not fail me, nor his counsel, nor his love. In his strength I will dare, and dare, and dare, until I die. I will go now to the common people, and let the love in their eyes comfort me for the hate in yours. You will all be glad to see me burnt; but if I go through the fire I shall go through it to their hearts for ever and ever. And so, God be with me!"[1]

We have only to ask ourselves a series of questions which could go on for ever. Would we, in the end, rather be Saint Joan, or the men who burned her? Would we, in the end, rather be Socrates, or the men who compelled him to drink the hemlock? Would we, in the end, rather be Paul, or Nero who condemned him? Would we, in the end, rather be Jesus, or the Jewish authorities who compassed his death?

J. R. Lowell has a poem on the apparent defeat and ultimate victory of goodness.

"Once to every man and nation comes the moment to decide,
    In the strife of Truth with Falsehood, for the good or evil side;
    Some great cause, God's new Messiah, offering each the bloom or blight,
    Parts the goats upon the left hand and the sheep upon the right,
    And the choice goes by for ever 'twixt that darkness and that light.

[1]George Bernard Shaw, *Saint Joan*, Scene v.

Careless seems the great Avenger, history's pages but
    record
One death-grapple in the darkness 'twixt old systems and
    the Word;
Truth for ever on the scaffold, Wrong for ever on the
    throne,
Yet that scaffold sways the future, and behind the dim
    unknown,
Standeth God within the shadow, keeping watch above
    his own."

The lesson of the Resurrection – and the ultimate lesson of history – is that if a man wishes to be on the winning side, he must be on God's side, because, in the last analysis, goodness is always stronger than evil.

(ii) *The Resurrection teaches us that in the end love is stronger than hate.* It was the hatred of men which crucified Jesus. Had there been no Resurrection, it would have proved hatred the strongest force in the world; but the Resurrection is the proof that love is stronger still. It is a fact of life, which men seem always unable or unwilling to learn, that hatred begets nothing but hatred. If a person injures us and we injure him back, it simply means that a train of bitterness and anger is let loose which will go on and on. But if we refuse to hate, we bring a new element into the situation, the power of love, and love, the Resurrection proves, is in the last analysis the strongest power in the world.

Edward Denny sang of Jesus:

"Thy foes might hate, despise, revile,
    Thy friends unfaithful prove:
Unwearied in forgiveness still,
    Thy heart could only love."

It was that inexhaustible, undefeatable love which made Jesus the conqueror of men's hearts and the Saviour of the World. An American poetess wrote about the Resurrection.

"I heard two soldiers talking,
    As they came down the hill,

> The sombre hill of Calvary,
> Bleak, and black and still.
> And one said, 'The night is late,
> These thieves take long to die.'
> And one said, 'I am sore afraid,
> And yet I know not why.'
>
> I heard two women weeping,
> As down the hill they came;
> And one was like a broken rose,
> And one was like a flame.
> One said, 'Men shall rue
> This deed their hands have done.'
> And one said only through her tears,
> 'My Son! My Son! My Son!'
>
> I heard two angels singing
> Ere yet the dawn was bright;
> And they were clad in shining robes,
> Robes and crowns of light.
> And one sang, 'Death is vanquished.'
> And one in golden voice,
> Sang, 'Love hath conquered, conquered all,
> O earth and heaven rejoice!' ''

The Resurrection is the proof that love is the greatest conquering force in the world.

(iii) *The Resurrection teaches us that in the end life is stronger than death.* When the Jews had crucified Jesus, and he was laid in the tomb, they said to themselves: "That is the end of him." But it was not the end of him, for the Resurrection came and showed that life is stronger than death. Nothing can stop the force of life. A growing tree can split a concrete pavement. During the war a church was all set out on a Saturday afternoon for the harvest thanksgiving service on the Sunday. In the centre of the display was a sheaf of corn. That night came one of the worst of all the air raids; and on the Sunday the church was a heap of ruins. The winter came, and then the spring. And someone in the spring-time noticed something. On the rubble where that church had once stood, little green shoots of corn were growing; they flourished through the summer; and in the autumn there was a patch of corn. Not all the bombs and destruction could stop the force of life. Jesus said: "Because I live, you will live also" (John 14 : 19). The lesson of the Resurrection is that life is stronger than death and that Jesus has promised us a share in that life.

Jesus and the Resurrection

But the Resurrection also did something for Jesus.

(i) *It vindicated the claims of Jesus*. During his ministry Jesus never foretold the Cross without also foretelling the Resurrection. Always he ended his predictions of the last terrible times with the confident assertion that he would rise again on the third day.[1] The Resurrection was the proof that his claims were true. It was in fact the Resurrection which convinced the disciples that Jesus was indeed the Son of God. The gospel of the early church was the gospel of the Resurrection, for the Resurrection was the final proof that Jesus was the person whom he had claimed to be.

(ii) *The Resurrection liberated Jesus*. So long as Jesus was in the body, he was subject to all the limitations of the body. He could be in only one place at a time; he could reach only a limited number of people with his voice; he could touch only a limited number of lives. But with the Resurrection he was set free to work everywhere throughout the whole world. John Masefield has a play about the death and Resurrection of Jesus. In it Procula, Pilate's wife, was interested in Jesus. She had been anxious to stop Pilate sending Jesus to death.[2] She sent for the centurion who had been in charge of the crucifixion and who had ended on his knees confessing that Jesus was the Son of God.[3] His name was Longinus. Procula asked Longinus what had happened at the crucifixion. "He was a fine young fellow," he answered, "but when we were finished with him he was a poor broken thing upon a cross." "So you think that he is finished?" said Procula. "No, madam," answered Longinus, "I do not. He is set free throughout

[1]Matthew 16 : 21; 17 : 22, 23; 20 : 18, 19; Mark 8 : 31; Luke 9 : 22.
[2]Matthew 27 : 19.
[3]Matthew 27 : 54.

the world where neither Jew nor Greek can stop his truth." The Resurrection was the setting free of Jesus. No longer was he confined to Palestine. His sphere of influence and activity was now the whole earth.

The Resurrection and ourselves

But the Resurrection has also the most tremendous consequences for our own life and living. The great, basic truth of the Resurrection is that *Jesus is alive,* not just a figure in a book but a living presence. There is all the difference in the world between *knowing* a person and *knowing about* a person. The difference between Jesus and other great figures of the past is that we may *know about* them but can never *know* them; whereas it is not enough to *know about* Jesus; we must *know* him. The essential truth of the Resurrection is that Jesus not only *was*; he *is*.

John Greenleaf Whittier wrote:

"And warm, sweet, tender, even yet
    A present help is he;
And love has still its Olivet,
    And faith its Galilee."

Another poet wrote:

"Shakespeare is dust, and will not come
    To question from his Avon tomb,
And Socrates and Shelley keep
    An Attic and Italian sleep.

They see not. But, O Christians, who
    Throng Holborn and Fifth Avenue,
May you not meet, in spite of death,
    A traveller from Nazareth?"[1]

Francis Thompson wrote a poem in which he described the Christian experience when things go wrong. The last two verses are:

"But (when so sad thou canst not sadder)
    Cry – and upon thy so sore loss

[1]Quoted by J. S. Stewart, *The Strong Name*, p. 52.

Shall shine the traffic of Jacob's ladder
Pitched betwixt heaven and Charing Cross.

Yea, in the night, my Soul, my daughter,
Cry – clinging heaven by the hems;
And lo, Christ walking on the water
Not of Gennesareth, but Thames!"[1]

The truth of the Resurrection is that Jesus is alive,

The consequences for life are incalculable. It means that all life is lived in his presence and under his eye. That presence must always be our inspiration to goodness and our defence against temptation.

The Resurrection has consequences which go beyond life.

In the end comes death. Walter Savage Landor has a prose poem which he puts into the mouth of Aesop. He desires that in the life of Rhodope "The Summer may be calm, and the Autumn calmer, and the Winter never come." He is told that that can never be. "Laodameia died; Helen died; Leda, the beloved of Jupiter, went before. There are no fields of Amaranth on this side of the grave; there are no voices, O Rhodope, that are not soon mute, however tuneful; there is no name, with whatever emphasis of passionate love repeated, of which the echo is not faint at last."[2] There is beauty there, but also despair. When H. G. Wells was within a few days of his seventieth birthday, he made a speech to the P.E.N. Club. He was already the author of at least eighty-five books. He said: "I feel as though I were still in the nursery playing with my nicest toys, and nurse opens the door and says, 'Come now, George, it's bedtime; put these toys away.' Well, it will soon be time to put these toys away and there is still so much to be done." There is whimsicalness there, but at the back of it the haunting thought of the finality of death. Landor wrote in an epigram:

"I strove with none, for none was worth my strife.
Nature I loved, and after nature, art;

[1]Francis Thompson, *The Kingdom of God*, '*In no strange land.*' The poem will be found in *The Oxford Book of Christian Verse*, p. 516.
[2]Quoted by H. Greenhough Smith, *Odd Moments*, pp. 9, 10.

> I warm'd both hands before the fire of life;
> It sinks, and I am ready to depart."

Robert Louis Stevenson had it:
> "I have trod the upward and the downward slope;
> I have endured and done in days before;
> I have hoped for all and bade farewell to hope;
> And I have lived and loved and closed the door."

In every one of these sayings there is the idea of death as the end. But when that great saint and preacher F. B. Meyer received news that he had not long to live he wrote to a friend: "I have just heard to my surprise that I have only a few more days to live. It may be that before this reaches you I shall have entered the palace. Don't trouble to write; we shall meet in the morning." The difference is there for all to see. For the Christian death is the way to the morning; for others, it is the way to the dark. And the difference is Jesus. The great truth of the Resurrection is that we believe in one who conquered death and who has promised us a share in his victory.

We can be certain on the evidence of the Resurrection. The Resurrection is the proof that the values of God are the strongest things in this world and can never be destroyed. The Resurrection was the vindication and the liberation of Jesus. The Resurrection for us is the assurance of the presence of the living Christ all through life, and beyond life, into death, and beyond death, into life everlasting.

BIBLIOGRAPHY

There is a vast literature on the miracles, and books on the miracles are written from every point of view. We give here a list of books which we have found most useful; others have been mentioned in the footnotes.

Books on the Miracles

A. B. Bruce, *The Miraculous Element in the Gospels*
E. O. Davies, *The Miracles of Jesus*
R. H. Fuller, *Interpreting the Miracles*
J. Laidlaw, *The Miracles of our Lord*
C. S. Lewis, *Miracles*
A. Richardson, *The Miracle Stories of the Gospels*
F. R. Tennant, *Miracle*
J. M. Thompson, *Miracles in the New Testament*
R. C. Trench, *Miracles*
J. Wendland (translated by H. R. Mackintosh), *Miracles and Christianity*

Lives of Christ in which the Miracles are treated

G. Bornkamm, *Jesus of Nazareth*
R. Bultmann, *Jesus and the Word*
M. Dibelius, *Jesus*
A. Edersheim, *The Life and Times of Jesus the Messiah*
F. W. Farrar, *The Life of Christ*
M. Goguel, *Jesus the Nazarene*
C. Guignebert, *Jesus*
O. Holtzmann, *The Life of Jesus*
T. Keim, *Jesus of Nazara*
J. Klausner, *Jesus of Nazareth*
Xavier Léon-Dufour, *The Gospels and the Jesus of History*
D. Smith, *In the Days of His Flesh*

Standard Commentaries on the Gospels and on Acts

In many, if not most, cases the most helpful material on the miracles is in the commentaries on the New Testament books in which the individual miracle stories are told. Titles in various commentary series are listed below. On the Synoptic Gospels as a whole, see C. G. Montefiore, *The Synoptic Gospels.*

MOFFATT COMMENTARIES
Matthew : T. H. Robinson
Mark : B. Harvie Branscomb
Luke : W. Manson
John : G. H. C. Macgregor
Acts : F. J. Foakes-Jackson

WESTMINSTER COMMENTARIES
Matthew : P. A. Micklem
Mark : A. E. J. Rawlinson
Luke : L. Ragg
Acts : R. B. Rackham

PELICAN NEW TESTAMENT
COMMENTARIES
Matthew : J. C. Fenton
Mark : D. E. Nineham
Luke : G. B. Caird
John : J. Marsh

TYNDALE COMMENTARIES
Matthew : R. V. G. Tasker
Mark : R. A. Cole
John : R. V. G. Tasker
Acts : E. M. Blaiklock

A & C BLACK COMMENTARIES
Matthew : F V. Filson
Mark : S. E. Johnson
Luke : A. R. C. Leaney
John : J. N. Sanders and
B. A. Mastin
Acts : C. S. C. Williams

TORCH COMMENTARIES
Matthew : G. E. P. Cox
Mark : A. M. Hunter
Luke : W. R. F. Browning
John : A. Richardson
Acts : R. R. Williams

NEW CENTURY BIBLE
Matthew : D. Hill
Luke : E. Earle Ellis
John : B. Lindars
Acts : W. Neil

There is an excellent commentary on *Acts* by F. F. Bruce in the 'New International Commentary Series'. There are massive commentaries by R. Bultmann on *John*, by E. Haenchen on *Acts*, and by R. E. Brown on *John* 'The Anchor Bible'.

All these commentaries are on the English New Testament.